Le Cordon Bleu

DESSERT
TECHNIQUES

LAURENT DUCHENE & BRIDGET JONES

CASSELL

Created and Produced by
CARROLL & BROWN LIMITED
20 Lonsdale Road
London NW6 6RD

Managing Editor Laura Price
Editor Salima Hirani

Managing Art Editor Adelle Morris
Designers Leslie Feagley, Julie Bennett

Art Director Chrissie Lloyd

Production Manager Wendy Rogers

IT Manager John Clifford
IT Executive Paul Stradling

Photographers David Murray, Jules Selmes

A CASSELL BOOK
This edition first published
in the United Kingdom by

CASSELL plc.
Wellington House
125 Strand
London WC2R 0BB
www.cassell.co.uk
First published 1999

British Library Catalogue-in-Publication Data
A catalogue record for this book is available from the
British Library

ISBN 0-304-35120-2

Reproduced by Appletone, England
Printed and bound in Italy by Officine Grafiche de
Agostini, Novara

Contents

INTRODUCTION 6

FRUIT DESSERTS 9

ICED DESSERTS 31

CUSTARDS, CREAMS & WHIPS 45

SOUFFLES, MOUSSES & MERINGUES 55

SOFT CHEESE DESSERTS 73

BATTERS & OMELETTES 83

BASIC TECHNIQUES 97

CAKES & GATEAUX 129

PASTRIES 151

GRAINS 181

PETITS FOURS 191

FINISHING TOUCHES 197

GLOSSARY 214

INDEX 216

ACKNOWLEDGEMENTS 224

INTRODUCTION

Whatever your level of culinary knowledge or area of expertise, you can achieve dessert perfection simply by following the chefs of the famous Le Cordon Bleu Culinary Institute as they reveal their secrets and styling of the sweet course.

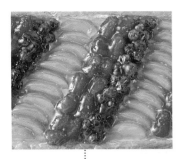

AS THE PARTING GIFT of your meal, the dessert course should be a visual and sensual triumph of harmonious perfection that complements the tastes and flavors of the other courses in your meal. *Le Cordon Bleu Dessert Techniques* brings the expertise of Le Cordon Bleu's 32 Masterchefs – from culinary institutes in France, Great Britain, Japan, Australia and North America – into your kitchen. The amazing craft of the Pâtissière is unveiled and stripped of its mystery in the pages of this remarkable book. Le Cordon Bleu is renowned for achieving the highest standards of culinary finesse, particularly in creating the sweet course for stylish menus. In this book, leading chefs from Le Cordon Bleu pass on their expertise and recipes for dessert success.

THIS BOOK IS THE ULTIMATE GUIDE to help you master the art of the sweet course. In the coloured central section, the opening pages pinpoint items of equipment that are important in dessert preparation, with advice on their usage and how to choose them. Following this guide to the specialized area of the *batterie de cuisine*, the rest of the chapter illustrates the basic techniques that are used repeatedly in the preparation of ingredients. Those who are not entirely confident in the kitchen will appreciate the notes on the fundamental elements of fruit preparation, making pastries, using sugar and chocolate and making a variety of sauces, icings and fillings. The chapter also focuses on the ease with which many desserts can be achieved with correct techniques and attention to details.

CHAPTERS ARE ORGANISED by dessert type, so that within each chapter there is a range of ideas, from the straightforward to the complex. A broad spectrum of classic desserts are covered, from frozen specialities and fruit desserts to dishes prepared with cheese or others based on sponge cakes, gâteaux and yeasted mixtures. Technique-led guidance forms the backbone of the chapters. From illustrating the fundamentals of classic and contemporary desserts to displaying the many ways in which simple methods form the basis for elaborate creations, the information progresses so

naturally within each section that the novice is never in any doubt as to how to approach a technique, yet those with more culinary confidence who may not wish to follow the step-by-step instructions may simply use the photographs as an *aide memoire* to prepare desserts that are familiar—or to inspire the creation of new ones. At each stage, there are examples of the ways in which simply prepared items can be presented in the form of a high-quality sweet course.

AS A SOURCE OF INSPIRATION, *Le Cordon Bleu Dessert Techniques* is superb. Studying the quality of the finished dishes and the standard of craft is, in itself, an education. Each page is meticulously designed to display the food, not only to show how irresistible the dish can be made to look, but also to ensure that the preparation detail is clearly visible and easy to emulate. Step-by-step photographs are flanked by information boxes and innovative ideas to inspire adventurous cooks who may like to explore the cornucopia of possibilities for each area of dessert cookery. Even with more advanced methods, concise instructions ensure that every stage is perfectly clear.

LE CORDON BLEU'S renowned and meticulous attention to detail – from the benchmark basics through to specialized procedures – all are demonstrated in a way that will encourage cooks of all abilities to experiment. The combining of ingredients, the marrying of basic components and the creativity and flair of finishing touches all stimulate the imagination. Innovative presentation of classical desserts is very much a feature of this book. You will find that ideas are clearly laid out and easy to adapt to suit changing seasons and different occasions.

WHEN YOUR CONFIDENCE in the mastery of the basic skills is brimming, Le Cordon Bleu chefs present *Les Pièces de Résistance* – a pinnacle of gourmet achievement for each chapter, taking the techniques and creating desserts that look and taste superb. These chef's specialities represent the extent to which the methods can be explored and developed. Here we see the chefs at work, creating those superlative desserts that every cook dreams of creating, and every diner of eating – and all the know-how is here for the taking.

AN INVALUABLE COLLECTION of classic recipes is contained in this volume – from superb vanilla ice cream or melt-in-the-mouth meringues to instructions for making crisp and juicy fruit fritters that will delight family and friends; this forms a kitchen library every cook should own. Throughout its pages, *Le Cordon Bleu Dessert Techniques* passes on exacting standards gathered from years of unmatched culinary experience – standards which have made Le Cordon Bleu *the* culinary institute.

PRESENTATION AND DECORATION are essential factors in preparing the most visual course of the meal. The final chapter of this book takes an in-depth look at the chefs' secrets for consistently achieving exacting standards. The twist that makes a fantastic chocolate curl; the flick of a sifter for the lightest dusting of sugar; and the steady touch of a piped decoration: all are explained in the chapter on finishing touches. While decoration is not always the focus, planned presentation is essential for style.

THE INTERNATIONAL CHEFS of Le Cordon Bleu are dedicated to sharing the arts of cuisine and pâtissière with their students. With decades of experience and scores of awards behind them, they travel the world giving practical demonstrations, participating in festivals and acting as gastronomic ambassadors; not only for the traditional disciplines of classic French cuisine, but also for the breathtaking storehouse of ingredients, skills and culinary traditions spanning the globe. Renowned for over a century for their exceptional results in teaching chefs, Le Cordon Bleu are the educational frontrunners, taking international cuisine into the 21st century, and have been selected by the Ministry of Tourism for the People's Republic of China to train their elite chef's in Paris. Le Cordon Bleu has also signed a joint venture with the Australian Government to train, in a new Cordon Bleu school, Australian chefs for the Millennium Olympics in Sydney.

HOW TO USE THIS BOOK

Le Cordon Bleu Complete Dessert Techniques opens the doors of Le Cordon Bleu to novices and experienced cooks alike. Each chapter allows you to choose the basis for your dessert and offers a range of options, from simple to complex.

Once you have decided upon a style of dessert you will find yet more choices for the look and flavour of your dish. The basics chapter in the center of the book offers a refresher course on the equipment and techniques needed to

prepare ingredients to their initial stages. To allow you to give your dessert the perfect finishing touch, the last chapter focuses on decorations and is full of both contemporary and classic ideas for presenting your dish.

FRUIT DESSERTS

FRUIT SALADS

MOLDING FRUIT

POACHING FRUIT

GRILLED & FRIED FRUIT

BAKED FRUIT DESSERTS

BREAD & FRUIT SWEETS

DRIED FRUIT DESSERTS

FRUIT SALADS

A fruit salad can be a simple alternative to a rich dessert or a sophisticated combination of complementary fruit and flavourings. Use prime-quality produce balanced with the right level of sweetness for superb results.

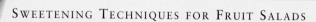

MAKING SIMPLE MIXED FRUIT SALAD

A poorly arranged fruit salad is a true waste of decorative potential. An eye for colour can create splendid arrangements, as here, with small whole plums, slices of peeled kiwi fruit and mango, whole raspberries and halved strawberries. Prepare a light syrup (see page 108), allow to cool, then macerate the fruit in it for at least 30 minutes before assembling the fruit salad. Use fruits that do not discolour when exposed to air.

FLAVOURING FRUIT SALADS

WHOLE SPICES

Cinnamon sticks and cloves may be added to oranges, apricots and strawberries. Sprinkle the fruit with caster sugar and chill for several hours.

CARDAMOM SEEDS

Green cardamoms add a fresh, exotic flavour to fruit. Split 2 cardamoms and crush the black seeds in a mortar with a pestle. Add to the syrup or sprinkle over the fruit.

Try soaked fresh figs and guava with honey, lime juice and a sprinkling of crushed cardamom seeds.

VANILLA

A vanilla pod can be used to flavour a light syrup for fruit salad. Alternatively, vanilla sugar can be used to macerate fruit. Vanilla works very well with berries and bananas.

HERBS

Mint, bay, lemon verbena or lavender add much flavour to syrups or when macerating fruit with sugar. Refreshing mint and lemon verbena are good with mixed fruit, grapes, grapefruit, kiwi and melon. The warm flavour of bay leaves complements stone fruit, such as peaches, apricots, guava and nectarines, and also works well with pears. Use lavender sparingly with grapes, pears, pineapple, melon or distinctly flavoured fruit.

SWEETENING TECHNIQUES FOR FRUIT SALADS

- **Juicy fruits**
  Sprinkle caster sugar to taste over cut oranges, kiwi fruit, apricots or pineapple and allow to macerate for at least 1 hour. The sugar dissolves in the fruit juice to form a delicious light syrup.

- **Uncut or non-juicy fruits**
  Sprinkle a little icing sugar over summer berries, melon or stone fruit. Allow the fruit to macerate for at least 1 hour before serving.

- **Firm fruits**
  Sprinkle lemon or lime juice over nectarines or peaches, bananas, star fruit or figs, and trickle a little clear honey over them.

- **Soft fruit and berries**
  Trickle pure maple syrup over papaya, blueberries and lychees. Allow the fruits to macerate for a minimum of 30 minutes before serving.

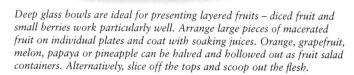

Deep glass bowls are ideal for presenting layered fruits – diced fruit and small berries work particularly well. Arrange large pieces of macerated fruit on individual plates and coat with soaking juices. Orange, grapefruit, melon, papaya or pineapple can be halved and hollowed out as fruit salad containers. Alternatively, slice off the tops and scoop out the flesh.

MOULDING FRUIT

Victorian cooks were often experts at creating glistening fruit jellies and the popularity of these jewel-like desserts continues today. Fruit juice or wines may be set with gelatine to complement fruit and keep it in place.

SETTING FRUIT

Fruit can be set in moulds to beautiful effect. Set layers of different types of fruit, whole and sliced, or a single large piece. A thin layer of fruit can form the base on which to set a mousse, cream or charlotte.

INDIVIDUAL FRUIT MOULDS

For individual portions, whole pieces of fruit, either large or small, can be set in ramekins, dariole moulds or appropriately sized basins. Fruit can also be halved, sliced, diced and segmented, and arranged attractively in small moulds.

Prepare the fruit, discarding any seeds. Here, sliced grapes are placed on a set liquid based on cider, covered with more liquid and reset. Peeled, sliced oranges, with pith removed, form the next layer. The jelly can be left plain, or decorated with crystallized fruit or zest.

SETTING FRUIT IN LAYERS

Pour a thin layer of jellied liquid (see page 128), here a combination of light syrup and white wine, into the base of the mould and chill until set. Arrange the fruit on top of this, spoon over another layer of liquid and set again. Add further layers of fruit (each one set separately). A mousse or cream can also be set in the mould.

SETTING LARGE FRUIT

To mould a large piece of fruit or whole fruit, set a thin layer of liquid in a mould, then add the fruit. Here, a peach is set in a liquid made of a light syrup, port and gelatine. Set the liquid in two stages so the fruit does not float.

ANGULAR EFFECTS

Striking irregular effects can be achieved by supporting dishes or moulds at an angle until the liquid has set. Here blackcurrants are poached in a syrup made with red wine and set when cooled.

1 Pour in the syrup and add the fruit. Sit the mould at the desired angle with an edge raised and chill.

2 Apply the second layer. Here, to complement the blackcurrants, a jellied liquid made of grape juice flavoured with peppermint liqueur is added. Decorate the finished jelly with some fresh blackcurrants and sprigs of mint, if desired.

Fresh Fruit Minestrone

Simple, yet beautiful to look at and refreshing to eat, a variety of cut summer fruit is steeped in a spiced fruit marinade, set over ice and served with a quenelle of iced yogurt. This special salad needs to be prepared well in advance to allow the fruit to absorb the flavours.

PREPARATION PLAN

▸ Prepare the marinade at least three hours ahead or the day before serving.
▸ Cut up fruit.
▸ Make the iced yogurt.

For the marinade
2 vanilla pods
400 ml water
350 g sugar
300 ml orange juice
1 lemon
1 banana
30 g basil

•••

For the fruits
1 Granny Smith apple
2 kiwis
200 g apricots
200 g strawberries
Fresh basil
Lemon juice, for sprinkling

•••

For the iced yogurt
425 ml natural or plain yogurt
100 g sugar
80 ml whipping cream (mixed, not whipped)

•••

Sprig of basil for decoration

1. Before you prepare the syrup for the marinade, peel and slice the lemon but not the banana as this will discolour very quickly once peeled. Set the lemon slices aside and cut the vanilla pods in half lengthwise to release the flavour more easily. Place the water, sugar and vanilla pods in a saucepan and bring to the boil. Remove from the heat and add the orange juice and the lemon. Blend ingredients together well in a blender. Peel and slice the banana before adding it to the marinade in the blender along with the basil. Blend again until the mixture is rich, thick and smooth. Set the marinade aside.

2. Prepare the fruit. Peel the apple, then core and slice, cutting thick rings first and then slicing down through the rings to form chunks. Sprinkle or brush the apple chunks with a little lemon juice to prevent discolouration. Peel the kiwi fruit. You may find that it is easiest to peel a kiwi fruit with your fingers, like a banana, rather than with a knife because less of the flesh is removed in this way. Cut the kiwi fruits into chunks of a similar size to your apple pieces. Cut the apricots in half and twist to remove the stone. Peel and cut into chunks. Hull the strawberries and slice in half.

3. Add the prepared fruit to the marinade and finally the basil, finely sliced. Allow the fruit to sit in the marinade for at least a few hours before serving.

4. If you have one, put all the ingredients for the iced yogurt in a sorbet machine. Otherwise, mix, do not whip, the ingredients together in a bowl and chill in the freezer for half an hour. Continue chilling and mix every 15 minutes until the yogurt is smooth yet firm enough to hold its shape when moulded.

5. Fill a large bowl with crushed ice and set the serving bowl of marinated fruit on top of the ice. Shape the iced yogurt into an oval and arrange on top. Add a decorative sprig of basil and serve.

What's in a Name?

Used in a figurative sense, minestrone means a mix-up or confusion and, as such, is an ideal description of dishes that contain a jumble of ingredients, each playing a distinct part in the finished dish. The culinary term is most famously applied to a soup that is renowned for the wide variety of vegetables and pasta shapes it contains. However, the term can be equally accurately applied to this delicious fruit salad with its own confusion of fruits.

POACHING FRUIT

Poached fruit can be used to fill pastries or pancakes, to accompany a mousse, cream or iced dessert, or served alone, either hot or cold. Select firm fruit, newly ripened, for the best results.

POACHING FRUIT

Poached fruit is coated with syrup (see page 108), which is reduced to a thick glaze for large fruit. (Increase the amount of sugar for sharp fruit.) Add some lemon or orange rind and lemon juice. Red or white wine or cider can be used in place of water. Use a light syrup for fruit that needs long cooking, which will become sweeter as the liquid evaporates.

1 Add the prepared fruit to the syrup. Make sure there is enough syrup to cover the fruit.

2 Heat to simmer. For large fruit which require longer cooking, cover the pan. Turn them occasionally so they cook evenly.

3 Drain the fruit and boil the liquid until reduced, either to a heavier syrup, for fruit such as apricots and plums, or to a thick glaze to coat large fruit such as peaches or pears.

CREATING INTENSE FLAVOURS

Cinnamon sticks, cloves, green cardamoms, vanilla, fresh root ginger, bay leaves, lavender sprigs, citrus rind or unblanched almonds are all suitable ingredients for flavouring poaching liquids. Simmer the condiments in the liquid before adding the sugar to create an intense flavour.

2 Drain the fruit and reduce the syrup to a thick glaze. Use this glaze to coat the fruit. Allow to cool. Fill the fruit with whipped cream flavoured with ginger syrup and decorate with preserved stem ginger and crystallized lime rind.

1 Simmer fresh root ginger and lime rind in dry cider for 15 minutes. Stand for 15 minutes, then add sugar to make a syrup. Use this to poach cored dessert apples or oranges.

MAKING FRUIT COMPOTES

Fruit served in its cooking liquid, sometimes slightly reduced, is a compote. Berries, such as strawberries, raspberries or blackberries are most commonly used for compotes. Sharp berries, such as blackcurrants and cranberries, require a larger proportion of sugar, which should not be added at the start of cooking to avoid causing the fruit skins to toughen. Once cooked, leave a compote to stand for 10 minutes before serving hot, or allow to cool completely.

1 Place the fruit in a pan and add the flavourings – here, orange rind and a vanilla pod are used. Add some sugar (roughly 175 g for 500 g fruit) and some liquid – red wine is used here (roughly 150 ml). If cooking sharp berries, such as red- or blackcurrants and cranberries, begin with a smaller proportion of sugar, approximately 50 g.

2 Simmer gently, stirring the fruit carefully until the sugar dissolves and the fruit is just tender. Leave the compote to stand for about 10 minutes. Flavour with 4 tbsp cassis, if desired, and serve with Crème Anglaise.

3 Sharp berries require a little further cooking. Stir in 150 g sugar at this stage and continue to simmer gently until the sugar has dissolved. If there is too little liquid, add a little more sugar to release the fruit juices.

COMBINING FRUIT IN COMPOTES

When combining fruit in a compote, make sure firm fruit is part-cooked before adding tender or small fruit. For instance, guavas should be quartered and poached for about 8 minutes before adding soft fruit. Less firm fruit, such as papaya, should be poached for 3 minutes before soft fruits are added.

The softest fruits, such as soft berries or the physalis and stoned lychees shown here, should be added to poached hard fruits, then cooked gently for 2 minutes.

SERVING COMPOTES

- *Serve hot as a filling or a topping for omelettes, crêpes, waffles or sponge puddings.*
- *Serve hot with creamy rice pudding, semolina or baked custard.*
- *Serve hot in pies and tarts.*
- *Serve cold with ice cream, sorbet or mousse.*
- *Serve cold as a filling for biscuit cups, tartlets or flans (sable or shortcake).*
- *Serve cold, topped with spun sugar.*

GRILLED & FRIED FRUIT

Select firm, newly ripened fruit for frying or grilling, macerating it first in juice flavoured with spices. Cook fruit rapidly under a preheated grill or over a high heat to develop flavour while retaining texture.

SIMPLE GRILLED FRUIT

Macerate fruit in citrus juice with sugar and flavourings (such as whole spices or small amounts of ground spice) for approximately 30 minutes before grilling. If you are using fruit that discolours, make sure it is thoroughly coated in juice and cover the bowl closely with clingfilm while the fruit macerates. Bananas can be grilled either whole, or sliced into halves along the middle. Pineapples should be sliced thickly. Peaches, nectarines, pears, apples, papaya and guava should be halved.

1 Drain the macerated fruit (reserving the juices) and pat dry on kitchen paper. Brush the pieces of fruit with melted unsalted butter and place them on a rack over a grill pan.

2 Make a small quantity of glaze for the fruit: heat the reserved juices with a little sweet cider or wine, adding honey, maple syrup or sugar to taste. Flavour this with some brandy or a liqueur, if desired.

3 Grill the fruit under a high heat until lightly browned. Turn once and brush with butter. Sprinkle with sugar and grill briefly until lightly caramelized. Serve immediately, with the hot juices spooned over.

MAKING FRUIT KEBABS

Small whole fruit or neat chunks of fruit make pretty kebabs. Grapes, strawberries, physalis and cherries can be skewered intact; halve dates, figs, apricots and plums; cut peaches, nectarines, tamarillo or apples into wedges; cut pineapple, mango, papaya and guava into chunks. Try poached kumquats. Serve kebabs alone, or arrange on a lightly sweetened fruit coulis (see page 113), marbled with Chocolate Sauce (see page 115) or cream, with toasted brioche spread with brandy butter (see page 115), on Waffles or Griddle Pancakes (see pages 87) with maple syrup.

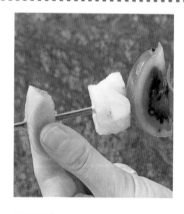 

1 Thread the fruit on short metal skewers or on satay sticks soaked in cold water for 10 minutes.

2 Baste 4 portions with 60 g unsalted butter mixed with the juice of 1 orange or lemon and 2 tbsp sugar. If the fruit is macerated, baste with marinade mixed with a little melted butter.

*Make small **kebabs** and serve in pairs for attractive presentation.*

MAKING A FRUIT BRULEE

Caramelized sugar on cream or yogurt makes a delicious topping for fruit. Fruit brûlées can be made large, or in ramekins for individual portions.

Arrange the washed, peeled and sliced fruit in serving dishes and cover with whipped double cream or Greek-style yogurt. Top with a thick layer of soft brown sugar and chill for several hours. Just before serving, place under a hot grill until the sugar has caramelized lightly and the cream or yogurt has melted over the fruit. Serve immediately.

VARYING FRUIT BRULEE

Most fruits are delicious brûléed. Try sliced peaches and halved strawberries and grapes as here, or concentrate on a more formal seasonal mixture such as summer berries, apple and pear, or exotic fruits.

PAN-FRIED AND FLAMBEED FRUIT

Flambéed fruits take on an intense flavour. Use brandy, rum, a fruit-based liqueur or a fortified wine. Warm the alcohol separately, ignite it with a taper, then pour it over the fruit.

1 Cut large fruit into wedges or slices. Sprinkle with caster sugar and a little ground cinnamon, grated nutmeg or ground mixed spice.

2 Melt a thin layer of unsalted butter in a frying pan. Turn the fruit in the butter over a medium to high heat until they are lightly browned.

3 Heat a little brandy, rum, Grand Marnier or similar alcohol for a few seconds in a separate pan, set it alight and pour it over the fruit. The flame will quickly die down.

BAKED FRUIT DESSERTS

Fruits can be baked alone, with sugar and butter or a more substantial filling. They may be cooked en papillote – wrapped in paper. Toppings can be added, such as a simple crumble or a creamed sponge.

SIMPLE BAKED APPLES

Cooking apples (Bramley's Seedling or similar) are sharp in flavour and soft in texture when baked. Dessert apples (Granny Smith's or Cox's Orange Pippin) are sweeter and more firm. Hollow out the core before filling – use sugar and a nut of butter as the basic filling. Add chopped dried fruit or nuts, cinnamon, mixed spice or grated citrus rind for additional flavour if desired.

1 Core the apples and sprinkle with lemon juice. Score the skin around the middle to prevent it from bursting during cooking.

2 Place the apples in a buttered ovenproof dish, fill with brown sugar and dot with butter. Bake at 200°C for 45–50 minutes.

IDEAS FOR STUFFING FRUIT

- *Add dried fruit (chopped if large), ground cinnamon or mixed spice, chopped nuts and grated citrus rind to the ricotta cheese.*
- *Mix sponge cake crumbs with a little grated lime rind and moisten with lime juice. Use this as a filling for papaya and serve with clotted cream.*
- *Mix fresh white breadcrumbs with some chopped walnuts, soft brown sugar and a generous sprinkling of ground cinnamon. Use to fill apples and serve with Crème Anglaise (see page 116) or with poached blackcurrants.*

STUFFED SOFT FRUIT

Baked soft fruits have an altogether different texture to apples. Nectarines, guavas and papayas can all be stuffed using this method and peaches work particularly well. Almond macaroons bring a deliciously contrasting crunchiness to soft baked fruit.

1 Prepare the stuffing first. Moisten some crushed almond macaroons with a little sherry, then stir this into some ricotta cheese. Add a touch of chopped preserved ginger to pep up the flavour of the stuffing.

2 Sprinkle halved, stoned peaches with lemon juice. Place in a buttered ovenproof dish. Use a small spoon to pile the filling into them. Bake at 180°C for 15–20 minutes, until tender and lightly browned.

STUFFED POACHED APPLES OR PEARS

To stuff and bake apples or pears, poach them lightly in syrup first (see page 14), which allows them to become tender during cooking and stops the flesh discolouring.

1 Halve and core the fruit, sprinkle it with lemon juice and poach in light syrup for about 5 minutes, or until just tender. Drain and place in a buttered ovenproof dish.

2 Moisten some chopped candied pineapple, walnuts and raisins with rum. Fill the poached fruit with this and bake at 180°C for 15 minutes. This texturally contrasting filling complements the fruit.

FRUIT PARCELS

Fruits baked 'en papillote' maintain much of their moisture and flavour. Mingle fruit flavours by wrapping several types of fruit together. Heighten the sweetness with sugar. A nut of butter added just before baking enriches the result.

2 Place the fruit on the middle of the foil, fold into a neat packet, fold the edges to seal and place on a baking dish. Bake at 190°C for about 30 minutes, until the guavas are tender.

1 Butter a double-thick rectangle of foil. Prepare the fruit. Here, nectarines and guavas are to be flavoured with some whole cardamom pods and brown sugar.

FRUITS FOR PARCELS

- *Combine halved bananas with firm strawberries and chunks of fresh or canned pineapple. Sprinkle with vanilla sugar and a little orange juice.*
- *Use quartered dessert apples and prunes, a little brandy, soft brown sugar and add a couple of whole cloves to each parcel. Sprinkle the*

finished parcel with toasted, flaked almonds.
- *Try figs with fresh nectarines. Add two split cardamoms to each parcel and trickle honey over the fruit. Serve with Greek-style yogurt.*
- *Combine rhubarb and mango and flavour with a cinnamon stick, a strip of orange rind and brown sugar.*

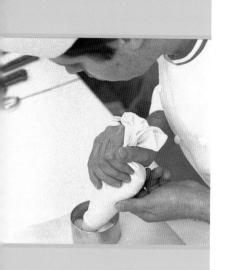

Spiced Pears

A truly Cordon Bleu treatment of a perennial favourite — pears cooked with wine — features pears first poached in a sugar syrup then pan-roasted with sweet spices, served atop a dacquoise ring topped with ganache and accompanied by a chocolate-and-red-wine sauce.

PREPARATION PLAN

- Poach the pears in advance. These can be made up to two days in advance and kept in the refrigerator until required.
- Preheat the oven to 170°C.
- Prepare and bake the dacquoise base.

For the dacquoise
70 g ground almonds
75 g icing sugar
2 tbsp flour
4 egg whites
3 tbsp granulated sugar

■ ■ ■

For the ganache
100 g bitter chocolate
100 ml cream
2 tbsp butter

■ ■ ■

For the sauce
½ bottle red wine
5 flowers star anise
200 g couverture chocolate
100 ml syrup

■ ■ ■

For the "roast" pears
4 pears, poached in sugar syrup
½ lemon
40 g honey
2 tbsp butter
Four spices: ground pepper,
cinnamon, cloves, nutmeg

■ ■ ■

Star anise
Redcurrants
Vanilla pods
Blackcurrants
Cinnamon sticks

Make the dacquoise mixture: mix together the ground almonds, icing sugar and flour. Whip the egg whites using a wire whisk. When they are almost at soft peak stage, add the granulated sugar. Whip until peaks form then gently fold in the almond, sugar and flour mixture.

Spoon the dacquoise mixture into a piping bag; pipe out four discs the same circumference as your ring mould, making the outside edges slightly thicker than the rest of the disc to act as a rim. Make an attractive flower-like shape by building up the edges with balls of dacquoise. Bake the dacquoise discs for approximately 15 minutes in a 170°C oven until golden brown. Remove from the oven and allow to cool on a metal rack.

Next, prepare the ganache: finely chop the chocolate. Warm the cream in a saucepan over a low heat then, as the cream comes to the boil, add the chocolate. Carefully mix with a wooden spoon until the chocolate has completely melted into the cream leaving a rich and creamy chocolate sauce. Add the butter and stir until smooth.

Heat the red wine in a saucepan with the star anise over a medium heat and bring to the boil. Cook until the wine has reduced by half. Drop in the couverture chocolate, add the syrup and bring to the boil again. Cook until the chocolate has completely melted. Allow to cool.

Spread the ganache in the centre of the dacquoise discs and place in the refrigerator to chill and harden. Meanwhile, pan-roast the pears: heat the butter, honey and spices in a pan. Add the pear halves and allow to cook for 5 minutes over a low flame.

Drizzle the red wine sauce around the edge of the centre of four warmed plates. Place a dacquoise disc in the centre of the sauce with two warm pear halves on top. Decorate with red- and blackcurrants, star anise, vanilla pods and cinnamon. Serves 4.

Peel the pears, slice them in half and remove the core, leaving the stalks in place for presentation. Rub with the lemon half to prevent discolouration. Make a sugar syrup (see page 108) with 250 g sugar and 500 ml water and bring to the boil. Add the pear halves, poach for 10–15 minutes, drain and set aside.

PLUM CRUMBLE

80 g unsalted butter
160 g plain flour
30 g caster sugar
1 kg firm plums, halved
and stoned
100 g sugar

Preheat the oven to 180°C. Rub the butter into the flour and stir in the caster sugar. Stone and halve the plums and place them in a fairly deep ovenproof dish, sprinkling the sugar between layers of fruit.

Sprinkle the crumble over the top. Do not press the crumble down as this will compact it and make it heavy. Bake for approximately 45 minutes, until crisp and golden on top.

MAKING FRUIT CRUMBLE

Being quick and simple to make, fruit crumbles are a classic family dessert. Try using and combining different fruit. Serve crumbles hot, with warm Crème Anglaise.

1 For a simple crumble topping, rub unsalted butter into plain flour until the mixture resembles fine breadcrumbs. Stir in the caster sugar.

2 Place a layer of fruit in an ovenproof dish and sprinkle with sugar. Repeat until all the fruit and sugar are used. Sprinkle on crumble mixture and bake until golden and crisp.

INDIVIDUAL FRUIT CRUMBLE

Fruit crumbles may also be prepared in individual, easy-to-serve portions. Use either individual soufflé dishes or ramekin dishes. Cut the fruit finely and pack it into the bottom of the dish well so that there is plenty of fruit to topping. Note that the cooking time will vary between approximately 20–30 minutes, depending on how substantial the helpings are.

CRUMBLE TOPPINGS

ROLLED OATS

Add 50 g rolled oats and the grated rind of 1 orange to 100 g plain flour. Substitute 100 g crushed almond macaroons for the sugar.

CHOCOLATE

Chop 100 g good-quality plain chocolate and add to the crumble mix. (Avoid using cooking chocolate.)

NUTS

Add 100 g finely chopped nuts, such as walnuts or toasted hazelnuts.

ALMOND

Omit the sugar and add 100 g almond macaroons instead.

FRUITS FOR CRUMBLES

Have a go at combining the fruits below with the alternative crumble mixtures (below, left) for some tasty variations.

BLACKCURRANTS
. . . .
Try blackcurrants with a chocolate-crumble topping.

DRIED PEACHES
. . . .
Mix ready-to-eat dried peaches with rhubarb.

PEARS
. . . .
Combine pears with nectarines.

EVE'S PUDDING

Tempting Eve's pudding is a homely sweet of apples topped with a light and deliciously creamy sponge. The method works equally well with other fruits, so try varying it throughout the year, using seasonally available produce. (See the variations below for some ideas.)

1 Peel, core and slice 500 g cooking apples. Place in a deep ovenproof dish – ideally a soufflé dish. Sprinkle with lemon juice and 100 g caster sugar.

2 Preheat the oven to 160°C. Prepare a half quantity of Steamed Sponge Pudding mixture (see page 144) and spread it lightly over the fruit. Bake for 1–1¼ hours, until the pudding has risen and is set.

VARYING EVE'S PUDDING

- *Use sliced rhubarb and add 1 tbsp ground ginger to the sponge with the flour.*
- *Sprinkle dried elderflowers or elderflower cordial on to a fruit-base of fresh gooseberries.*
- *Skin and slice peaches for the fruit. Add a few drops of rosewater to the sponge mixture and sprinkle on some flaked almonds before baking.*
- *Replace 2 tbsp flour with 2 tbsp desiccated coconut in the sponge mixture. Use tropical fruits such as mango or papaya.*
- *Try dark soft fruits, such as blackberries and black-currants with a light lemon sponge.*

BREAD & FRUIT SWEETS

Bread may seem an unglamorous dessert ingredient, but many classic recipes make excellent use of it. For memorable results, select fine quality bread – but not too fresh and doughy. Trim the crusts and cut even slices.

SUMMER PUDDING

Making this classic British dessert requires a little forward planning – allow time for pressing it overnight, so that the fruit juices are thoroughly soaked into the bread and the pudding is set in its shape well.

SUMMER PUDDING

Approximately 12 bread slices, with crusts removed
250 g blackcurrants and/or redcurrants, preferably a mixture
150 g sugar
250 g mixed berries, such as strawberries, raspberries, mulberries and blueberries
2 tbsp water

Set the pudding in a deep 1.25 litre pudding basin. Line the basin neatly with the bread slices, trimming off the excess bread. Reserve the neatest slices for when you come to cover the fruit filling.

Place the blackcurrants and redcurrants in a pan with the sugar. Add 2 tbsp water and cook gently, stirring occasionally until the sugar has dissolved and the juice runs from the fruit. Simmer for 5 minutes, then remove from the heat. Cut any large strawberries into halves or quarters, then add them to the currants with the other berries.

Spoon some of the juice from the mixture into the basin lined with bread, then fill it with the fruit, pressing the filling down well. Top with bread and cover with a saucer. Stand the basin on a dish to catch any spillage and place a heavy weight on top of the saucer. Chill overnight. Invert on to a flat platter and remove the basin just before serving.

MAKING SUMMER PUDDING

A traditional pudding basin is the perfect shape for this dessert. Make sure you position the bread neatly for an attractive finish.

1 Line the basin with bread slices. Begin with a circle of bread that is cut to the right size to fit the base, then overlap slices evenly around the side.

2 Lightly cook the currants with sugar until plenty of juice has been yielded. Mix the raw berries with the currants and spoon some of the juices over the bread before filling the basin.

3 Make sure that the fruit is packed well into the pudding basin. Then cover the fruit with bread, ensuring it is completely covered with an even layer.

4 If there is any juice remaining, spoon this over the top layer of bread. Stand the basin in a dish to catch any overspill of juice, cover and weight, then chill overnight. Remove from the refrigerator when ready to serve. If there is any juice pooled on the dish, spoon it over the pudding when it has been unmoulded, particularly over any bread which has not soaked up the juice.

5 Hold a flat serving platter over the basin and turn both simultaneously.

6 Place the platter on a table and lift off the pudding basin very carefully, so as not to disturb the surface of the pudding. Decorate with fresh berries and serve immediately.

VARYING SUMMER PUDDING

A variety of fresh, frozen or canned fruit can be used in place of the summer berries shown here. Colour is important, as without it, the bread tends to look insipid. If you wish to use pale fruits, make a syrup (see page 108), simmer some orange rind in it and use it to cook the fruit. Try the following suggestions:

▪ *Autumn Pudding*
Poach diced pears in a cider syrup until tender, then add blackcurrants and stoned, quartered plums for about 1 minute.

▪ *Winter Pudding*
Pre-soak dried fruit, such as apricots, peaches, mango, figs and prunes overnight in unsweetened apple juice until plump. Drain them, reserving the juice, and slice. Cook peeled, cored and diced apple in the juice with the grated rind of 1 orange until tender. Mix in the soaked fruit.

EXOTIC FRUIT PUDDING

Fragrant exotic fruits may be prepared as for Summer Pudding (see previous page). Make a syrup flavoured with mixed citrus as the base for the firm fruits, which should be cut finely.

1 Squeeze the juice from 1 lime, 1 lemon and 1 orange. Cut the fruit into chunks. Bring the juice and shells to the boil with 300 ml water, cover and simmer for 30 minutes.

2 Strain the liquid and boil for 2 minutes with 100 g sugar. Cool slightly. Add 500 g fruit: diced melon, mango, pineapple, papaya and guava; halved lychees or physalis. Assemble as for Summer Pudding to complete.

Tropical colours and flavours give this pudding its charm. It can be decorated with pieces of sliced fruit and served with whipped or clotted cream. **Exotic Fruit Pudding** *and Summer Pudding can also be made in individual ramekin dishes or pudding moulds.*

INDIVIDUAL SCANDINAVIAN CHARLOTTES

This classic dessert of fried breadcrumbs and fruit is cooked in individual dishes, such as standard sized ramekins. Use good quality fruits for the best results. Serve Scandinavian Charlottes chilled, with ice cream or whipped cream.

1 Cook 100 g fresh white breadcrumbs and 1 tsp ground cinnamon in 75 g unsalted butter until crisp and golden. Stir in 50 g soft brown sugar and cook for a few seconds.

2 Stew 600 g fruit, such as the plums here. Cook to a thick pulp (but not a purée), adding sugar to taste. Use apples, apricots, black-currants or a fruit mixture.

3 Base-line six ramekins with baking parchment. Layer the breadcrumbs and fruit in the dishes. Begin and end with the breadcrumbs. Cool, then cover and chill for several hours.

4 Loosen the puddings with a knife and invert on to plates. Remove the baking parchment and serve.

BAKED FRUIT CHARLOTTE

In a cooked version of the Summer Pudding method, crisp, golden bread encases tender fruit in this family pudding. Serve hot, with cream, yogurt or warm Crème Anglaise (see page 116).

1 Trim the crusts off 4–5 bread slices, halve them, then cut off an acute angle with a round cutter to form curved-ended wedges.

2 Arrange the wedges in the base of a generously buttered charlotte mould, then press them down.

3 Line the side of the mould with a neat layer of bread, overlapping the slices to ensure there are no gaps in the bread layer. Brush the bread with melted unsalted butter.

4 Peel, core and slice 500 g cooking apples. Cook with 100 g sugar until tender (not pulpy). Add 50 g raisins, 4 peeled, sliced peaches and the grated rind of 1 orange. Once softened, place the fruit in the mould.

5 Butter bread triangles on one side and use to top the fruit, buttered-side down. Brush with more butter and bake at 180°C for 1 hour, until golden. Unmould and serve.

DRIED FRUIT DESSERTS

Widely used with other ingredients, dried fruits come into their own when
they take centre stage. Buy high quality produce in sealed packets. Ready-
to-eat dried fruits, such as apricots and prunes, do not require soaking.

MAKING DRIED FRUIT COMPOTE

*Any variety of dried fruit may be used, either alone or mixed.
This compote, made of 100 g cherries and 250 g ready-to-eat
peaches, can be served warm or chilled with many desserts.*

Heat 300 ml dry white wine
with 100 g sugar and 50 g
blanched, slivered almonds.
Once the sugar has dissolved,
add the dried fruit. Cover and
simmer gently for 20 minutes.
Stir in 4 tbsp either brandy or
kirsch and set aside to cool.
Serve this compote with an
appropriate dessert such as a
light vanilla cheesecake or a
steamed sponge, or on toast
flavoured with cinnamon and
icing sugar and topped with
clotted cream.

FRUIT IN ALCOHOL SYRUP

*This tasty alcoholic preserve can be stored for up to a year. Use it as a topping for cream-filled
tartlets or baked custard tartlets, or serve with ice creams or chilled soufflés. It also makes a
good accompaniment for pancakes, waffles or steamed sponge puddings.*

2 Place the ready-to-eat
dried fruits, such as
apricots, peaches, papaya
and pineapple in a sterilized
preserving jar. Any mixture
of complementary fruits
may be used – try adding
apple rings and figs. Place
a cinnamon stick and a few
cloves in with the fruit for
added flavour.

1 Dissolve 200 g sugar in
200 ml water to make a
syrup. Remove from the heat
and add 600 ml either brandy
or rum. Allow to cool.

3 Pour the syrup over the
fruit. Shake the jar to
ensure all the air bubbles are
removed. Cover and store in
a cool, dark place for at least
one month before use.

PRUNES IN ARMAGNAC

This is a classic method of transforming prunes into a fabulous, if somewhat alcoholic, fruit preserve. Traditionally, ordinary dried prunes were used. Once the preserve is ready to eat, it may be served with a wide variety of desserts or on its own as a simple end-of-meal treat.

Pack stoned, ready-to-eat prunes in a large preserving jar and cover with Armagnac or another brandy. Ensure that there are no air bubbles in the jar, seal it tightly and leave for at least a month. Store for up to one year.

Brandy-preserved prunes can be served in brandy-snap baskets filled with mascarpone, with toasted flaked almonds and crystallized orange zest (see page 205).

MAKING MINCEMEAT

This festive British preserve should be prepared at least one month before use, preferably three months ahead of time. This allows the flavours time to develop.

MINCEMEAT

100 g candied citron and orange peel
100 g blanched almonds
250 g each of currants, raisins and sultanas
500 g cooking apples, peeled and cored
Grated rind and juice of 1 orange and 1 lemon
250 g soft brown sugar
1 tsp ground cinnamon
1 tsp grated nutmeg
1 tsp ground mixed spice
200 ml brandy
100 ml dry sherry
150 g shredded suet

Chop the citron and orange peel, the almonds, currants, raisins, sultanas and apples. Mix with the orange and lemon rind and juice in a large bowl. Stir in the sugar, spices and alcohol. Leave to macerate for 2–3 days, stirring occasionally.

Stir in the suet. Spoon into pots, pressing down well. Seal, label and store in a cool place. Makes approximately 2.5 kg.

1 Chop all the fruit, peel and nuts. Mix with the citrus rind and juice in a large bowl, then stir in the sugar, spices, brandy and sherry. Cover and leave to stand for 2–3 days, stirring once or twice a day.

2 Mix in the suet and spoon the mincemeat into sterilized preserving jars. Press it down well with a spoon. Seal tightly, label, and store in a cool, dark place.

MINCE PIES

These traditional Christmas treats are simple to make once the mincemeat has been prepared.

1 Add the grated rind of 1 orange to Pâte Sucrée (see page 122). Roll out the pastry and cut circles to line patty tins. Fill to two-thirds full with mincemeat, dampen pastry edges with egg wash (see page 123) and press on pastry circles as lids.

2 Using a sharp knife, make a neat hole in the top of each pie and brush with milk. Chill the pies for 30 minutes, then bake at 180°C for 25 minutes. Cool in the tin for 10 minutes to allow the pastry to set, then transfer on to a wire rack to cool.

As with mincemeat, Christmas Pudding should be made at least one month before it is consumed, to allow the flavours plenty of time to blend and mature. The basic pudding recipe can be varied slightly to suit your particular taste. For example, chopped prunes, dried figs and/or apricots can be added. Crystallised or chopped candied ginger and candied pineapple are succulent additions. A few drops of pure oil of bitter almonds can be added, but take care not to add more or the flavour will dominate the pudding.

Serve with Brandy Sauce (see page 000), Hard Sauce (see page 000) or whipped cream.

CHRISTMAS PUDDING

350 g currants
250 g each of raisins and sultanas
100 g candied citron and orange peel, finely chopped
Grated rind and juice of 1 orange
100 g ground almonds
1 tsp ground cinnamon
1 tsp grated nutmeg
1 tsp ground mixed spice
150 g dark soft brown sugar
200 g shredded suet
200 g fresh white breadcrumbs
150 g plain flour
2 eggs
100 ml stout, such as Guinness
4 tbsp brandy or rum
2 tbsp black treacle

Grease two 1 litre pudding basins. Cut double thick circles of baking parchment and foil large enough to cover the tops of the basins.

Mix the currants, sultanas, raisins, candied peels, orange rind, almonds, spices, sugar and suet in a large bowl. Stir in the breadcrumbs and flour.

Beat the eggs, then stir in the stout, orange juice, brandy or rum and treacle. Mix the liquids with the dry ingredients until they are well combined. Divide the mixture between the two basins, pressing it down well, cover with parchment and foil, folding the foil securely on the rims of the basins to prevent any steam from entering.

Steam the puddings over boiling water for 6 hours, topping up the water when necessary. Uncover, then cover loosely with kitchen paper and leave to cool. Cover with fresh foil and baking parchment. Wrap tightly in polythene bags and store in a cool place. Steam the puddings for 2 more hours before serving. Makes two puddings, each serving 8

1 Stir the fruit and sugar with crumbs and flour. ADD A

2 Beat the eggs then add the wet ingredients. ADD A LINE

3 Mix the liquids and the dry ingredients until thoroughly combined.

ICED DESSERTS

SORBETS & GRANITAS

·

ICE CREAMS

·

PARFAITS & BOMBES

·

ICE CREAM GATEAUX

·

ICED SOUFFLES

·

SHAPING ICE CREAM

·

ICE BOWLS

SORBETS & GRANITAS

Based on fruit or wine syrup, or smooth fruit purée, sorbets and granitas combine punchy flavours with a cleansing iciness, making them ideal for summertime desserts or as between-course palate cleansers.

PINK CHAMPAGNE SORBET

400 g sugar
400 ml water
1 bottle Pink Champagne
Juice of 1 lemon

Dissolve the sugar in the water over a low heat, then bring the syrup to the boil. Stir in the wine and lemon juice. Set aside the wine syrup to cool. Freeze in a sorbetière until smooth, firm and white. Serve at once, or transfer to a container and freeze. Serves 12.

Simple Syrup Sorbets

Omit the wine for fruit syrups. For citrus sorbets, add the juice and thinly pared rind of 3 limes, lemons or oranges to 1 litre water with the sugar. (Add the juice of 1 lemon to orange syrup mix. For grapefruit sorbet use 2 fruit. Add 6 mint sprigs to lemon juice for mint.) Strain once cooled. Apricot, peach or mango sorbets use 1 litre fruit juice instead of water. Add the juice of 1 lemon.

FREEZING SORBET

To obtain a smooth texture, sorbet must be frozen rapidly so that few ice crystals form. Constant churning breaks down ice. A sorbetière both freezes and churns simultaneously.

An electric sorbetière or ice cream machine churns the sorbet constantly during freezing until smooth and firm. A food processor is the best alternative. Chill the bowl and blade before use and set the freezer to fast-freeze. Place the mixture in the freezer until a wide, frozen rim has formed on the surface, then remove and blend until smooth.

*Mango slices and a twist of lime give **mango sorbet** a tropical finish. Scooped melon makes an ideal bowl for **melon sorbet** with a mint crown. A zig-zag trim and candied zest on **orange sorbet** provides refreshing brightness.*

PIPING SORBET

Once prepared and slightly softened, sorbet can be piped for decorative effects. Chill the piping bag and nozzle beforehand.

HOLLOWED FRUIT
Pipe sorbet into fruit shells and freeze before serving. Alternatively, pipe sorbet into chilled serving glasses and freeze until required.

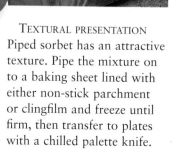

TEXTURAL PRESENTATION
Piped sorbet has an attractive texture. Pipe the mixture on to a baking sheet lined with either non-stick parchment or clingfilm and freeze until firm, then transfer to plates with a chilled palette knife.

MULLED WINE GRANITA

175 g caster sugar
Pared rind of 1 orange
80 ml orange juice
2 tbsp lemon juice
1 x 8 cm cinnamon stick
2 cloves
130 ml water
750 ml Burgundy or other red wine
Candied julienne of orange rind or mint sprigs to decorate

Place the sugar, orange and lemon juice, rind, cinnamon and cloves in a saucepan. Pour in the water and wine and heat gently, stirring, until the sugar has dissolved. Bring slowly to the boil, reduce the heat and simmer for 2–3 minutes. Set aside until cold.

Strain the mulled wine through a fine sieve into a shallow freezer container. Freeze until firm. Chill eight servings glasses. Scrape the granita into crystals and spoon them into the chilled glasses. Decorate with candied julienne of orange rind and mint sprigs. Serves 8.

FRUIT PUREE SORBET

Sorbets that are made from fruit purée are light and refreshing. Prepare 500 ml smooth fruit purée, such as raspberry, blueberry, peach, strawberry, mango, papaya, nectarine or melon. Make a syrup with 175 g sugar in 150 ml water and stir into the purée. Refrigerate until cold, then freeze the sweetened purée in an electric sorbetière or a food processor as described (see opposite page).

GRANITA

Crunchy, finely crushed ice crystals are the signature of this cooling Italian dessert. A syrup with a full, punchy flavour is essential and fruit juice or wine, white or red, may be used with, or instead of, water. While strong and sweet espresso coffee is the secret of the classic coffee granita, delicate aromatic teas can be used to make refreshingly light granita. Herbs and spices can give crunchy ices interesting flavour twists. Try mint or lemon balm with lemon, bay with apple juice, or mulling spices with red wine.

SPOONING
The syrup can be frozen and the granita scraped off in crystals when it is served.

SERVING
Chill glasses in advance. If possible, frost them in the freezer. Portions of granita should be modest, so long-stemmed glasses with small bowls or small cupped dishes are ideal.

FORKING
Freeze the syrup until half frozen. Then crush the ice crystals using a fork and mix them with the unfrozen syrup. Repeat this process several times, until the mixture is evenly frozen in small crystals, giving it a 'slushy' appearance and texture.

Strawberry Vacherins

The traditional meringue and cream dessert is here given a new twist. Individual meringue nests, filled with strawberry sorbet and topped with fresh berries and redcurrants and a further spoonful of sorbet, are set afloat on baked crème brûlée custard, flavoured with thyme.

PREPARATION PLAN

▶ Create the meringue nests.
▶ Prepare the strawberry sorbet.
▶ Cook the crème brûlée custard.
▶ Apply a coating of whipped cream and sponge crumbs to the meringue nests.

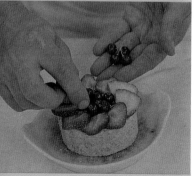

For the Italian Meringue
250 g sugar
60 ml water
5 egg whites

• • •

For the strawberry sorbet
300 g strawberries
150 ml water
150 g sugar
Juice of 1 lemon

• • •

For the thyme crème brûlée
125 ml milk
1 tsp dried thyme
6 egg yolks
100 g sugar
350 ml cream

• • •

Sponge crumbs
Whipped cream for coating
A little sugar for caramelizing
400 g strawberries
Redcurrants
Thyme

1 Prepare an Italian Meringue with the sugar, water and egg whites (see page 68). Transfer to a piping bag and pipe small discs on to circles marked on baking parchment with a small plain nozzle. Pipe one or two layers to form a rim around the edge and smooth the outside with a palette knife. Cook for about 1 hour at 100°C.

2 Make the sorbet. Clean and trim the strawberries and purée them in a food processor. Remove the puréed fruit and strain through a metal sieve. Bring the water and sugar to the boil. Allow to cool. Mix the fruit, syrup and lemon juice together. Turn the mixture into a sorbetière (see page 32) and churn until smooth and frozen. Alternatively make the sorbet by hand. Clean and trim the strawberries

and chill the bowl and blade of a food processor. Place the strawberries in the bowl and process the fruit to a smooth paste. Set the freezer to fast-freeze and place the mixture in it until a wide, frozen rim has formed on the surface. Remove them from the freezer and blend again until smooth. Repeat this process until your sorbet reaches the required consistency then remove from the food processor bowl and return to the freezer until ready to use.

3 Prepare the crème brûlée. Bring the milk to the boil, add the thyme and infuse for 10 minutes. Whisk the egg yolks with the sugar, whisk in the cream, the infused milk, then strain. Fill shallow porcelain dishes (13 cm wide and 3 cm deep) to a depth of 5 mm and bake at 90°C for 10 minutes. Remove from the oven and set aside to cool.

4 Coat the outside edges of the meringue nests with a layer of whipped cream and roll them through a layer of sponge crumbs to coat the cream.

5 Dredge the surface of the crème brûlée custards with sugar and caramelize the sugar with a blow torch. Alternatively place the custards under a hot grill until the sugar forms a crisp golden brown crust.

6 Slice more strawberries and set aside. Fill the centres of the meringue nests with the strawberry sorbet and arrange the strawberry slices around the rim of the nest. Fill the centre of the strawberry circle with redcurrants. Place ½ scoop of sorbet on top and garnish with thyme. Place the filled meringue on the crème brûlée and serve immediately.

What's in a Name?

Vacherin is also the name given to several cow's milk cheeses that have a soft texture and washed rind. The dessert is said to resemble the cheese in shape and colour – hence the name.

ICE CREAMS

Ice cream has an elusive quality of understated richness. When frozen, creamy, well-flavoured mixtures are light on the palate. Transformed by sophisticated presentation, they can make spectacular finales.

PREPARING RICH VANILLA ICE CREAM

A vanilla custard enriched with whipped cream makes good ice cream which can be flavoured in many ways. Freezing the mixture in a sorbetière or ice cream churn gives the best results. A good standard can also be achieved in a food processor, but the ice cream mixture has to be processed frequently for a smooth result.

1 Prepare 1 quantity Crème Anglaise (see page 116) and cool it in a bowl set over a container of ice, stirring continuously to prevent a skin from forming on the surface.

2 Keep stirring the mixture continuously to ensure a smooth texture. Whip 250 ml whipping cream very lightly and fold this into the custard until they are evenly combined.

3 Churn and freeze the custard in a sorbetière. Or use a food processor (see page 32), freezing the custard in a chilled container that is large enough to allow it to spread thinly and freeze quite quickly.

VARIATIONS ON A BASIC ICE CREAM

CHOCOLATE OR COFFEE
....

Blend 2 tbsp cocoa powder or 1 tbsp instant coffee with 2 tbsp icing sugar and 3 tbsp boiling water. Cool, then stir into the chilled custard. Alternatively, melt the chocolate or coffee in the milk when preparing the custard.

WHISKY AND GINGER
....

Add 4 tbsp whisky to the chilled custard. Fold in 50 g chopped candied or stem ginger before the final freezing.

RATAFIA
....

Fold in 100 g crushed ratafia biscuits before the final freezing.

4 Process the mixture until smooth and thick, then place in a container and freeze until firm.

FRUIT ICE CREAM

Fruit purées with whipped cream make a good alternative to custard for ice cream. They tend to freeze hard, so sweeten well, whisk in egg whites or mix in alcohol for softer results.

1 Prepare 300 ml fruit purée and sieve to remove seeds. Add lemon juice to less acidic fruits, such as strawberries, blueberries or, as here, ripe cherries. Sweeten with 2–4 tbsp icing sugar, depending on how sweet the fruit is.

2 Whip 300 ml double cream until it stands in soft peaks, then fold it into the fruit purée. Freeze the mixture in a sorbetière or in the freezer, whisking it several times until smooth.

RIPPLES

To make a ripple, part-mix Rich Vanilla Ice Cream with an ice cream of a contrasting flavour and colour. Powerful in both look and taste, blackcurrant ice cream is ideal.

Cut and fold equal quantities of the two ices together just before the final freezing. If frozen ice creams are used, soften them slightly so that they can be rippled easily.

CRUSHED MERINGUE FOR SOFT RESULTS

WITH PREPARED ICE CREAM
Add 100 g crushed cooked meringue and the desired quantity of chocolate chips to vanilla ice cream and mix well. This gives the ice cream sweetness and a soft texture.

WITH HOMEMADE ICE CREAM
Make blackcurrant ice cream following the steps for Fruit Ice Cream (above, left). Fold in the crushed meringue after the cream. This mixture may be frozen until firm without churning or whisking

PARFAITS & BOMBES

Parfaits are distinctively smooth and creamy frozen syrup desserts. Bombes provide an exciting way of presenting ice creams. These chilled summer sweets may be served individually or enjoyed in a combination dessert.

PREPARING A PARFAIT

1 Prepare a syrup by boiling 100 g sugar in 50 ml water to the soft-ball stage (see page 108). Whisk together 1 egg and 5 yolks. Add the syrup slowly in a thin stream, whisking until cold and thick.

2 Whip 500 ml double cream until it stands in soft peaks. Fold this into the egg and syrup mixture, making sure that all the ingredients are thoroughly mixed before proceeding to the next step.

3 Tape collars of non-stick parchment around four 8 cm metal rings, ensuring they rise 2 cm over the rims. Stand the rings on a baking sheet lined with parchment and pour in the mixture to the height of the collars.

4 Level the surface with a palette knife and freeze until firm. The parfaits are easily unmoulded by briefly wrapping a hot tea-towel around the rings once the collars are removed.

*A neat collar of broken nuts gives a contrasting texture and apricot slices provide an attractive splash of colour. Arrange the slices around the **parfait** and drizzle a little caramel across them. Try different moulds for varying effects, such as a loaf or fluted tin. Stick to clean shapes as **parfait** may be removed from these more easily than from intricate moulds.*

FLAVOURING PARFAIT

VANILLA

Add 1 vanilla pod or a pinch of vanilla powder to the eggs when whisking.

CHOCOLATE

Instead of 1 egg and 5 yolks, use simply 3 yolks. Melt 150 g good-quality plain chocolate and fold this into the parfait mixture before adding the whipped cream.

RUM AND GLACÉ FRUIT

Soak 175 g mixed chopped glacé fruit and peel in rum for at least one hour, until soft, then drain and fold into the parfait mix before adding the cream.

BRANDY OR LIQUEUR

Before whipping the cream, add 5 tbsp brandy, Grand Marnier or cassis.

HAZELNUT

Fold in 100 g finely ground toasted hazelnuts before adding the cream.

COFFEE

Add 100 g coarsely crushed, roasted coffee beans to 150 ml milk and heat gently. Just before the milk begins to boil, remove from heat, cover and set aside until cold. Strain through a fine sieve into the cream before whipping.

SERVING PARFAIT

Try these different serving suggestions for plain parfait.

- *Sprinkle on a thick layer of fine-quality cocoa before unmoulding. Serve with Chocolate Sauce (see page 115). Decorate with White Chocolate Caraque (see page 203).*
- *Place on circles of thin, liqueur-moistened sponge and decorate with piped whipped cream and fresh fruit. Serve with a Melba Sauce (see page 115).*
- *Serve with a Fruit Coulis (see page 113). Add sugar or chocolate shapes (see page 198) to decorate.*

MAKING PERFECT BOMBES

The layers of contrasting colours and flavours in bombes appeal to both eye and palate. Use soft, freshly-made ice cream. Fold in chunks of fresh fruit if desired, reserving some for decoration. Create either horizontal layers, or domed layers to echo the mould shape. Ensure that each layer is of an even thickness for a neat presentation. Parfait may substitute for a layer of ice cream to create a variety of textures.

1 Stand the bombe mould in a bowl of ice. Using a metal spoon, spread freshly-made Vanilla Ice Cream (see page 36) around the mould in an even layer. Make the Blackcurrant Parfait whilst the first layer is freezing (which will take about 45 minutes).

2 Once the first layer is firm, level the top with the rim of the mould using a sharp knife. Fill the recess with the second layer up to the rim. Cut a circle of non-stick parchment to the same size as the lid and place it on top of the ice cream before closing, and freeze as before.

BOMBE MOULD

A traditional bombe mould is a bell-shaped, curved metal vessel with a base stand and lid. Some have a screw in the base that may be tightened once filled. Unscrewing allows air into the mould which releases the frozen bombe. A deep, freezer-proof basin of an appropriate shape may be used in place of a traditional mould.

ICE CREAM GATEAU

Ice cream gâteau is easy to prepare, yet looks spectacular. Use a layer of parfait for both visual and textural contrast and add the finishing touches just before serving.

GATEAU WITH A SPONGE BASE

Use a thin layer of light sponge (see page 118), cut to the same size as the mould for the base. Here Rich Vanilla Ice Cream (see page 36) is flavoured with 225 g finely chopped skinned pistachio nuts for the top layer and a Chocolate Parfait forms the other layer. Once frozen, unmould the dessert on to a chilled platter, decorate and refreeze.

1 Spoon the first layer, here, pistachio ice cream, into the base of the mould. It is important to make the layers even in depth, so do not over fill the mould with the first layer. Freeze until firm.

2 Once the first layer is firm, spoon in the second layer – here, chocolate parfait. Run the spoon over the surface of the parfait to make it smooth and even in preparation for the next layer.

3 Place the thin sponge (moistened with a drizzling of a liqueur such as Crème de Cacao) on top of the chocolate parfait layer. Cover the gâteau and freeze. When ready, unmould the gâteau by inverting the mould and wrapping a warm tea towel around it.

4 Decorate the gâteau by spreading a thin layer of whipped cream around the side and pressing on skinned, chopped pistachio nuts. Cover the top with cream and pipe on some Ganache (see page 111). The gâteau can be returned to the freezer at this stage and transferred to the refrigerator about 20 minutes before serving. Finish it with chocolate decorations (see page 198).

ICED SOUFFLES

An iced soufflé is basically an uncooked dessert soufflé. Without gelatine as a setting agent, it is frozen until firm, but the mixture retains a light, airy texture that works wonderfully with fruit flavours.

ICED SOUFFLES

Use the proportions for a standard chilled soufflé (see page 56), omitting the gelatine. Mousse mixtures (see page 61) also freeze well, giving the required firm but aerated texture. Prepare a 1.5 litre soufflé dish as for a chilled soufflé (see page 56).

1 Prepare 350 ml fruit purée (see page 113). (Lemon purée is used here.) Fold in 1 quantity Italian Meringue (see page 68). Whip 400 ml double cream until it stands in soft peaks and fold it into the mixture.

2 Tape a collar of acetate around the rim of the soufflé dish so that it rises a couple of centimetres above the rim. Turn the mixture into the dish so that it reaches the top of the acetate collar.

3 Dip a palette knife in warm water, shake off the excess and smooth the top of the soufflé mixture. Freeze until the soufflé is firm – for about 2 hours, depending on your freezer.

PREPARING INDIVIDUAL SOUFFLES

Prepare small soufflés in ramekin dishes rather than individual soufflé dishes, which tend to be too large for desserts. In ramekins, the soufflé freezes quickly and is easy to serve. Scale down the size of the decoration for individual portions. For example, use a small nozzle for piping cream, or small fruits such as redcurrants, raspberries, blueberries, crystallized violets, sugared, kumquats or chocolate-coated coffee beans.

4 About 20 minutes (or less, if possible) before serving, peel away the collar and smooth the sides. Pipe on whipped cream and chill until ready to serve.

SHAPING ICE CREAM

**Making ice cream is only half the work. Beautiful presentation adds
greatly to the pleasure to be gained. Use these techniques to fire your
imagination and also to shape sorbets, parfaits, soufflés and mousses.**

TEXTURED SCOOPS

*Prepare more ice cream than is needed, to allow for perfect presentation and freeze in a deep
container. Keep a baking sheet or plastic tray lined with non-stick parchment
handy on which to place the ice cream once shaped.*

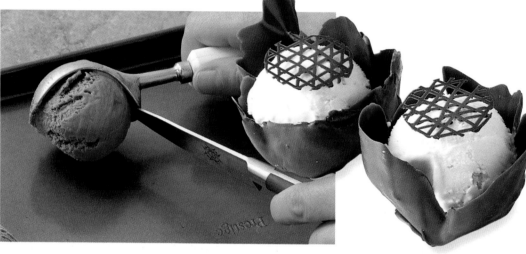

1 Dip the scoop into cold
water and shake off the
excess. Press the scoop down
firmly into the ice cream at a
slight angle. When it is firmly
embedded in the ice cream,
give the scoop a complete
twist, then pull it up
with more pressure
on the open side of
the scoop.

2 Hold the scoop close to the baking sheet and jerk the
wrist to loosen the ice cream. If it fails to free itself, use
the point of a knife to encourage it on to the baking sheet.

*Ice cream scoops sit perfectly
in chocolate cups (see page 202)
and are topped with finely piped
chocolate lattices.*

QUENELLES

*Use two metal spoons to
make quenelles or smooth
ovals. This technique takes
a little practice to perfect.*

*Serve ovals of contrasting flavoured
ice cream on crisp **tuile**
biscuits.*

1 Dip a spoon
in cold water,
shake off the excess,
then slide it sideways
down into the ice
cream. Turn it upwards
and lift simultaneously.

2 Use a second spoon
to shape the top of
the oval. Once in shape,
twist it gently to loosen it
from the first spoon and
slide it sideways on to a
baking sheet.

CUTTING SHAPES

Freeze ice cream in a baking tray for an even slab from which to slice and stamp shapes. To remove the ice cream, invert the tray and wrap it in a warm tea towel.

1 Mark out the positions for all the cuts on the slab, then apply even pressure on to the knife. Rinse the knife in hot water between each cut.

2 Cut the strips in one direction, then in the opposite direction. Take care not to move the strips as you work – this will result in misshapen diamonds.

SLICING

Ice cream frozen in a loaf tin or oblong mould can be sliced into neat shapes. A straight-sided, shallow container with sharp square angles around the base creates a good shape for slicing. Base-line the mould with non-stick parchment. Slice the ice cream on a chilled board, then transfer the slices to a lined baking sheet and freeze until firm before serving.

Rinse a large chef's knife in hot water. Apply pressure with one hand, then gradually apply more pressure with the other hand to slice through the ice cream. This creates slices with smooth sides. (Avoid using a sawing action.) Rinse the knife in hot water and wipe it between each cut.

STAMPING SHAPES

Stamping creates ice cream shapes with wonderfully clean lines. Use the same stamp to cut matching biscuit shapes and sandwich the ice cream between these.

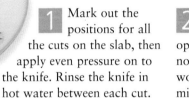

Use a metal cutter rinsed with hot water to stamp out shapes. Leave them in position. Using a knife with a small point, cut away the mixture surrounding the stamped shapes.

ICE BOWLS

Delicate flowers and leaves suspended in a bowl made of ice make a
beautiful container in which to serve fresh fruit, ice creams and sorbets.
With care, an ice bowl can be used more than once.

MAKING AN ICE BOWL

There are moulds available that have
been specially designed for making
ice bowls, consisting of two
plastic bowls that clip
together, leaving a gap in
which to pour the water
and place the flowers.
Ordinary freezerproof
bowls work just as
well. Try making
individual ice bowls
with small bowls.

1 Use two freezer-
proof bowls, one
slightly smaller than the
other. Pour a little water into
the larger bowl, add some
flowers, ferns or petals, such as
pansies and geranium leaves,
and freeze until hard.

2 Stand the smaller bowl
on the ice. Weight it to
stop it from floating, then
pour some water between
the bowls and add more
flowers. Freeze until hard.
Repeat the process until
the gap between the bowls
is filled with flowers in ice.

3 If necessary, wipe the
inside of the inner bowl
with a hot cloth, then wrap
the cloth around the outer
bowl to release the ice bowl.
Store the ice bowl in the
freezer until ready for use.

SAVING AN ICE BOWL

Stand the ice bowl on a
platter to take it to the table,
serve, then return the bowl
to the freezer immediately.
With ice bowls, the contents
should be removed as soon
as possible. If you intend to
save an ice bowl and are
using it to serve ice cream,
try and avoid getting traces
of ice cream stuck to the
bowl by making sure that
the scoops of ice cream are
frozen separately, until they
are quite firm, before placing
them in the bowl. Scrape off
any small traces of ice cream
with a rigid plastic spatula.

CUSTARDS, CREAMS & WHIPS

BAKED CUSTARDS
·
MOULDED CUSTARDS
·
FOOLS, CREAMS & WHIPS

BAKED CUSTARDS

With custards, the proportion of egg yolk and white to milk determines the texture – whites set custard while yolks make it creamy. Using whole eggs with yolks makes it easier to unmould desserts when chilled.

TURNED-OUT BAKED CUSTARD

The classic Crème Caramel (bottom, left) is simple yet sophisticated, with the emphasis on gentle cooking. If the heat is too high when cooking a custard, it will separate and curdle. To rescue it, remove from the heat and beat with a spoon or whisk until blended. For Crème Caramel, prepare a caramel (see page 109) with 100 g sugar and 60 ml water. Make a custard with 2 eggs, 2 egg yolks, 30 g caster sugar, ½ tsp vanilla extract and 500 ml milk. Fill the moulds as below and bake at 160°C for 40 minutes. Cool and chill overnight. Makes 4.

1 Pour caramel into the moulds when it is deep golden in colour. Roll the moulds around to coat the insides evenly.

2 Pour in the custard and bake them, standing the moulds in an inch of water to prevent curdling at the sides before the centres are set.

FLAVOURING CUSTARDS

ORANGE

Infuse the grated rind of 1 orange in the hot milk for 30 minutes. Serve orange custard with fine strips of crystallized julienne of orange (see page 205) and some orange segments (see page 104).

COFFEE

Add 2 tbsp coffee essence to the eggs or infuse 50 g coarsely crushed beans with the milk for 30 minutes. Strain the milk before adding to the eggs. Serve with Crème Chantilly (see page 116) and decorate with mint and chocolate-coated coffee beans.

CHOCOLATE

Stir the hot custard into 100 g melted high-quality plain or bitter chocolate. Bake for 40 minutes.

ALMOND

Heat 225 g blanched almonds with the milk until it is just about to boil, then set aside until cold. Purée the milk and nuts together in a blender, then strain the milk mixture through a fine sieve before using it to make the custard.

RICH BAKED CUSTARDS

To make soft, creamy custards, use either egg yolks or a small proportion of whole egg. For Petits Pots de Crème, which are baked in ramekins, use 5 yolks to 500 ml milk or single cream. For a Crème Brûlée, (shown right) combine 5 yolks with 500 ml double cream. Once chilled, top the custards with a thick layer of brown sugar and place under a hot grill until caramelized. Once cooled, the topping forms a crisp crust.

FLAVOURED BAKED CUSTARD

To make a custard with a distinctive tang, use 150 ml freshly squeezed orange juice with 350 ml milk and 50 g caster sugar. Bake for 40 minutes at 160°C. For a more exotic flavour, replace the milk with coconut milk. Use it for an unusual Crème Caramel. Prepare it in individual serving dishes, as here. Serve coconut custard with fresh tropical fruit and Crème Chantilly laced with a touch of rum.

1 Make the custard as for Crème Caramel (see previous page). Heat 100 ml double cream with 400 ml canned coconut milk until hand-hot, then stir it into the eggs.

2 Pour the custard into a greased shallow dish, or six 150–200 ml ramekins and bake, standing the dishes in an inch of water, at 160°C until set – for 30–40 minutes. Pour into six 150 ml ramekins and leave to cool, then chill overnight. Decorate before serving with an exotic fruit salad.

SPICED CUSTARD

To spice up a British-style baked custard, sprinkle on grated nutmeg before cooking. Traditional Indian custards are spiced with cardamom and saffron and use whole eggs and melted butter for added richness and firmness of texture, to balance the spices. This type of custard is served chilled, cut into neat shapes. Spiced custard may be baked in ramekins and decorated with whipped cream and nuts.

Here, it is poured, about 2 cm deep, into an 18 cm square tin and decorated with crushed pistachio nuts before being baked. Once chilled, it is cut neatly into diamond shapes to serve.

1 Scrape the seeds from 2 green cardamoms and grind them to a fine powder in a mortar. Add about ⅛ tsp saffron strands and grind together to a make a slightly sticky powder. Stir in 2 tbsp hot water.

2 Lightly whisk 3 eggs with 100 g caster sugar. Stir in 75 g melted unsalted butter, 250 ml single cream and then the spice mixture. Pour into an 18 cm square tin and bake at 160°C for 30–40 minutes, until golden on top and set. Cut into shapes and decorate. Cool and chill.

*An exotic baked **Coconut Custard** served with a tropical fruit salad. **Spiced Custard** topped with crushed pistachio nuts and delicate shreds of gold leaf.*

FRIED BAKED CUSTARD

Baked custard is delicious fried and served with a fruit sauce or compote (see page 15). Make a custard as for Crème Caramel, using 3 eggs and 2 yolks. Bake for 40 minutes at 160°C in a large, 2.5–3 cm-deep oblong or square mould. Cool and chill overnight. Cut into fingers, squares or diamonds.

1 Coat the custard with a mixture made of flour, 2 beaten eggs and 60 g dry white breadcrumbs. Apply a second layer if needed, so the pieces are well coated. Chill for 30 minutes, or longer.

2 Fry the fritters in 175 g clarified butter. Work over a fairly high heat to cook the coating quickly. Turn them halfway through cooking (when they are crisp and golden underneath) using two palette knives, or a fish slice and knife. Drain on kitchen paper and serve.

BAKED-CUSTARD PUDDING

Bread and Butter Pudding is a classic hot custard pudding. Use good-quality bread, such as a traditional loaf or brioche, for perfect results. Single cream may be used in place of milk for a rich pudding and chopped dried apricots or peaches are excellent alternatives to sultanas.

1 Make a Crème Caramel (see page 46) omitting the 4 egg yolks. Cut bread shapes (here, a 150 g brioche loaf is used) and butter them on one side. Arrange them buttered side down in a straight-sided ovenproof dish, sprinkling sultanas between bread layers. Then pour in the custard.

2 Allow the pudding to stand for 30 minutes before baking at 160°C for 1 hour, until set and lightly browned. Sprinkle with caster sugar and serve hot.

TRADITIONAL QUEEN OF PUDDINGS

Custard	Meringue	
200 ml milk	3 egg whites	Make a custard (see page 46) but with the above proportions. Mix the breadcrumbs with the rind in a 1 litre ovenproof dish. Pour the custard in, cover and set aside for 30 minutes. Bake the custard at 160°C for 1 hour or until set. Spread a layer of jam over the cooked custard. Make a French Meringue (see page 68) and pile this on top of the pudding. Bake for a further 15–20 minutes.
300 ml single cream	100 g caster sugar	
25 g caster sugar	2 tbsp good-quality jam	
1 tsp natural vanilla extract		
3 egg yolks	This old-fashioned pudding uses whites left over from preparing custard to make a meringue topping. Here the classic custard is enriched by using cream as well as milk.	
100 g white breadcrumbs		
Finely grated rind of 1 lemon		

MOULDED CUSTARDS

Custard may be set with gelatine as an alternative to baking. This method offers many possibilities – flavoured custard may be served alone as a chilled dessert, or prepared in complementary layers to colourful effect.

PREPARING A CLASSIC BAVAROIS OR BAVARIAN CREAM

Crème Anglaise enriched with whipped cream and set with gelatine forms the classic French bavarois, which is set in a mould. A charlotte set in a mould lined with sponge fingers is one of the best known bavarois desserts. To unmould, wrap with a warm teatowel or dip the mould in warm water for 10 seconds, then invert on to a plate.

1 Dissolve 15 g powdered gelatine in 3 tbsp water and stir this into 1 quantity warm Crème Anglaise (see page 116). Pour into a bowl and allow to cool.

3 When the custard begins to set and has the texture of thick syrup, whip 225 ml double cream until it stands in soft peaks and fold into the custard.

2 Pour the custard through a fine sieve into a bowl sitting in iced water.

4 Rinse a 1.5 litre mould with cold water and dry. Pour in the bavarois. Chill until set. Unmould on to a serving platter.

FLAVOURING BAVAROIS

RICH CHOCOLATE
Cocoa may be used, but for a rich result, stir the hot Crème Anglaise into 200 g melted high-quality plain or bitter chocolate.

ALMOND
Heat 225 g blanched almonds with the milk until just about to boil, then set aside to cool. Purée in a blender and strain through a fine sieve. Add a few drops of bitter almond essence or oil of bitter almonds for more flavour.

ROSE
Omit the vanilla essence and add 3 tbsp rose water to the milk for the Crème Anglaise.

FRUIT BAVAROIS

In place of custard, fruit purée forms the base for fruit bavarois. Add egg yolks for a rich result, especially if using strong-flavoured fruit, such as blackcurrants.

Prepare 500 ml sweetened fruit purée. The blackcurrant bavarois here is sweetened with 225 g sugar to 1 kg fruit. Stir in 4 tbsp liqueur (for blackcurrants, use cassis), and 15 g gelatine dissolved in 3 tbsp water. Whip 225 ml double cream to soft peaks and fold in. Make a syrup with 3 tbsp caster sugar and 50 g water. Beat the syrup with 3 egg yolks in a bowl over hot water until thick and pale, then gradually stir in the sweetened fruit purée. Spoon fruit bavarois into serving glasses or a mould and chill until set. Decorate with whipped cream and fresh fruit.

SURPRISE BAVAROIS

Use two or three bavarois of different flavours for this presentation method. The dessert may be set in small loaf tins or oval or round moulds. Decorate the desserts when unmoulded by piping on reserved bavarois mixture, whipped or chocolate cream, and top with frosted rose petals, miniature roses or fresh fruit to complement the flavours of the bavarois.

1 Coat a mould with the first mix, here vanilla, level the top and chill.

2 When the first bavarois layer is chilled to a firm consistency, spoon in soft raspberry bavarois to fill the mould three-quarters of the way. If you wish to add a third layer, chill this one first.

3 Place some raspberries into the second layer and cover with sponge. Chill until completely set, then invert on to serving plates, unmould and decorate. Serve immediately.

THREE-FRUIT BAVAROIS

Orange and raspberry bavarois mixtures are here combined with a layer of sliced bananas. The orange flavoured mixture is the basic bavarois but the milk is infused with pared orange rind and the Crème Anglaise has 4 tbsp orange liqueur added to it along with the gelatine. When preparing layered bavarois, remember to adjust the quantities for each mixture to avoid making too much for the size of the mould used.

1 Line the greased mould with a strip of sponge fingers (see page 119). Pipe in the first layer of bavarois, here orange. Chill until set. Pipe the second layer to an equal depth as the first and chill again until set.

2 Once the second layer is firm, add a layer of sliced bananas. Top with sponge fingers and invert on to a serving plate. Sprinkle the top and sides with icing sugar and decorate with fresh fruit and a sprig of mint.

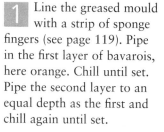

FOOLS, CREAMS & WHIPS

**Creams and whips are soft desserts that are set. Fools are simply unset
fruit creams. As light in texture as the name suggests, whips are also wonderfully rich, being made with cream or whipped custard.**

FRUIT FOOLS

*Fruit fools are fruit purée
enriched with whipped cream
and sweetened with icing
sugar. Allow 300 ml double
cream to 250 ml fruit purée,
sweetened to taste.*

1 Melon makes delicious
fool. If you want to
serve the fool in the shells,
cut the fruit decoratively.
Discard pips and purée the
flesh in a blender. Add fresh
mint leaves if desired.

2 Turn the purée into a
bowl and stir in icing
sugar to taste. Fold in the
whipped double cream and
chill in fruit shells. Serves 4.

SIMPLE FRUIT CREAMS

*Fruit creams can be made from custard, yogurt or soft cheese
bases. Here, Crème Pâtissière (see page 116) is used for apple
cream. Flavour the Crème Pâtissière with a few drops of oil
of bitter almonds or natural almond flavouring before folding
in the purée and whipped cream. Spoon the fruit cream into
serving dishes and chill before serving.*

Make Crème Pâtissière with
250 ml milk, ½ vanilla pod,
60 g caster sugar, 3 yolks,
10 g plain flour and 10 g
cornflour. Add the almond
flavouring. Fold in 300 ml
apple purée. Whip 200 ml
double cream to soft peaks
and fold in.
Serves 4.

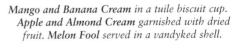

LIGHT ALTERNATIVES

*A low-fat soft cheese such as
Quark can be used for light
fruit creams. For the Mango
and Banana Cream shown here,
flavour 200 g soft cheese with
½ tsp vanilla extract. Purée
2 ripe bananas with a dash of
lemon juice and stir into the
cheese. Add icing sugar to taste.
Fold in 250 ml crème fraîche
and the finely diced flesh of
1 mango. Chill before serving.*

*Mango and Banana Cream in a tuile biscuit cup.
Apple and Almond Cream garnished with dried
fruit. Melon Fool served in a vandyked shell.*

Entremet Contemporain

In the Middle Ages, an entremet was a spectacular end to a meal, sometimes accompanied by music, juggling and dancing. This modern version is flavoured with caramel sauce and mousse and complemented with a hazelnut cream.

PREPARATION PLAN

- Preheat oven to 200°C.
- Prepare and bake ladyfingers and sponge cake.
- Cook caramel sauce and mousse.
- Assemble cake and chill to set.
- Decorate.

For the ladyfingers and sponge cakes
20 egg yolks
500 g sugar
20 egg whites (cook at 200°C)
500 g flour
25 g hazelnuts

• • •

For the caramel sauce
300 g sugar
80 g glucose
150 ml water
A pinch of salt
360 ml condensed milk
6 g vanilla extract

• • •

For the caramel mousse
75 ml water
40 g powdered gelatine
290 g caramel sauce
520 g whipping cream

• • •

For the hazelnut whipped cream
1.2 litres whipping cream
90 g icing sugar
600 g grilled hazelnuts, cooked through
and finely ground

• • •

For the caramel syrup
10 ml caramel sauce
10 ml water

• • •

Caramel glaze
Whole grilled hazelnuts
Chocolate curls

1 Prepare the ladyfingers and sponge cakes. Whisk the egg yolks and half the sugar until pale and tripled in volume. Whisk the remaining sugar and egg whites into a meringue. Fold the meringue and flour in alternate batches into the yolk mixture, starting and finishing with meringue. Place into a piping bag fitted with a No.8 nozzle and pipe a 10 x 40 cm strip of sponge diagonally on to a silicone-lined tray. Coarsely chop the hazelnuts and sprinkle on to the sponge strip. On to the same tray, pipe two 20 cm diameter discs of sponge for the cake, then bake at 200°C for 20 minutes.

2 Meanwhile, prepare the caramel sauce. Make a dark caramel with the sugar, glucose and 60 ml water (see page 109). Add 90 ml water and a small pinch of salt to arrest the cooking. Once cooled, add the condensed milk and the vanilla.

3 Next create the caramel mousse. Heat the water to 60°C and add the gelatine then 290 ml of the caramel sauce. Allow to cool to 28°C. Meanwhile, whip the cream. Once the caramel reaches the desired temperature, fold in the whipped cream.

4 Now make the hazelnut whipped cream. Whisk the cream, mix in the icing sugar and fold in the ground, grilled hazelnuts.

5 To assemble the dessert, cut the strip of ladyfinger sponge in half lengthways and use it to cover the sides of the ring mould. Place one sponge disc in the base, imbibe with caramel syrup (made by mixing the remaining caramel sauce with 300 ml water) then half-fill with caramel mousse. Cover with the second disc of sponge and imbibe this with caramel syrup also. Fill the ring to the top with hazelnut cream then smooth the top with a palette knife. Place in the refrigerator for at least six hours to set or in the freezer for two hours.

6 Remove the mould. Make a caramel glaze. Boil 150 g sugar and 75 ml water until reduced to a deep caramel. Arrest cooking with a few tablespoons of cold water. Cool the glaze a little before use. Spread it over the top of the dessert without disturbing the surface. Make chocolate curls (see page 201). Place on the cake and add whole, grilled hazelnuts.

Syllabub and *Flummery* are both served chilled. Here, the former is with piped whipped cream and candied peel and the latter, with frosted rose petals. *Zabaglione* is served hot in warmed glasses with sponge fingers.

LIGHTLY SET CREAMS – FLUMMERY

Creams can be thickened with a starch such as arrowroot or cornflour, or set lightly with gelatine; in some recipes both are used. Blancmange is an almond-flavoured cooked cream and flummery, shown here, is its chilled version – a set almond cream which is enriched with whipped cream.

1 Heat 100 g blanched almonds, 50 g sugar and 300 ml milk until just boiling. Cool, purée and strain. Dissolve 15 g gelatine in 3 tbsp water. Add to the milk with 1 tbsp orange flower or rosewater.

2 When the almond milk begins to set, with the texture of heavy syrup, whip 300 ml double cream to soft peaks and fold it in. Spoon into dishes and chill until set. Serves 4.

WHIPPED CREAM–SYLLABUB

An old English recipe, syllabub is simple and, although rich, quite refreshing. It can be swirled on trifle or over fresh fruit. Layer it in a bowl with sherry-moistened sponge and fruit as an alternative to trifle. Serve crisp, light biscuits with syllabub.

1 Mix 75 g caster sugar, 100 ml either medium or sweet sherry and 2 tbsp brandy with the finely grated rind and juice of 1 lemon. Chill, then pour the mixture into 300 ml double cream in a bowl, stirring with a whisk.

2 Whip the cream mixture until it is light and thick and holds the trail of the whisk in soft swirls. Transfer to 6 dishes and chill for up to 2 hours before serving. (If it stands for any longer it will separate.)

WHIPPED CUSTARD–ZABAGLIONE

Italian zabaglione, similar to the French sabayon, is a rich dessert of egg yolks whipped with sugar and Marsala, served hot, with sponge finger biscuits. The quantity of sugar and type of wine can be varied to make the dessert less sweet.

1 Whisk together 4 egg yolks and 40 g caster sugar over warm water until thick, pale and warm. Add 100 ml Marsala, whisking continuously.

2 The mixture is ready when it is pale, thick and light. Lift the whisk and the mixture should hold a trail as it falls in ribbons. Pour into warmed serving glasses and serve immediately.

SOUFFLES, MOUSSES & MERINGUES

COLD SOUFFLES
·
BAKED SOUFFLES
·
MOUSSES
·
MERINGUE

COLD SOUFFLES

Cold soufflés owe their light texture to whisked egg whites and whipped cream. For an attractive finish and in imitation of their hot counterparts, tape a collar to the dish, allowing the soufflé to stand above the rim.

LEMON SOUFFLE

2½ leaves or 2¼ tsp powdered
gelatine
4–6 tbsp water
200 g caster sugar
Grated rind and juice
of 2 lemons
3 eggs, separated
250 ml double cream

Prepare a 1 litre soufflé dish. Sprinkle the powdered gelatine in 2 tbsp water and allow it to become spongy, or soak the leaf gelatine in cold water.

Dissolve 100 g caster sugar in 2 tbsp water in a saucepan, then boil to soft-ball stage (see page 108). Heat the lemon juice to boiling, cool slightly, then dissolve the gelatine in it. Whisk the egg yolks with the lemon rind and pour in the syrup in a thin stream, whisking continuously until pale and creamy. Fold in the gelatine dissolved in the lemon juice.

Boil a syrup of the remaining 100 g caster sugar and 2 tbsp water to soft ball stage. Whisk the egg whites until stiff, then gradually whisk in the syrup to make an Italian Meringue (see page 68). Whip the cream lightly until it is thick but not stiff, then fold it into the yolk mixture. Fold the meringue into the yolk mixture.

Turn the mixture into the dish and level the top with a palette knife dipped in water. Chill for several hours until set. Peel away collar and decorate.

MAKING A SET SOUFFLE

1 For a cold set soufflé, secure a double-thick band of baking parchment or a piece of acetate cut to the correct shape around the dish to stand 3–5 cm above the rim.

2 To make the soufflé mixture, whisk the egg yolks with the lemon rind and pour in the syrup in a thin stream, whisking continuously until pale and creamy. Follow the recipe (above left) to complete the mixture.

3 Turn the mixture into the prepared soufflé dish and smooth the top with a palette knife dipped in warm water. Chill to set, then carefully peel back the acetate from the set soufflé, lifting it up off the rim of the dish as you peel it away from the soufflé.

FINISHING SET SOUFFLES

Here, finely chopped pistachio nuts are applied to the side and piped cream finishes the top.

1 Press nuts on to the side using a palette knife. Stand the dish on parchment to catch falling nuts.

2 Pipe rosettes of cream around the top edge: start with opposite rosettes then pipe more in between.

CHOCOLATE SOUFFLE CUPS

To make 12 edible chocolate cups (see page 202), use 500 g plain chocolate. Make the cups in cases with straight, almost upright sides, such as plastic drinking cups or muffin cases. Chill, then fill with soufflé mixture once set.

1 Tape double-thick bands of baking parchment around the set cases, leaving a collar of 2–4 cm. Place on a baking tray and fill with 1 quantity white chocolate soufflé (see below, right). Chill until set.

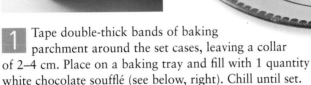

INDIVIDUAL SOUFFLES

Set individual cold soufflés in ramekin dishes and decorate as for large soufflés. Here coffee soufflé is dredged with icing sugar which is then branded with a hot metal skewer to produce a striking criss-cross pattern on the surface and provide a hint of a slightly bitter taste. Crushed Amaretto biscuits are applied to the side. A delicious alternative to these biscuits is chocolate-coated coffee beans.

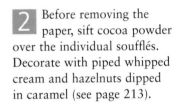

2 Before removing the paper, sift cocoa powder over the individual soufflés. Decorate with piped whipped cream and hazelnuts dipped in caramel (see page 213).

SIMPLE SET SOUFFLES

ORANGE
. . . .
Use one large orange instead of the lemons.

COFFEE
. . . .
Use 100 ml very strong black coffee instead of lemon juice and rind. Dissolve the gelatine in the coffee.

PRALINE
. . . .
Add 100 g praline (see page 109), ground to a fine powder in a food processor, to the yolk mixture instead of the lemons. Dissolve the gelatine in a little water. Add 2 tbsp Frangelica liqueur with the gelatine.

CHOCOLATE
. . . .
Add 60 g melted plain bitter or white chocolate to the yolk mixture and use only 2 leaves of gelatine or 2 tsp of powdered gelatine. Omit the lemons.

57

BAKED SOUFFLES

A baked soufflé is the ultimate last-minute dessert, requiring confidence and timing. The Crème Pâtissière base can be made in advance but the final preparation, baking and serving are all performed in one sequence.

MAKING BAKED SOUFFLES

Heat causes a soufflé to rise, as it encourages the air in the light soufflé mixture to expand. The egg in the mixture sets the shape and holds it up. Dusting the dish with sugar allows the soufflé to cling to it and rise successfully.

1 Grease the soufflé dish with butter, then dust with caster sugar, tipping out the excess sugar.

2 Prepare the Crème Pâtissière base and stir in the flavourings, here lemon rind, Malibu and coconut. Allow to cool slightly.

*A good **baked soufflé** rises a couple of centimetres above the rim of the dish, with an even shape and a crisp, golden brown top surface.*

3 Prepare the Italian Meringue at the last minute and fold in. Turn the mixture into a prepared soufflé dish.

4 Run your thumb around the inside of the rim of the dish, cleaning a narrow channel to allow the mixture to rise cleanly and evenly.

COCONUT SOUFFLE

250 ml milk
1 vanilla pod
50 g caster sugar, plus extra for dusting dish
4 eggs, separated
30 g plain flour
15 g cornflour
Grated rind of 1 lemon
3 tbsp Malibu
25 g desiccated or fresh coconut
Unsalted butter for greasing dish
Icing sugar to decorate

Grease a 1.5 litre soufflé dish and dust it with caster sugar. Prepare a Crème Pâtissière (see page 116) using the milk, vanilla, 30 g caster sugar, egg yolks, plain flour and cornflour. Stir in the lemon rind, Malibu and coconut. Cool slightly.

Use the remaining caster sugar and egg whites to make an Italian Meringue (see page 68). Fold the meringue into the Crème Pâtissière mixture. Run your thumb around the inside rim of the dish – this will prevent the mixture from sticking to parts of the dish when rising, so it rises evenly. Bake at 190°C for 15–20 minutes, or until the soufflé is risen, set and golden. Serve immediately, dusted with icing sugar.

SMALL BAKED SOUFFLES

For six individual soufflés, use 250 ml sugared, buttered soufflé dishes in place of a large dish. Bake the small soufflés for approximately 15–20 minutes.

1 Fruit may be placed in the dishes. Poached cherries are good with a soufflé flavoured with kirsch. Either canned or bottled cherries, drained of their juices, may be used.

2 Stand the dishes on a baking tray for easy handling. For a glazed finish, dust the soufflé tops with icing sugar 2–3 minutes before the end of cooking. Work quickly so that the soufflés do not collapse.

SOUFFLES IN HAZELNUT CUPS

Chocolate and hazelnut are two flavours that particularly work well together. Here, a crisp hazelnut crust provides a pleasing contrast for creamy baked chocolate soufflé.

1 Line standard-sized patty tins with hazelnut Pâte Sucrée (see page 122) and bake blind for about 10 minutes at 200°C. Cool on a wire rack. Reduce the oven temperature to 190°C.

2 Place the pastry cups on a baking tray. Fill the cups with soufflé mixture flavoured with chocolate (see overleaf) and run the tip of your little finger around the inside edge of the cups.

3 Bake for about 12–15 minutes and serve immediately. Use a metal slice to transfer the cups to plates, taking care not to disturb the soufflé fillings.

VARIATIONS

VANILLA SOUFFLE

Omit the rind, Malibu and coconut. Use 1 tsp vanilla extract in place of a pod. Use vanilla sugar. Bake in a buttered, sugared 1.2 litre dish at 190°C for 15 minutes.

APPLE SOUFFLE

Use Calvados instead of Malibu. Omit the coconut and fold in 50 g apple purée. Bake in a 1.2 litre dish at 190°C for 25–30 minutes.

CHOCOLATE SOUFFLE

Omit Malibu and coconut. Mix 25 g cocoa with 50 ml boiling water. Use 200 ml milk for Crème Pâtissière. Halve other ingredients. Bake in a 1.2 litre dish at 190°C for 25 minutes.

HOT FRUIT SOUFFLES

Fruit shells are excellent containers for baking hot soufflés. Orange cups are ideal but any other fruit with a skin tough enough to withstand baking can be used, such as lime, lemon and grapefruit.

1 Use 6 oranges, weighing roughly 175 g each. Slice about a third off the top of each orange and trim the base so that the fruit stands neatly. Scoop out the flesh, leaving a neat edge on the shell.

2 Follow the Coconut Soufflé recipe (see page 58), using orange rind instead of lemon and Cointreau or Grand Marnier instead of Malibu. Omit the coconut. Spoon into the orange shells. Bake at 190°C for about 10–12 minutes. Serve at once.

SOUFFLE-TOPPED PINEAPPLES

Top fruit with soufflé mixture, or use it to fill fruit shells. Try halving small pineapples and filling them with fruit chunks. Miniature pineapples can be scooped out as for oranges. Here, 2 pineapples are used, weighing roughly 1.19 kg each (including the leaves).

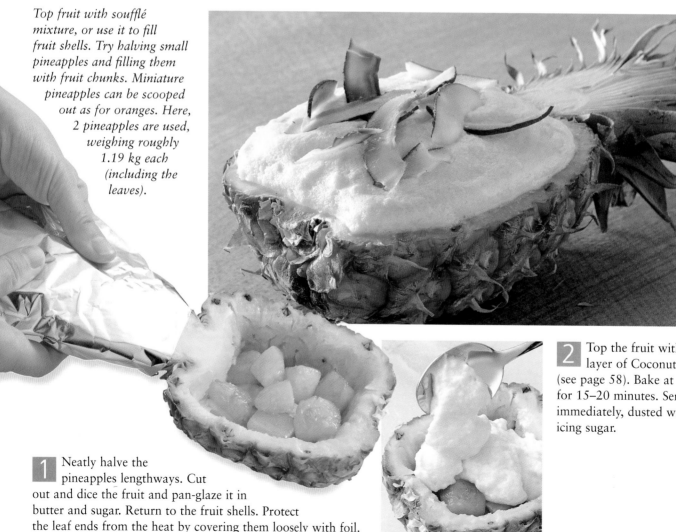

1 Neatly halve the pineapples lengthways. Cut out and dice the fruit and pan-glaze it in butter and sugar. Return to the fruit shells. Protect the leaf ends from the heat by covering them loosely with foil.

2 Top the fruit with a layer of Coconut Soufflé (see page 58). Bake at 190°C for 15–20 minutes. Serve immediately, dusted with icing sugar.

MOUSSES

Faultless mousse requires a little practice. Ensure success by perfecting certain techniques – for folding in ingredients, judging the setting point of gelatine mixtures and achieving an ideal texture when whipping cream.

MAKING CHIBOUSTE MOUSSE

Chibouste is Crème Pâtissière lightened with whisked egg whites or meringue. It is used as the base for the Lemon Mousse shown here.

1 Beat the cooled Crème Pâtissière until smooth. Stir in the dissolved gelatine.

Mousse looks very elegant in short-stemmed serving glasses with large, cupped bowls. Serve with crisp, light biscuits if desired.

2 Fold in the Italian Meringue and spoon the mousse into serving dishes, then chill for several hours.

3 Decorate with piped whipped cream and crystallized strips of lemon peel (see page 205).

LEMON MOUSSE

250 ml milk
4 eggs
240 g caster sugar
20 g cornflour
Grated rind and juice of 1 lemon
3 leaves gelatine or 2¾ tsp powdered gelatine
6 tbsp water

Use the milk, egg yolks, 40 g caster sugar and cornflour to make a Crème Pâtissière (see page 116). Stir in the lemon rind and cover with clingfilm, then leave to cool until just warm.

Soak the leaf gelatine in water or dissolve the powdered gelatine in 2 tbsp of the water until it is spongy. Heat the lemon juice to boiling, cool slightly, then dissolve the drained leaf or sponged gelatine in it.

Use the remaining sugar and the water to make an Italian Meringue (see page 68). Beat the Crème Pâtissière, then stir in the dissolved gelatine. Fold in the meringue. Spoon the mousse into glasses or serving dishes and chill until set. Serves 8.

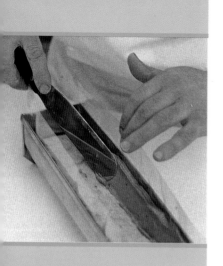

Chocolate Suprème

Layers of sponge are sandwiched with chocolate mousse and vanilla cream and then moulded into a log shape. A decorative spine of assorted nuts separates the two halves of the topping – a rich chocolate glaze and a coating of powdered cocoa.

PREPARATION PLAN

- ▶ Preheat the oven to 180°C.
- ▶ Prepare and bake the sponge.
- ▶ Make the chocolate mousse and vanilla cream.
- ▶ Create the log shape.
- ▶ Arrange the toppings and decorations.

For the dacquoise sponge
8 egg whites
60 g caster sugar
110 g finely ground almonds
110 g icing sugar
25 g flour

• • •

For the chocolate mousse
2 small egg yolks
40 ml syrup (made with 25 g sugar/25 ml water)
80 g chocolate
150 ml whipping cream

• • •

For the vanilla cream
85 ml milk
2 vanilla pods
20 g sugar
2 egg yolks
1 tsp cornflour
1 tsp custard powder
15 g powered gelatine
100 g Italian Meringue
100 ml double cream

• • •

For the chocolate glaze
180 g chocolate
200 ml whipping cream
40 g sugar
40 g glucose
30 g butter

• • •

Cocoa powder
Assorted whole nuts

1 First prepare the dacquoise sponge. Whisk the egg whites and add the sugar to make a meringue. Sieve all of the dry ingredients together then gently fold into the egg whites. Spread evenly on to a baking sheet lined with baking parchment. Bake in a 180°C oven for approximately 20 minutes. Allow to cool.

2 Prepare the chocolate mousse. Whisk the yolks. Cook the sugar and water to 120°C, slowly pour on to the egg yolks and continue whisking until cool. Melt the chocolate to 35°C and fold into the yolk mixture. Whip the whipping cream, quickly fold it into the yolk mixture and stir to incorporate. Chill.

3 For the vanilla cream, heat the milk and split vanilla pods. Whisk the yolks and sugar, add the cornflour and custard powder, then mix in a little of the milk, warmed, and blend. Add the remaining milk and bring to simmering point. Remove from the heat, add the gelatine and cool. Whip the double cream, fold it and the Italian Meringue into the mixture and chill.

4 Line a curved mould with acetate leaving 5 cm excess overhanging. Pipe a layer of chocolate mousse following the mould's curve. Cut the sponge into two strips, each the length of the mould but narrower. Place one on top of the piped chocolate mousse. Pipe more chocolate mousse to fill any gaps around the sponge and smooth it up the sides of the mould.

5 Pipe a layer of vanilla cream on the sponge and between the coated sides. Add the second strip of sponge. Fill any gaps with vanilla cream and freeze.

6 Retaining the acetate, unmould the dessert on to a cake board. If it is too long to handle, cut it in half. Cut the acetate along the top length and remove one half of it. Dredge the open half of the cake with cocoa powder then remove the rest of the acetate.

7 Prepare the chocolate glaze. Roughly chop the chocolate and place in a bowl. Gently warm the cream with the sugar and glucose in a saucepan. Pour this over the chopped chocolate and as it begins to melt, gradually stir in the butter until all the chocolate has melted and the glaze is smooth. Cool to 40°C then ladle the glaze over the second half of the cake using the diagonal line of the cocoa powder as a guide and leave to set. Arrange a selection of nuts along the top, then chill and serve.

DARK CHOCOLATE MOUSSE

High-quality plain chocolate is enriched with egg yolks and lightened with whites. The bitter chocolate sets the mousse. Use 450 g chocolate, 30 g unsalted butter, 100 g caster sugar and 6 eggs, separated.

1 Melt the chocolate with the butter in a large bowl over hot, not boiling, water. Remove from the heat.

2 Use half the sugar and 4 tbsp water to make a syrup, boiling to soft ball stage (see page 108). Cool slightly, then pour into the yolks, whisking continuously.

3 Using a spoon, fold the melted chocolate into the egg yolks. Make sure the melted chocolate is cool before you add the yolks, or they will begin to cook.

4 Use the remaining sugar, 4 tbsp water and egg whites to make an Italian Meringue (see page 68). Beat 2 tbsp of meringue into the chocolate mixture, then fold in the rest of the meringue. Turn the mixture into 12 coffee cups and chill.

*Coffee cups make ideal containers for serving either **dark** or **white** chocolate mousse. Strong, stunning colour contrasts can be made with the decoration, such as the dark chocolate caraque and the leaves made from white chocolate shown here.*

WHITE CHOCOLATE MOUSSE

This mousse is set with chocolate and lightened with whipped cream; the result is soft and creamy.

1 Melt 100 g white chocolate in a bowl over hot water and stir in 50 ml hot double cream. Allow to cool until it begins to thicken slightly.

2 Whip 200 ml whipping cream and fold it into the chocolate. Transfer to serving glasses or dishes and chill.

SIMPLE FRUIT MOUSSE

A full-flavoured fruit purée (see page 113) can be used instead of Crème Pâtissière or chocolate. Whipped cream enriches the purée and produces a light, creamy texture. Italian Meringue (see page 68) can be added for a light, aerated texture and a wonderfully delicate flavour. Gelatine is the setting agent.

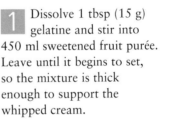

1 Dissolve 1 tbsp (15 g) gelatine and stir into 450 ml sweetened fruit purée. Leave until it begins to set, so the mixture is thick enough to support the whipped cream.

2 Whip 300 ml double cream until it stands in soft peaks. Stir 2 tbsp of this into the fruit mixture before folding in the rest. Turn into serving dishes and chill. Decorate with fruit once chilled. Serves 4.

If decorating with fruit, use small amounts as too much will sink into the mousse. Here, two raspberries and a sprig of mint are ample.

SERVING IDEAS

There are many ways of serving mousse: in biscuit or chocolate cups, as a filling for gâteaux or in pastries. The following are simple suggestions.

■ *Mousse in a biscuit crust*
Prepare a chocolate biscuit crust in a flan dish (see page 80) and fill with lemon mousse (see page 61). Alternatively, replace the lemon with 2 limes for a delicious lime mousse. Decorate with grated chocolate. Individual flans and tartlets can also be prepared in this way.

■ *Matching mousses*
Combine in serving glasses mousses of complementary colours and flavours, such as white chocolate and apricot, mango or raspberry. Prepare and chill the chocolate mousse before making the fruit mousse. Use chocolate caraque or piped cream and fruit to decorate.

■ *Moulded mousse*
Mould fruit mousse in plain or fluted moulds. Set pieces of fruit in a thin layer of fruit juice jelly in the base of a plain mould, to form a decoration when the mousse is inverted and unmoulded.

Nid d' Abeille

Honey, and a ring of honeycomb-patterned rectangles, transform a dacquoise, cream and meringue confection, into a delicious beehive. The summery allusions are reinforced by a decoration of seasonal fruits and more of the honeycomb.

PREPARATION PLAN

- ▶ Preheat the oven to 180°C.
- ▶ Cook the peaches and the dacquoise base.
- ▶ Prepare the filling and assemble the cake.
- ▶ Create the honeycombs and garnish when the cake is cold.

For the dacquoise base
8 egg whites
80 g sugar
100 g ground almonds
150 g icing sugar
50 g flour

• • •

For the Italian meringue
150 g honey
2 egg whites, whisked

• • •

For the honey cream
2½ gelatine leaves
230 g Crème Pâtissière, warmed
750 ml whipping cream

• • •

For the honeycombs
60 g butter
50 ml cream
80 g sugar
40 g honey
60 g sliced almonds

• • •

500 g (canned) peaches
50 g butter
80 g honey
100 g wild strawberries or raspberries
100 g redcurrants
Apricot jam

1 Prepare the dacquoise. Whisk the egg whites with the sugar. Mix together the ground almonds, icing sugar and flour before carefully folding into the egg whites. Pipe two discs on to a baking sheet lined with baking parchment or wax paper and bake for 20 minutes at 180°C.

2 Heat the butter and honey. Add the peaches with their syrup. Cook over a low heat for approximately five minutes. Slice the cooked peaches

3 Now prepare the Italian meringue and honey cream. Cook the honey to 118°C and fold into the whisked egg whites. Set aside. Immerse the gelatine in a bowl of cold water. Once softened, remove the gelatine and stir into the warmed Crème Pâtissière (see page 116), then place in the refrigerator to cool. Whisk the whipping cream until semi-whipped and fold into the chilled Crème Pâtissière. Fold in the slightly warm Italian meringue and use immediately.

4 To assemble the cake, carefully trim the edge of both discs of dacquoise so they fit into a ring of a slightly smaller size. Place one disc inside the ring and carefully spread with half of the honey cream. Sprinkle liberally with most of the sliced peaches and half the fresh fruit. Place the second dacquoise disc on top and spread with the remaining honey cream. Gently press more peach slices and fresh fruit into the cream (reserving some for decoration) and smooth off the top using a palette knife. To set, place in the freezer for 2 hours or in the refrigerator for 6 hours before decorating.

5 Prepare the honeycombs. Combine the butter, cream, sugar and honey in a saucepan and cook until the syrup begins to colour slightly. Add the almonds and pour on to a baking sheet lined with baking parchment or wax paper. Place in a 170°C oven for 5 minutes. Remove from the oven and immediately cut into uniform rectangles the height of your cake. Work speedily as the honeycombs will quickly solidify.

6 Brush the top of the chilled, set cake with melted apricot jam to give it shine. Gently overlap the honeycomb rectangles around the edge. Decorate with the remaining fruits and honeycombs.

MERINGUE

Meringue – simply sweetened, stiffly whisked egg white – is used in many desserts, both uncooked and cooked. Make sure the whites are completely yolk-free and the equipment is grease-free, for good volume once whisked.

THREE TYPES OF MERINGUE

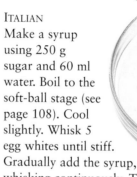

FRENCH
Use 115 g sugar to 2 egg whites. Whisk the whites until stiff and dry. Gradually whisk in half the sugar, then fold in the remainder. Use for shaping and drying out in the oven or for poaching.

SWISS
Use 125 g sugar to 2 egg whites. Whisk the whites and sugar together in a bowl over barely simmering water. Keep turning the bowl for even results. Use this meringue for piping and shaping.

ITALIAN
Make a syrup using 250 g sugar and 60 ml water. Boil to the soft-ball stage (see page 108). Cool slightly. Whisk 5 egg whites until stiff. Gradually add the syrup, whisking continuously. This meringue is very firm and glossy. Use for piping, as a quickly browned topping or to lighten mousses.

PIPING MERINGUE

FILLING THE BAG
Spoon the meringue into the bag, holding it in one hand. Twist the bag just above the nozzle or support it in a jug, pulling the sides of the top of the bag down over the rim of the jug.

SMOOTH ROUNDS OR OVALS
Use a large plain nozzle and hold the bag at a slight angle to the board. Squeeze it firmly, barely lifting the bag to form a smooth shape.

EVEN DISCS
Draw a circle on parchment and turn it over. Use the shape, visible through the paper, as a template. Choose the nozzle according to the size of disc you require. Hold the bag vertically and pipe from the middle outwards.

NESTS
Pipe small discs with a small star or plain nozzle. Pipe one or two layers to form a rim around the edge. For larger nests use a large nozzle to create a thicker rim.

SHAPING MERINGUE

Prepare your template – draw the outline of the shape you require clearly on baking parchment and turn it over. Pile the meringue into the middle of the shape, then spread it with the back of a metal spoon. For a Pavlova, hollow out the middle to create a nest-shape.

PAVLOVA

3 egg whites
175 g caster sugar
1 tsp white wine vinegar
or fruit vinegar
1 tsp cornflour
300 ml double cream,
whipped
Mixed fresh fruit, such as
strawberries, raspberries,
pineapple and kiwi fruit

Use the French Meringue method (see opposite) for the Pavlova base. Fold in the vinegar and cornflour with the second half of the sugar. Shape into a 20 cm nest (see left). Bake at 150°C for 1 hour. Turn the oven off and leave the meringue inside to cool. Fill with cream and fruit no earlier than 1 hour before serving.

BAKING OR DRYING OUT MERINGUE

Meringue can be baked very briefly at high temperatures (220–250°C) to brown the surface. To dry out meringue slowly, bake at 100°C for 1–3 hours, depending on texture required, or leave at 60°C for 5 hours or longer. To maintain a very low temperature for a long period of time, wedge the oven door ajar with a wooden spoon handle if possible. Place the meringue in tins or on trays lined with baking parchment for cooking.

COATING MERINGUE

A moist filling will soften meringue. These tips show how to coat meringue to protect it from moistness and retain its crisp, crumbly texture.

BRUSHING
Brush melted chocolate under and inside nests. Use either plain or white chocolate, depending on the decorative results you require.

DIPPING
Dip meringue shapes into melted dark chocolate for a smooth layer of chocolate and a striking contrast of colours and tones.

*Meringue nest filled with fresh fruit. Coated **meringue shapes** filled with dark and white chocolate mousses, decorated with cocoa or caramel.*

69

Exotic Rice Imperatrice

A dish truly fit for an emperor! A crown of fresh fruit-topped sponge is filled with creamy rice pudding and exotic fruit and smothered in swirled, toasted meringue. The base is neatened with a brim of delicate coconut biscuits.

PREPARATION PLAN

- ► Prepare the fruit sauce and sponge.
- ► Make a rice pudding (see page 182).
- ► Create the mould and the biscuits.
- ► Pipe and toast the meringue.

For the jellied sauce of mango and passion fruit
125 g pulp of passion fruit
125 g pulp of mango
35 g sugar
5 g gelatine

• • •

For the Génoise sponge
4 eggs
120 g caster sugar
120 g plain flour

• • •

For the cream of rice
200 g pastry cream
2 gelatine leaves
2 ml low-fat cream
100 g rice pudding

• • •

For the coconut tuiles
2 egg whites
75 g icing sugar
65 g grated coconut
50 g unsalted butter, melted

• • •

For the Italian meringue
250 g sugar
60 ml water
5 egg whites

• • •

Exotic fruits

For the mango and passion fruit sauce, blend the sugar and fruit pulp. Soften the gelatine, place in a bain marie, then fold in a quarter of the pulp. Warm, fold in the remaining pulp, pour into a tray and chill.

Prepare the sponge. Preheat the oven to 170°C. Break the eggs into a heatproof bowl and add the sugar. Stand the bowl over a saucepan of hot, not quite boiling, water and whisk until the mixture is pale and thick. Remove the bowl from the pan and continue whisking until cool. Sift the flour and fold it into the mixture using a large metal spoon or spatula. Use a figure-of-eight action, lifting the mixture over the flour to incorporate it without knocking out any air from the mixture. Pour into two greased tins, smaller in circumference than your final mould, and bake for 25 minutes or until risen and pale golden.

Make the cream of rice. Soak the gelatine in cold water. As it melts place in a bain marie then fold into the chilled pastry cream and whisk thoroughly. Quickly add the cream and fold in the rice pudding.

Fill a dome mould with rice pudding, smoothing it up the sides and leaving a hollow in the middle. Set one sponge circle, imbibed with the mango and passion fruit sauce, over the rice pudding.

With a round pastry cutter that is smaller than the dome mould, cut a disk of set jellied sauce and place on top of the sponge layer. Finish the mould with the rice pudding and the second disc of imbibed sponge. Chill and set.

Finally, prepare the coconut tuiles. In a large mixing bowl, whisk the egg whites until smooth. Stir in the sugar and grated coconut until evenly combined, using a wooden spoon. Stir in the melted butter and mix thoroughly. Spread the mixture evenly over a greased baking sheet and chill for 1 hour. Once fully chilled, bake at 160°C for 3 minutes. Remove from the oven and, whilst still warm and pliable, use a small pastry cutter to stamp out biscuits to the size you require and leave to cool.

Prepare the Italian meringue (see page 68). Use a piping bag fitted with a plain nozzle to pipe diagonal curves from the base to the top of the unmoulded dish. Pipe a rope of meringue around the top and scorch the meringue with a blow torch. Fill the top with exotic fruits and decorate with coconut tuiles.

ASSEMBLING A PYRAMID

A meringue pyramid looks spectacular on the table and usually elicits a comment or two. As impressive a showpiece as it is, it is actually quite easy to assemble. All that is required is a steady hand for neat, even piping. Dust the finished pyramid with cocoa and top with a pecan nut.

Prepare three to five meringue discs that decrease in size proportionally. Place the largest on a serving platter or stand. Brush with melted white chocolate and, once set, top with piped coffee cream. Brush the second disc with white chocolate and, once set, place the disk on top of the previous layer and pipe with cream. Continue in this way until the entire pyramid is assembled.

OEUFS A LA NEIGE

4 egg whites
125 g caster sugar

Poaching Syrup
1.5 litre water
300 g sugar
Crème Anglaise (see page 116)
Mint sprigs and caramel (see page 109) to decorate

Heat the water and sugar until the sugar dissolves, then bring to the boil and reduce the heat.

Whisk the egg whites and gradually add the caster sugar, whisking until smooth and stiff. Shape the meringue into ovals. Place them in the syrup and cook gently for 3–4 minutes. Remove and drain the meringues with a slotted spoon and place them on paper towels.

Pour chilled Crème Anglaise into serving bowls. Arrange the meringues on top. Decorate with caramel and mint.

POACHING MERINGUE

Use two spoons to form a quenelle shape or oval. Scoop the meringue on one spoon and use the second spoon to slide it off the spoon sideways in a neat oval, straight in to the barely simmering poaching liquid. Poach gently for 3–4 minutes.

FLAVOURING MERINGUE

CITRUS

Add the finely grated rind of 1 lemon, 1 orange or 2 limes to the stiff meringue, folding or whisking it in.

ESPRESSO

Fold in 1 tsp coffee essence into the prepared meringue just before shaping.

VANILLA

Add ½–1 tsp natural vanilla extract to Italian or Swiss meringue, whisking it in with the sugar.

SOFT CHEESE DESSERTS

MOULDED CHEESE DESSERTS
·
BAKED CHEESECAKES
·
CHILLED SET CHEESECAKES

MOULDED CHEESE DESSERTS

A high water content (which is later drained away) allows soft cheeses to be moulded. These creamy desserts can be served ungarnished to cleanse the palate, or flavoured and decorated to complement any meal.

CREMET DE TOURAINE

200 ml whipping cream
300 g cream cheese
Approximately 50 g icing sugar

Raspberry Coulis
400 g fresh raspberries
80 g icing sugar
Lemon juice to taste

Decoration
Mint leaves
Red berries, such as raspberries
or other soft fruit

Line 6 ramekin dishes with muslin. Whip the cream lightly over ice, add the cream cheese and continue to whip until the mixture is smooth and creamy. Stir in icing sugar to taste. Spoon the mixture into the dishes and chill for at least 1 hour or overnight.

Make a coulis (see page 113) using the raspberries and icing sugar, with a little lemon juice to taste. Unmould the Crémet de Touraine and serve with the coulis. Decorate with fresh red berries and raspberry coulis.

The classic moulded cheese dessert, **Crémet de Touraine,** *can be flavoured with grated lemon or orange rind. Here it is served with raspberry coulis and decorated with sugared redcurrants.*

INDIVIDUAL SOFT CHEESE MOULDS

Choose moulds with holes in the bottom, which are necessary for draining the cheese mixture. Heart-shaped ones are attractive. Cut the muslin into appropriately sized squares.

1 Line the moulds with muslin, leaving the excess hanging over the rims. Stand them on a tray or in a larger dish.

2 Whip the cream lightly in a bowl standing over ice. Add the cream cheese and continue to whip until smooth and creamy.

3 Mix in the icing sugar to taste, then spoon the mixture into the dishes. Chill for at least an hour or preferably overnight.

4 Unmould the cheese carefully on to plates and gently remove the muslin. Serve with fruit coulis – kiwi, apricot or blackcurrant, or with fresh fruit slices.

MAKING PASHKA

Traditionally, this Russian Easter speciality is pressed lightly in a tall, muslin-lined, perforated, pyramid-shaped mould. A well-cleaned, new flowerpot is an adequate alternative. Pashka is made with 2 egg yolks, 150 g caster sugar, ½ tsp natural vanilla extract, 500 g cream cheese, 150 ml soured cream, 50 g sultanas, roughly chopped, and 300 g mixed candied and crystallized fruits, such as cherries, angelica, citron peel and pineapple, plus extra to decorate.

1 Beat together the egg yolks, vanilla and sugar over hot (not boiling) water until pale and thick.

Pashka can be decorated with candied fruit and peel, crystallized fruit or candied angelica.

2 Take the bowl off the hot water and beat until cool. Beat in the cream cheese and soured cream gradually.

3 Add the candied and crystallized fruit to the mixture and spoon into a muslin-lined sieve which rests over a bowl.

4 To enable excess liquid to drain, place a small plate or saucer on top of the cheese and top with a weight.

CHEESE VARIATIONS

There are several different types of cheeses you can use for making moulded cheese desserts. They should be light flavoured fresh cheeses with a rich, creamy texture. These include both cow's and goat's cheeses and the different types available can vary considerably in fat content, texture and flavour. Try the following:

Cottage cheese
Cream cheese
Curd cheese
Fromage frais
Mascarpone
Ricotta.

5 Chill overnight. To mould cheese, press the mixture into four muslin-lined dariole moulds. Chill for 1½–2 hours. To unmould, cover with a plate and invert both plate and mould together. Lift off the mould and peel away the muslin.

Mascarpone Figs

Cheese and fruit are both popular ways of ending a meal; here, two exotic varieties are combined. The creamy texture of the mascarpone marries well with the sweetness of the figs and both are set off by a deliciously crunchy cinnamon shortbread.

PREPARATION PLAN

▶ Prepare the shortbread biscuits, which can be made up to a couple of days before you assemble the dessert.

▶ Clean the figs with a damp cloth.

For the cinnamon shortbread
150 g butter
90 g caster sugar
30 g almond powder or finely ground almonds
1 large egg
250 g flour
1 tsp ground cinnamon

■ ■ ■

For the mascarpone cream
125 g mascarpone
250 ml double cream
50 g sugar
Pinch of ground cinnamon

■ ■ ■

For the caramelized figs
150 g sugar
1 cinnamon stick
2 stems rosemary
6 figs
Juice of 1 lemon

■ ■ ■

Rosemary

1 Prepare the cinnamon shortbread. Cream the butter and caster sugar together, then add in the ground almonds and then the egg. Sift the flour and cinnamon together and incorporate them into the creamed mixture. Stir until smooth and place in the refrigerator. When chilled, remove from the refrigerator and roll out the dough to a thickness of approximately 2–3 mm. Cut out 8 rectangles of about 8 x 5 cm. Bake in a 160°C oven for about 15 minutes until golden brown.

2 To prepare the mascarpone cream, whip the double cream with the sugar until it is thoroughly mixed and then incorporate the mascarpone, little by little, until the mixture has a smooth, rich, creamy texture. Add the cinnamon at the end and mix thoroughly. Leave to one side until ready to use.

3 Finally prepare the figs. In a sauté pan, cook the sugar with the cinnamon stick and the rosemary just until the mixture begins to caramelize. Add the figs and then the lemon juice. Cook on a low heat for a few minutes, stirring regularly until the figs begin to brown, then remove from the heat. Leave the figs whole for now so they retain their heat.

4 Using two spoons, shape the mascarpone cream into 8 quenelles of the same size. Take one piece of shortbread and place 2 quenelles of the mascarpone cream on it. Then lay another shortbread biscuit on top. Repeat with the rest of the biscuits.

5 Cut the figs in half lengthwise and place 3 warm fig halves on top of each upper biscuit. It is best to halve and place the figs once all of the biscuits are prepared to stop them from becoming cold during the preparation. Place the fig-topped shortbread on a small plate and spoon a little of the pan juices from the sautéeing over the figs and around the plate. Decorate with rosemary and serve immediately while the figs are still warm.

What's in a Name?

A rich double- or triple-cream cheese made from cow's milk, mascarpone hails from the Lombardy region of Northern Italy. It ranges in texture from that of a light clotted cream to the firmness of unchilled butter.

Although mainly sold unflavoured, in Italy's Friuli region a local speciality is to flavour mascarpone with anchovies, mustard and spices, but it is most widely sold sweetened with fruit. With its delicate flavour, mascarpone is versatile enough to take on board many flavours, but is equally delicious when served alone or simply topped with fruit.

Baked Cheesecakes

When baking cheesecake, aim for a slightly dry texture, rather than moist and heavy. Serve rich baked cheesecake with the classic accompaniments of poached or stewed fruit and generous spoonfuls of soured cream.

Baked cheesecake can be dusted with icing sugar and served with fresh fruit and a drizzle of fruit coulis, such as the raspberry coulis here.

MAKING BAKED CHEESECAKE

Plain cheesecakes are delicious, but for those who like a little extra flavour, add 75 g finely chopped citron peel and 100 g sultanas before folding in the egg whites, then bake as normal.

1 Line the base of a thoroughly greased springform tin with Pâte Sucrée, pushing it right to the edge of the tin. Prick well, chill and bake blind.

2 Prepare the filling. Fold in the egg whites at the last minute. The resulting mixture should be soft and light, similar in consistency to a whisked sponge.

BAKED CHEESECAKE

Pâte Sucrée (see page 122) made with 200 g flour, 130 g butter, 80 g caster sugar and 1 egg yolk

Filling

4 eggs, separated
100 g caster sugar
250 g cream cheese
250 g curd cheese or quark
Grated rind of 1 lemon
60 g plain flour
4 tbsp soured cream
Icing sugar to sift

Make the Pâte Sucrée and use to line the base of a greased 25 cm springform tin. Prick the dough and chill for 30 minutes, then bake for 10 minutes at 170°C.

Beat the egg yolks and caster sugar together until pale and creamy. Beat in the cream and curd cheeses (or quark) and the lemon rind gradually. Sift the flour over the mixture and beat it in, then fold in the soured cream.

Whisk the egg whites until stiff and fold into the mixture. Turn into the pastry case and bake at 160°C for 1½ hours, until deep golden and set. Leave to cool in the tin. Chill for several hours and sift with icing sugar before serving.

3 Pour the filling mixture evenly over the Pâte Sucrée base. Bake until it has risen and is deep golden. The centre should feel set and slightly springy.

4 Remove from the oven, place on a support and leave to cool in the tin. This type of cheesecake tends to shrink back on cooling.

INDIVIDUAL CHEESECAKES

The basic cheesecake mixture can be baked in pastry cases, Yorkshire pudding tins or muffin tins to make cheese tarts in individual portions. Alternatively, metal rings can be used. Stand the rings on a baking sheet. 1 quantity Pâte Sucrée as made for baked cheesecake (see left) and ½ quantity cheesecake filling (see left) will line and fill 12 muffin tins.

BASE VARIATIONS

- *Line the tin with thinly rolled pastry with the excess overhanging the edge. Add the filling and cover it with the overhanging pastry to form a complete case, trimming of the excess.*
- *Bake a thin layer of whisked sponge (see page 118) in the tin.*
- *Bake a thin layer of sweet yeast dough in the tin.*

1 Grease the muffin tins well and line with Pâte Sucrée. Trim the pastry to the tops of the tins, then part-bake the bases for about 10 minutes.

2 Spoon the mixture into the cases so they are two-thirds full. Add a little blackcurrant jam and bake for about 25–30 minutes at 160°C. Decorate once cold.

ALMOND RICOTTA CHEESECAKE

Pâte Sucrée (see page 122) made with 225 g plain flour, 100 g ground almonds, oil of bitter almonds, 130 g butter, 80 g caster sugar and 1 egg yolk

Filling

4 eggs, separated
100 g caster sugar
500 g ricotta cheese
Juice and grated rind of 1 lemon
60 g plain flour
1 tsp natural vanilla extract
150 g mixed dried and candied fruit
100 g ground almonds
Flaked almonds and icing sugar to decorate

Make Pâte Sucrée, adding 100 g ground almonds with the flour and a few drops of oil of bitter almonds with the yolk. Grease a 25 cm springform tin and line with pastry.

For the filling, beat together the egg yolks and caster sugar until pale and creamy. Beat in the cheese, lemon juice, rind and vanilla extract slowly. Sift in the flour, then beat. Add the ground almonds and fruit. Whisk the egg whites until stiff and fold into mixture. Turn into pastry case, sprinkle with flaked almonds, and bake at 170°C for 1¼ hours until deep golden and set. Leave to cool, then chill for several hours and sift with icing sugar before serving.

CHILLED SET CHEESECAKES

Cheesecakes which are unbaked and set with gelatine are comparatively modern additions to the culinary repertoire. They are invariably topped with fruit.

BISCUIT CRUSTS

Crushed biscuit bases are a very popular base for set cheesecakes. The crumbs are bound using melted unsalted butter and are pressed into a tin and chilled until firm. Digestive biscuits are ideal for this purpose – they are not too sweet and make a base with a good crumbly texture. Various other biscuits can be used on their own or combined with digestives. For example, try almond macaroons or chocolate-coated biscuits. Always buy good-quality biscuits.

1 Crush the biscuits in a plastic bag, tapping or rolling with a rolling pin. Alternatively, use a food processor, pulsing the power for even results.

2 Melt the butter in a saucepan and stir in the biscuits. Remove the base mixture and press into a tin, smoothing with the back of a metal spoon. Chill until firm.

MAKING A SET CHEESECAKE

The Lemon Cheesecake recipe is an excellent base for different fruit toppings. Or add chopped fresh fruit to the mixture. It is important to make the mixture as smooth as possible.

1 Boil the sugar and water to the soft ball stage, then whisk it into the egg yolks in a thin stream. Continue whisking until cool.

2 Beat together the cream cheese, lemon rind and juice. Stir in the dissolved gelatine. Mix this with the yolks gradually until smooth.

3 Fold in the whipped cream. Turn the filling mixture on to the biscuit base and chill until set.

LEMON CHEESECAKE

250 g digestive biscuits
130 g unsalted butter
160 g sugar
125 ml water
15 g powdered gelatine
6 egg yolks
Grated rind and juice
of 1 lemon
500 g cream cheese
400 ml whipping cream

Prepare a biscuit crust using the digestive biscuits and butter (see steps, left). Press this into a 25 cm springform tin and chill until firm.

Make a syrup. Dissolve the sugar in 80 ml of the water in a saucepan, then boil to the soft ball stage (see page 108). Whisk the egg yolks in a heatproof bowl, then pour in the syrup in a thin stream, whisking continuously until the yolk and syrup mixture is pale and creamy. Continue whisking until cool.

Dissolve the gelatine in the remaining water. Beat together the cream cheese, lemon rind and lemon juice, then stir in the dissolved gelatine. Stir the cheese mixture into the yolk and syrup mixture gradually.

Whip the cream until it stands in soft peaks and fold this into the mixture. Turn into the tin on the biscuit base, smooth the top so that it is level and chill for several hours, until firm.

80

FRESH FRUIT TOPPINGS

Peaches, berries and exotic fruit are ideal for topping lemon cheesecake. Prepare the fruit according to type. Use evenly sized fruits or pieces of fruit.

1 For an elaborate peach arrangement, start at the edge, overlapping fruit slices until most of the cake is covered. Work symmetrically.

2 Make the arrangement more dense towards the centre. Finish by applying an apricot or redcurrant glaze over the fruit slices.

POACHED FRUIT TOPPINGS

Fruits can be poached in light syrup. Once cooled, the fruit can be applied as a topping. Thicken the syrup with some arrowroot (to set it in a clear glaze) and pour it over.

1 Pipe a whipped cream border to neaten the edge of the cheesecake and contain the thickened syrup.

FLAVOURING CHEESECAKE

FRUIT PUREE
. . . .

Fruit purée may be used instead of the egg yolk mixture. Beat 160 g caster sugar with the cream cheese and lemon juice. Omit the lemon rind. Gradually beat in 300 ml fruit purée (apricot, strawberry or raspberry, for example) before adding the gelatine. Fold in the whipped cream as above.

LIME OR ORANGE
. . . .

The grated rind and juice of lime or orange may be used instead of lemon.

*The deep red of cherries contrasts beautifully with the creamy body of the **cheesecake**.*

2 Arrange the cold fruit on top of the cake and then carefully spoon over the cooled, but not set, syrup.

INDIVIDUAL FRUIT CHEESECAKES

A plain, thin whisked sponge, made as for Swiss Roll (see page 118), can be used as a base for lemon cheesecake (see page 80). For individual chilled fruit cheesecakes, cut the sponge to fit small moulds, such as metal rings.

1 Apply a light coating of sweet almond oil to 7.5 cm metal rings and stamp out sponge circles. Place the rings on a tray, keeping the sponge in place within them.

2 Moisten the sponge with spoonfuls of kirsch or another liqueur.

3 Top the sponge with fresh fruit, such as halved strawberries.

4 Fill with the lemon cheesecake mixture, ensuring the fruit is concealed, and chill. Loosen the cheesecakes from the rings with a thin-bladed knife, then lift off the rings. Transfer the cheesecakes to plates with a metal slice or palette knife.

*Decorate **individual cheesecakes** with sliced strawberries that have been glazed with warmed redcurrant jelly, piped whipped cream, and fine orange zest.*

BATTERS & OMELETTES

CREPES & PANCAKES
·
WAFFLES
·
BAKED BATTER PUDDINGS
·
FRITTERS
·
OMELETTES

CREPES & PANCAKES

Making a batter of perfect consistency and controlling the cooking temperature are two essential points for success when making delicate crêpes or pancakes.

MAKING LACY CREPES

Thin, rich batter is essential for French-style fine crêpes. The pan must be hot enough to set the batter quickly, but not too hot so as to brown it before the crêpe is firmly set. It is usually difficult to achieve an ideal temperature for cooking the first crêpe, which tends to brown before it is firm enough to turn without breaking.

 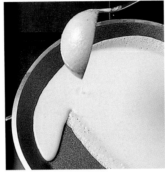  

1 Heat a little clarified butter or oil in a pan and pour off the excess. Hold the pan at an angle and pour in a little batter.

2 Tilt and swivel the pan as you pour to coat the base thinly and evenly with the batter.

3 When the crêpe is pale gold underneath, use a palette knife to loosen and turn it. Shake the pan to settle the crêpe.

4 Cook until golden on the second side. Turn on to parchment. Interleave crêpes with baking parchment to prevent sticking.

CREPE BATTER

100 g plain flour
½ tsp salt
3 eggs
1 yolk
175 ml milk
75 ml water
25 g clarified butter, melted, or 1 tbsp oil

Follow the basic technique for preparing batters (see page 125), adding the melted butter at the end. Cover the batter and chill for 30 minutes. If it is cooked immediately, it tends to either rise slightly or bubble. Check the consistency of the batter after standing and add a little milk if it is too thick.

Fans

SERVING CREPES AND PANCAKES

Choose delicate fillings for the finest crêpes and slightly more substantial fillings for thicker pancakes. Try some of the suggestions here.

- *A sprinkling of lemon juice and caster sugar.*
- *Fruit preserve or sauce.*
- *Grilled fruit.*
- *Poached or puréed fruit.*
- *Crème Pâtissière (see page 116), either plain or fruit flavoured.*
- *Melted chocolate and finely chopped toasted hazelnuts.*
- *Maple syrup.*
- *Heated thickened syrup from compotes.*
- *Crème Anglaise (see page 116).*
- *Cold ginger syrup (from a jar of stem ginger).*
- *Hot Chocolate Sauce (see page 115).*

FOLDING CREPES

The traditional shape for a folded crêpe is a fan. This is made by folding the crêpe in half, then into quarters. This presentation displays the filling. Other options are folding crêpes into pannequets or cigarettes, both of which enclose the filling completely.

Pannequets

PANNEQUETS
To fold crêpes into squares or pannequets, fold opposite sides inwards over the filling to meet in the middle. Then bring the bottom edge up to the centre and the top edge down to overlap.

CIGARETTES
For rolls or cigarettes, fold opposite sides inwards, but not all the way to the middle, then, starting at the bottom, roll the crêpe up towards the top. Take care not to squeeze out the filling as you roll.

Cigarettes

FRUIT-FILLED CREPES

Soft fruit, such as strawberries, should be sprinkled with icing sugar to taste. Grilled or fried fruit (see pages 16) are alternatives – try sliced grilled bananas or chunks of fried pineapple. Poached and puréed fruit (see pages 113) are ideal fillings. Place filled crêpes in a buttered ovenproof dish, dust with icing sugar and reheat briefly in the oven before serving.

CREPE PANS

Pans for pancakes and blini (see page 87) have shallow sides which slope widely, making it easy to turn the contents. Traditionally, they are made of thick cast iron to spread the heat evenly. They must not be washed, but should be seasoned with a little oil, rubbed with salt, wiped out, heated with some oil and wiped again. After use, wipe with clean oil on kitchen paper. If necessary, scour with salt and wipe clean with oil.

COOKED FRUIT
Spoon the filling, here cherry compote (see page 15), on a quarter of each crêpe. Fold in half, then into a quarter.

WHOLE OR CHUNKY FRUIT
Using a spoon, fill the crêpes carefully with pieces of whole fruit or fruit pieces. Do this directly before serving, so that the crêpes are not saturated with fruit juice.

LAYERED CREPES

Crêpes can be layered with fillings and served as a crêpe gâteau or a pancake stack. Spread firm fillings thinly to help keep the stack in shape, or use a metal ring mould or a loose-based tin to confine the crêpes. (Make sure the crêpes are cooked to the correct size for the tin.) Cook the batter as usual, then reduce the heat to cook the last crêpe so that it has a slightly paler colour. Place this one on the top of the stack and serve.

1 Spread firm fillings, such as ricotta and candied fruit, thinly. The crêpes can be layered on a baking sheet or in a tin or mould.

2 Place the pale crêpe on the top of the stack to give the dessert a light look. This also helps to highlight the topping.

3 Before baking, brush the top layer with a little hot syrup. Use lemon and Amaretto to glaze.

*Decorate **pancake stacks** with ingredients that suit the filling. Ricotta and candied fruit are here complemented with a sprinkling of toasted almond flakes and icing sugar. Try flavoured sauces, melted chocolate or honey.*

SOUFFLE CREPES

Soufflé and crêpes work well together in terms of flavours, and this dessert looks quite spectacular. Cook the pancakes in advance, and prepare the soufflé filling at the last minute.

Spoon some soufflé mixture on to a crêpe, slightly off centre, and fold the crêpe almost in half over it. Once filled, place the crêpes in a buttered shallow ovenproof dish. Apply a light dusting of icing sugar over the pancakes and bake them at 220°C for about 5 minutes, until the soufflé is risen and just set. Serve immediately.

CREPE FILLINGS FOR GATEAUX & SOUFFLES

- *Sweetened fruit purée. Serve with Crème Chantilly or Crème Anglaise.*
- *Sweetened chestnut purée mixed with 2 tbsp rum and whipped double cream. Serve with chocolate sauce.*
- *Ricotta cheese with fresh chopped or candied fruit. Serve with a fruit sauce or flavoured syrup.*

For a vanilla flavour, make a Vanilla Soufflé (see page 60), reducing the milk to 300 ml and using 4 eggs to produce a slightly firmer mixture which will not run out of the crêpes. Any of the flavoured soufflés, similarly adapted, can be used as fillings for crêpes. Serve the dessert with a fruit sauce or a hot fruit compote.

GRIDDLE PANCAKES

225 g plain flour
1 tsp cream of tartar
½ tsp bicarbonate of soda
25 g caster sugar
2 eggs
Approximately 300 ml milk,
buttermilk or single cream
50 g butter, melted

Sift the flour, cream of tartar and bicarbonate of soda into a bowl. Stir in the sugar. Make a well in the dry ingredients, add the eggs and gradually work in the milk, buttermilk or single cream and melted butter to make a smooth, thick batter. Cook the batter as soon as it is prepared (see steps, right).

COOKING GRIDDLE PANCAKES

These small, thick pancakes, known as drop scones, Scotch pancakes or American pancakes, are traditionally served at teatime with butter and caster sugar. For a special breakfast or dessert, serve them with pan-glazed poached fruit, particularly tangy varieties – try pan-glazed apple wedges with Crème Anglaise or Crème Chantilly, sprinkled with ground cinnamon.

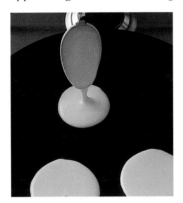  

1 Grease a hot griddle with clarified butter. Hold a dessertspoonful of batter high above the griddle (so it falls into a neat circle) and drop the batter, holding the spoon vertically.

2 Cook the pancakes until the batter is blistered with bursting bubbles and just set, but still slightly moist on top. Then turn and cook the second side until golden.

3 To keep the pancakes warm until all the batter has been cooked, place them in a heated dish lined with a warmed tea-towel and cover.

4 Cook 225 g cranberries with 4 tbsp port until tender. Stir in 175 g sugar and 2 peeled, cored and diced eating apples. Cook until the apples are tender.

5 Carefully top each pancake with cooked cranberry and apples. Serve them dusted with caster sugar or icing sugar.

BLINIS

120 g plain flour
12 g baking powder
1 egg
30 g sugar
125 ml milk
30 g softened butter

Sieve the flour and baking powder into a bowl and add the egg and sugar. Mix these together as you slowly add the milk and then the softened butter. Heat a little oil in a pan and, using a dessertspoon, drop in some batter. Cook as for griddle pancakes, above. Serve straight away with a selection of sweet and fruit toppings.

Orange Crêpe Gâteau

This spectacular cake is assembled from individual crêpes, which are moulded and filled with a Cointreau-laced orange cream and then topped with an apricot glaze. For a grand finale, spoon more Cointreau over the top and set alight.

PREPARATION PLAN

▶ Prepare the batter in advance and keep refrigerated for up to 24 hours until ready to use.

▶ Take the zest for the orange cream from one of the oranges and keep the orange covered to avoid drying out.

For the crêpe batter
100 g plain flour
4 eggs
2.5 g salt
70 g sugar
200 ml milk
100 g double cream
30 g melted butter
2 tbsp beer

■ ■ ■

For the orange cream
200 ml single cream
20 g icing sugar
Zest of ½ an orange
1 tbsp Cointreau

■ ■ ■

For the apricot glaze
100 g apricot jam
50 ml water

■ ■ ■

**4 oranges
2 tbsp Cointreau**

1 Make the crêpe batter. Mix together the flour, eggs, salt and sugar. Gradually incorporate the milk and cream and then the melted butter. Mix the beer in thoroughly and leave to one side.

2 For the orange cream, pour the cream into a chilled bowl and whisk in the icing sugar. Just before the cream begins to form firm peaks, add the grated orange zest and then the Cointreau. Mix together and refrigerate.

3 Peel the oranges and separate the segments. Clean them of pith and remove the membranes. Set to one side, lightly covered with a cloth or bowl.

4 Cook the crêpes in a non-stick pan. If the batter is too thick you can dilute it by mixing in a little milk before cooking. Heat a small amount of butter in the

pan. Spoon 1–2 tbsp of crêpe batter into the hot pan and tip the pan to ensure there is an even coating of batter in the bottom of the pan. Cook for about 2–3 minutes, until the edges of the crêpe lift cleanly from the pan and the underside is golden brown. Turn the crêpe and cook for a further 2–3 minutes until golden on both sides. Repeat with the rest of the batter, making at least 12–14 crêpes in all. When all the crêpes are made, place them in a warm oven while you prepare the mould.

5 Set aside 3–4 crêpes and several orange segments for the finishing touches. Prepare a 12 cm charlotte mould. To aid unmoulding, line the mould with cling-film, leaving enough excess hanging over the edges of the mould to cover the top of the finished gâteau. Take 2 crêpes and line the mould, allowing their edges also to hang over the edges of the mould.

6 Fill a piping bag with the orange cream and pipe a layer of cream into the base of the lined mould. Press 3–4 orange segments into the cream and top with a crêpe, with the edges folded in to fit. Repeat until you just reach the top of the mould. Finish with a layer of cream and then fold the loose edges of the first two crêpes over the top. Follow this by folding the clingfilm over the top of the crêpes. Place in the refrigerator for 2–3 hours to chill thoroughly.

7 When ready to serve, prepare the apricot glaze. Gently heat the apricot jam in a saucepan until it begins to liquefy, then add the water and bring to the boil, stirring continuously. Remove from the heat and allow to cool a little while you unmould the gâteau and remove the clingfilm. Sieve the jam glaze and pour half the resulting liquid over the crêpe gâteau. Take the 3–4 crêpes that were set aside and either brush or dip them into the glaze one at a time, then pleat into pretty folded shapes and decorate the top of the gâteau with them. Add the reserved orange segments, tucking them into the folded pancakes on top of the gâteau. As you serve the gâteau, pour the remaining Cointreau over it and set alight.

FRUIT PANCAKES

*Perfect fruit pancakes should be slightly risen, crisp in places
and pleasantly juicy or tangy, depending on the fruit used.
Lighten the batter with egg whites and fold in pieces of fruit.
Prepare the fruit according to type, discarding tough skin,
cores and stones. Use 225 g fruit – apples, plums, pineapple,
cherries or blueberries, 75 g plain flour, 2 tbsp caster sugar,
100 ml single cream, 1 egg, separated, with caster, cinnamon
or icing sugar to serve. Serve fruit pancakes immediately as
they should be enjoyed freshly cooked.*

1 Sift the flour into a bowl and stir in the sugar. Mix in the cream and egg yolk to make a smooth thick batter. Fold the stiffly whisked egg white into the thick batter, but do not incorporate it thoroughly at this stage.

2 Fold in the prepared fruit, making sure it is distributed evenly in the batter. This action will ensure that the egg white is also evenly distributed.

3 Cook spoonfuls of the pancake and fruit mixture in hot clarified butter. Use the tip of the spoon to distribute the fruit evenly and attractively across the pancake before the batter has set.

4 Regulate the heat to suit the fruit. Firm fruits should have time enough to cook before the batter is set and browned underneath. Soft fruits, blueberries, for instance, should be cooked quickly. Use a spatula to turn the pancakes carefully.

FRUIT FLAVOURINGS

CITRUS FRUIT

Citrus fruits work well with this batter. Peel the fruit and remove all pith and pips and cut into small pieces. Try combining certain fruits, such as lemon and lime, orange and lemon. Tangerine pancakes make a good winter teatime treat. Add a little lemon juice to the batter for extra tang, if required.

DRIED FRUIT

Chop dried fruit into small pieces. They can be soaked in alcohol before cooking to add to the flavour. Try with raisins and sultanas, apricots with apples and mangos with papaya.

FRESH FRUIT

If you are using quite large fruit, cut it into smal pieces so that it can be evenly distributed around the pancakes mixture. For example, slice apples and plums thinly, cut small pineapple pieces and halve cherries. Small berries – blueberries and raspberries – can be used whole.

WAFFLES

As with griddle pancakes, waffle batter rises with the help of a raising agent such as self-raising flour, or with the addition of egg whites. The result is crisp and light.

WAFFLE BATTER

175 g plain flour
2 tsp baking powder
½ tsp salt
2 tsp sugar
2 eggs, separated
225 ml milk
85 g butter, melted

Sift the plain flour into a bowl with the baking powder and the salt, then stir in the sugar. Beat together the egg yolks, milk and butter in a separate bowl, then add this mixture to the dry ingredients and mix well. Whisk the egg whites until they are stiff and fold them into the waffle mixture. This waffle batter should be quite smooth and fairly thick.

WAFFLE IRONS

These double-sided cooking utensils give waffles their characteristic honeycomb appearance. Traditionally, they are made of cast iron, are heated on the hob and are turned half way through cooking. The electric waffle iron is more commonly used today. It has non-stick plates with a heating element on each side. Once the batter is poured in and the top plate closed, the batter cooks evenly. For using and cleaning waffle irons, follow the instructions provided by the manufacturer.

MAKING WAFFLES

Scandinavian waffles are often enriched with soured cream and served with berries and more soured cream. Americans enjoy waffles with syrup for breakfast. Try flavouring the batter with ground cardamom or cinnamon.

1 Pour the batter into one plate and tease it into the corners with the tip of a spoon. Close the cover and heat. With stove-top irons, cook for 2 minutes, then turn the iron to cook the second side.

2 Open the iron carefully and, if necessary, ease the waffle away from the top plate using a plastic utensil. (Do not scratch the non-stick surface by using a knife or other metal utensil.) Turn the waffle out on to a plate.

*Combine hot and cold – serve **waffles** with vanilla ice cream, a sprinkling of chopped nuts and chocolate sauce. Try pan-glazed tangerines, flamed in rum, with whipped cream and candied zest. Strawberry compote is delicious on waffles, served with clotted cream. Decorate with a sprig of mint.*

BAKED BATTER PUDDINGS

**A crisp, light batter studded with colourful and refreshing fruit makes
an attractive dinner party dessert. Being quick and easy to make, baked
batter puddings are also ideal for everyday meals.**

INDIVIDUAL BATTER PUDDINGS

*When preparing individual
portions, bear in mind that
batter cooks quickly in small
dishes, so firm fruits such as
pears should be poached first,
as shown here. For a zesty
flavour, poach them in light
syrup (see page 108) adding
the pared rind and juice of 1
orange. Pour the batter over
the fruit and bake at 180°C
for 30 minutes. Be creative
with your choice of fruit and
fruit combinations.*

1 Poach the pears gently
until just tender. Test
the softness by piercing with
a knife. Drain the pears.

2 Slice pears three-quarters through to the stalk ends. Place
the pears in buttered individual ovenproof dishes and fan
out the slices. Pour in the batter carefully and bake.

LARGE BATTER PUDDING

*Clafoutis, the classic French
batter pudding, is best served
warm to bring out the flavour
of the cherries fully. Cherries
are traditional, but any fruit
can be cooked in this way
(larger fruits may
require pre-
cooking).*

1 Ladle the batter over the
cherries in a buttered
shallow ovenproof dish.

2 Dredge the top of the
cooked pudding with
caster sugar while hot.

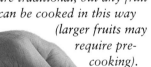

CLAFOUTIS

125 g plain flour
Pinch of salt
2 eggs
25 g caster sugar
300 ml milk
½ tsp natural vanilla extract
500 g cherries, stoned

Make a batter as on page 125
and stir in the vanilla extract.
Carefully ladle the batter over
the cherries in a buttered,
shallow ovenproof dish. Take
care not to disturb the cherries
so they float to the surface of
the batter. Bake at 180°C for
1–1¼ hours, until the batter
has set, risen and is golden in
colour. Dredge the top of the
hot pudding with caster sugar.
Allow the pudding to cool
slightly before serving it warm.

DECORATED BATTER PUDDINGS

Creamy custards or tangy fruit sauces and syrups complement baked batter puddings and can be used as decoration. Ice cream provides a superb hot-cold contrast. Here, crisp-baked apple puddings are shaped attractively in muffin tins.

1 Dip thin slices from a quartered, cored and peeled apple in lemon juice to prevent discolouration.

2 Arrange in deep, buttered muffin tins and pour in the Clafoutis batter (see opposite page). Bake at 180°C for 20–25 minutes.

3 While the apple puddings are cooking, dip unpeeled apple slices in a light caramel (see page 109) and place on non-stick baking parchment to set.

FRUIT FOR BATTER PUDDINGS

- *Apples, peeled, cored and halved, quartered or sliced.*
- *Halved and stoned fresh apricots.*
- *Pitted prunes soaked in brandy and drained.*
- *Gooseberries, served whole or peeled.*
- *Rhubarb, cut tender stalks into short lengths.*
- *Plums, halved and stoned.*

*Apple pudding is sprinkled with icing sugar and served with caramel-dipped apples. **Apricot batter pudding**, shaped in a Yorkshire pudding tin, is served with custard patterned with apricot coulis, with summer berries.*

FRITTERS

Different ingredients and preparation methods will produce dessert fritters in a range of interesting variations. Batter made with yeast has another character altogether – it has a distinctively light, spongy texture.

PREPARING FRITTERS

Prepare a light batter using 300 g plain flour, 2 tbsp potato flour, a pinch of salt, 250 ml light beer or lager and 2 eggs (see page 125). Stir in 1 tbsp oil. Use a two-pronged fork to dip fruit in the batter, allowing the excess batter to drain off. Heat the vegetable oil to 190°C to deep-fry the fritters. Drain, then turn in caster sugar.

1 Peel and cut the fruit, removing pips or stones. Drain well on kitchen paper, then dip into the batter.

2 Deep-fry the fritters for 2–3 minutes until crisp and golden. Once fried, drain well on kitchen paper.

3 Turn the fritters in caster sugar, giving them an even coating. Serve fritters immediately.

ORIENTAL COATED FRITTERS

Make a caramel (see page 109). Peel and cut the fruit (apples and bananas are used traditionally). Dip the fruit into batter and deep-fry until golden brown. While draining the fritters, dip the base of the pot of caramel in iced water to stop it cooking. Coat the fritters in caramel, drain, sprinkle with sesame seeds and serve at once.

STUFFED FRITTERS

Dried prunes and apricots steeped in brandy or liqueur are ideal for this dish. Mix ground almonds, a little icing sugar, a few drops of rose water and a touch of sherry into a stiff paste. Press an oval of the paste into each piece of fruit and roll in ground almonds. Dip in batter and deep-fry as before. Serve immediately.

*Serve a selection of **plain, coated** and **stuffed fritters** with an apricot coulis (see page 113) for a delicious family treat.*

YEASTED BATTER FRITTERS

Fritter batter that is made with yeast produces light fritters with a crisp, golden surface. Moistness and sweetness in the form of smooth honey syrup completes the recipe. The Greeks call their version of this dish Loukoumathes and the Turkish variety is Lokma. The Italians flavour these fritters with vanilla, nuts, lemon and candied peel. Traditionally, the batter is beaten with the flat of the hand.

*Honey syrup complements both the colour and flavour of **yeast fritters**.*

YEAST BATTER

175 g strong plain flour
1 tbsp caster sugar
¼ tsp salt
1 tbsp fast-action easy-blend dried yeast
100 ml water
100 ml milk
½ tsp natural vanilla extract

Mix the flour, sugar, salt and yeast in a bowl and make a well in the middle of these ingredients. Pour the water into this recess, then begin to stir in the dry ingredients gradually from the edges of the water. Once part of the dry ingredients are mixed with water, add milk and the remaining flour gradually. Add the vanilla with the last of the milk.

Beat the batter hard until smooth and elastic. Cover with cling film or a slightly damp tea-towel. Set aside to rise until doubled in volume.

Honey Syrup

Dissolve 100 g sugar in 100 ml water and boil for 2 minutes. Stir in the juice of ½ lemon and 175 g clear honey. Bring to a full boil, then remove from the heat.

FLAVOURING YEASTED FRITTERS

LEMON RIND
· · · · · · · ·

Add the grated rind of 1 lemon, 50 g finely chopped candied peel and an additional 1 tbsp caster sugar to the beaten batter and mix well before setting aside to rise. Dust the fritters with caster sugar before serving.

CURRANTS
· · · · · · · ·

Add 50 g currants and the grated rind of 1 lemon to the beaten batter and mix well before setting aside to rise. Dust with caster sugar and serve with lemon wedges – lemon juice enhances this mixture of flavours.

1 Beat the batter hard until smooth and elastic – it should have a stringy, stretchy texture. Cover the bowl and leave in a warm place until risen to twice its original volume.

2 Heat oil for deep-frying to 190°C. Dip two metal spoons in cold water, shake off excess liquid – this stops batter from sticking to them. Scoop up some batter with one spoon and use the other to slide this into the oil.

3 Fry the fritters until they have puffed up fully and are crisp in texture and deep golden in colour. Drain well on absorbent kitchen paper. Serve the fritters immediately with warm honey syrup.

OMELETTES

**Folded around a sweet filling, such as fruit, cheese or jam, an omelette
makes a substantial dessert. Light handling and speedy cooking are
essential for successful results.**

SETTING AND FOLDING AN OMELETTE

*Before cooking, prepare the filling and have a warmed plate ready for serving. Use clarified
butter and heat the pan thoroughly. For a large serving, use a 20 cm pan for 3 eggs with 1 tbsp
water. With a small pan, 2 eggs will be ample. Once cooked, slide on to the plate and serve.*

1 Lightly whisk the eggs and water, then pour them into the foaming butter in a very hot pan, tilting it to coat it evenly.

2 Cook the eggs over a high heat, lifting the sides of the omelette to allow any egg that is not yet set to run on to the hot surface.

3 Once the omelette is set, but moist on top, add the filling. Fold the omelette in half or roll it to enclose the filling. Serve immediately.

SOUFFLE OMELETTE

*A soufflé omelette
is made from
separated eggs.
The stiffly
whisked
whites are
folded into
the yolk
mixture.
Flash the
omelette
under a hot
grill to set
the top.*

*Fill **omelettes**
with fruit preserve
and a fruit coulis,
marmalade, fresh
fruit, soft cheese
or honey.*

1 Beat together in a bowl 2 egg yolks, 10 g caster sugar, 1 tbsp water and ¼ tsp natural vanilla extract. Whisk the egg whites until stiff and beat a small spoonful of this into the yolk mixture, then fold in the rest.

2 Cook the omelette in clarified butter over moderate heat until golden underneath. Set and lightly brown the top under a hot grill. Quickly add the filling, then fold the omelette in half and serve immediately.

BASIC TECHNIQUES

EQUIPMENT
·
FRUITS & NUTS
·
SUGAR SYRUPS
·
CHOCOLATE
·
ICINGS, PUREES & COULIS
·
SAUCES
·
CUSTARDS & CREAMS
·
SPONGES
·
PASTRY
·
BATTERS
·
BISCUITS
·
JELLIES & GELATINE

EQUIPMENT FOR DESSERTS

It is difficult to separate items of equipment that are particularly suitable for desserts from the general batterie de cuisine for preparing savoury dishes, although there are many items that are specifically designed for the preparation of desserts and fruit. Highly specialist pieces of equipment are explained when and where they are used throughout the chapters, particularly those on cakes, chocolate and sugar, but the following are helpful notes on selecting general equipment with dessert preparation in mind.

MEASURING EQUIPMENT

As for all cooking, accurate scales for weighing are essential, as is a clearly calibrated glass measuring jug for checking liquid volumes. Remember to stand your measuring jug on a level surface and view it from the side for an accurate reading. The following are also useful items for making desserts.

GATEAU DIVIDERS OR MARKERS Either as concentric rings or in the form of a wedge-shaped marker, these can be used for accurately measuring portions of round gâteaux. This is useful for applying symmetrical decorations as well as for marking wedges into icing or dredged sugar coatings.

METAL KITCHEN RULER Keep a 30–45 cm metal ruler exclusively for kitchen use. This is essential for measuring some pastry items and biscuits, and excellent for preparing chocolate decorations. A ruler is also useful for marking portions on oblong or square items, such as tray-baked desserts or gâteaux and tarts.

METAL MEASURING SPOONS Although good quality plastic spoons are perfectly acceptable for the majority of ingredients, metal is particularly useful for syrups and honey. Sticky ingredients will slide off a metal spoon that has been heated in boiling water and then dried.

THERMOMETER A sugar thermometer is useful for boiling syrups. Look for one which has a hook suitable for supporting the thermometer on the side of a pan. This will keep it in the liquid but away from the base of the pan.

VERSATILE UTENSILS

The following is a selection from the vast range that is available. As a general rule, invest in good-quality equipment, which may seem expensive, but will wear well and give consistently good results in the right hands.

APPLE CORER A cylindrical blade for cutting the centre cleanly out of apples.

BALLER For scooping balls of melon or other fruit, or for sorbets and ice creams. Available in a variety of sizes,

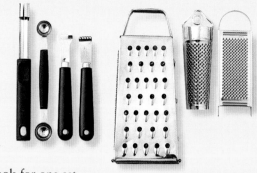

especially from specialist cookshops and chefs' suppliers.

CITRUS SQUEEZER A ridged cone on which to press and turn halved citrus fruit to extract juice. Look for one set over a fairly large container to catch the juices, with a strainer to separate pips.

DREDGER A container, usually of metal, with a perforated top for sprinkling flour, sugar, chocolate or other powder. A sieve can be used instead.

GRATER A box grater which will stand firmly on a board is a good investment. Look for one with several different blades, giving a choice of fine or coarse results.

ICE CREAM SCOOP There are two main types: firstly, a bowl-shaped scoop with a fine, blunt blade which 'flips' across the inside of the scoop to release ice cream. This gives a semi-circular, very rounded portion. A scoop with cutaway sides can be used for creating slightly softer shapes and this is usually the better choice as, with practice, full, rounded scoops can be formed. Look for a sturdy scoop which will cope with firmly frozen ices.

MARBLE SLAB A good investment if you frequently work with chocolate or fondant. A large marble surface is also ideal for pastry work.

NUTMEG GRATER A small, fine grater, sometimes with a compartment for storing a nutmeg. Mechanical nutmeg graters (with a compartment in which to place the nutmegs and a handle for winding them over a blade) can be an extremely disappointing waste of money.

PASTRY BRUSHES A good selection is essential, with a brush reserved for greasing with oil and others for glazing items, such as pastries.

PESTLE AND MORTAR Available in various sizes for grinding herbs and spices. Get one that is big enough: stone or porcelain are the best – wood may absorb flavours and metal can make the ingredients taste tinny.

ROLLING PIN The standard variety is made of solid, heavy wood. Marble or other stone rolling pins are cooler, making it easier to work with some doughs.

SIEVE Buy a fine, stainless steel sieve. A large one will allow foods to be worked around with a spoon when puréeing or removing seeds or skin.

SLOTTED SPOON For straining. A hole in the handle makes it easy to hang up.

SPATULA Look for a flexible plastic or rubber spatula for removing mixtures from bowls.

STONER OR PITTER For removing the stones from cherries or olives, this consists of a cherry-sized cup with a hole in the base through which a prong pushes out the stone.

VEGETABLE PEELER Look for a swivel-bladed peeler which can be used for thin paring.

WHISK A wire balloon whisk or similar is essential. Look for sturdy construction and a substantial handle that is comfortable. A miniature whisk is a useful tool. Electric whisking is a feature of most food processors.

WOODEN SPOONS These are useful and inexpensive. Throw them away when they become burnt or cracked: not to do so is a false economy.

ZESTER This consists of a line of small holes at the end of a blunt utensil. These are dragged over citrus fruit to remove short, fine strips of zest that are larger than coarsely grated, but smaller than strips removed using a canelle knife.

NOTES ON KNIVES AND CUTTERS

A range of good general-purpose, sharp knives is essential in every kitchen. You will need large and medium chef's knives for slicing, cutting and chopping.

BISCUIT AND PASTRY CUTTERS Hundreds of different models are available. The traditional round ones will probably be used more than the exotic animal and flower shapes, although the latter can also double as interesting cake decoration tools.

CAKE SLICE Buy both a large and a small one. Trying to balance a large piece of gateau on a narrow slice can easily lead to disaster.

CANELLE KNIFE This has a small dip or 'V' edge in the blade, designed to cut thin strips from fruit rind (or vegetables). Useful for cutting citrus rind or for scoring decorative marks into pears or apples.

FINE-BLADED KNIFE (SMALL) A small knife with a fine, narrow blade is useful for cutting decorative shapes into fruit and fruit rind. These are often sold as part of garnishing or decorating kits but better quality fine-bladed knives are often bought singly.

PALETTE KNIVES (LARGE AND SMALL) A palette knife has a blunt flat blade, with a rounded top. It is useful for spreading and smoothing ingredients such as cream and for detaching items such as biscuits from baking trays.

PARING KNIFE A small knife, similar to a chef's knife, is essential for preparing fruit. This should be a knife that you can hold comfortably and

manipulate easily to perform fiddly tasks, such as cutting the cores out of apple quarters.

PASTRY WHEEL Useful for cutting long strips of dough.

SCISSORS Make sure they are sharp, comfortable and made of stainless steel. Like good knives, good scissors are not cheap.

SERRATED KNIFE (LARGE) For slicing sponge cake into horizontal layers when making gateaux. This should have a long, straight blade with a rounded end. A large bread knife is ideal.

BOWLS AND BASINS

Professional cooks prefer stainless steel, but ovenproof glassware is the classic domestic alternative. Bowls and basins are often confused with each other: a bowl is a large and fairly wide-topped container; a basin is a small but deep container. A small bowl would have a wider top than a small basin. The classic British pudding basin has deep sides sloping to a narrow, slightly rounded bottom. Modern basins, used for mixing and cooking puddings, are slightly wider across the bottom: they are not quite as deep and their sides do not slope as sharply. Old-fashioned pudding basins have wide rims for attaching a cloth around the top to cover a steamed pudding, but with foil being the modern alternative to cloth, new basins have only a narrow rim. Having the correct bowl to hand makes the job of cooking infinitely easier.

MOULDS

GLASS MOULDS While these have a classic decorative appeal, metal are more practical, allowing heat to be applied for releasing moulded desserts.

PLASTIC MOULDS AND CONTAINERS These vary widely in quality. High-quality rigid containers with airtight lids are excellent, but flimsy ones will become misshapen and should be avoided. Some plastics may affect the taste of food.

PIPING EQUIPMENT

BAGS A plastic-coated fabric piping bag is a kitchen essential: a good bag can be sterilized or boiled after use and dried. It should give several years' wear. It will probably be necessary to have a few bags, cut to different widths at the base to accommodate various piping nozzles.

NOZZLES Large nozzles double up for savoury and sweet use. Plain nozzles in two or three sizes are useful for piping choux paste and meringue. Serrated nozzles are also used for piping whipped cream decorations on to gateaux and desserts. Small nozzles of the type used in cake decorating are fitted into paper piping bags rather than fabric bags. They are used for finishing petits fours and creating fine pipings on gateaux, for example.

PAPER PIPING BAGS For piping chocolate and icing. They can be purchased from cookshops and sugarcraft suppliers and are good for drizzling sauces for specific shapes and finishes.

OVENPROOF EQUIPMENT

There is a vast range from which to select. Good-quality items are the best value: high-quality metal bakeware will literally last a lifetime if treated correctly. This means washing and drying thoroughly after use and not exposing metals to sudden extremes in temperature, such as submerging an oven-hot tin into cold water. The following is a brief guide to standard items.

BAKING BEANS When baking a pastry shell 'blind', it should be filled with ceramic beans during cooking, available from cook shops. In the absence of these, lentils or other dried beans can be used. Do not use kidney beans: they are poisonous when raw.

BAKING SHEET Buy heavy baking sheets which are flat or slope down on three sides, but with a lip on the fourth side. This provides an edge to hold when removing the sheet from the oven, while delicate items can be removed by sliding them off the sheet rather than lifting them over a lip around the edge.

DARIOLE MOULDS Also known as castle moulds, these tins vary slightly in size. They have flat bottoms and deep, straight sides.

DEEP BAKING DISHES For making deeper baked puddings, such as fruit crumbles.

FLAN TINS Round, oblong or square, in a wide variety of sizes. These should have removable bottoms.

INDIVIDUAL TINS There is a wide variety, from classic British patty tins, used to make small tarts and cakes, to French tartlet tins which may be linked to form a tray or used individually. American-style muffin tins are deeper than patty tins, with steep sides at less of an angle.

LOOSE-BOTTOMED DEEP ROUND CAKE TIN A good basic tin for making sponges and cakes.

PIE DISH For making sweet, pastry-topped pies. The important feature is a flat rim on which to rest the pastry and a good depth for retaining fruit juices.

RAMEKIN DISHES Small, straight-sided round dishes, these are miniature soufflé dishes.

RING TIN For baking Savarin or ring-shaped cakes; also useful for setting cold desserts into ring shapes.

SHALLOW BAKING DISHES Rather like the gratin dishes used for savoury cooking, these have many uses, including baking fruit and batter puddings.

SMALL PUDDING MOULDS Slightly larger than dariole moulds, these tins are rounded at the bottom edge and have slightly sloping sides.

SOUFFLE DISHES Straight-sided round dishes, varying in size from individual soufflé dishes (larger than ramekins) to large, deep soufflé dishes.

SPRINGFORM TIN Not as deep as a standard cake tin, this type of tin has a spring clip to keep the side in place on the base. When the clip is released, the side loosens, leaving the contents free on the base. Useful for cheesecakes as well as baking. These have different types of bases which can be inserted instead of the standard one, for example a decorative base or a funnel insert for making ring cakes.

SWISS ROLL TIN A shallow, rectangular tin for baking thin sponges which can then be rolled with various fillings.

TIME-SAVING MACHINERY

BLENDER For making smooth purées and sauces. Also useful for grinding and crumbing dry ingredients. A hand-held blender is extremely useful for puréeing ingredients, such as poached fruit, without having to pour them into a special goblet. Some hand-held blenders also have whisk and chopper attachments, which are ideal for whipping cream or whisking a small number of egg whites and chopping nuts.

ELECTRIC BEATER A hand-held electric beater is a good basic piece of equipment for creaming mixtures, whisking egg whites, beating eggs and whipping cream.

FOOD PROCESSOR Completes a wide range of tasks, including puréeing, crumbing, blending dry ingredients and creaming. Attachments are available for extracting juice and whisking.

ICE CREAM MAKER Available as manual or electric models. Manual ones are hard work: of the electric ones, the smaller type will sit inside your freezer and make a few pints of ice cream, while the larger, self-contained models produce large volumes of excellent frozen desserts. These machines, also known as sorbetières, are available from specialist shops or suppliers.

APPLE AND PEAR PREPARATION

Hard fruits such as apple, pear and quince generally need to be peeled and cored before being used in desserts. All fruit should be washed carefully as the first step in preparation. Use citrus juice to prevent apples and pears discolouring when cut, and try to use them immediately after preparation. If possible, use stainless steel tools, as some metals will tarnish and may discolour the fruit.

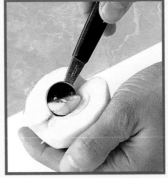

CORING WHOLE FRUIT
Push a vegetable peeler or corer into the stalk of an apple or the bottom of a pear and through to the other end. Twist to cut around the core, then gently pull it out.

CORING HALVES
Using a small knife, cut out both ends of the fruit. Halve it and cut around the core to loosen it. Then using a melon baller or spoon, scoop out the core and seeds.

PEELING
Core the whole fruit, then peel off the skin with a peeler, circling around the apple from top to bottom.

DECORATIVE PEELING
Using a canelle knife, peel away a thin strip of skin, spiralling down around the length of the fruit.

CUTTING RINGS
Core and peel your fruit, keeping it whole. Hold the fruit on its side and slice downwards.

CUTTING CRESCENTS
Peel and core the fruit but keep it whole. Cut it in half lengthwise, place each half, cut-side down, and cut crosswise into half moons.

DICING
Core, peel and slice the fruit into rings. Stack the rings and cut down through the fruit, holding the stack together. Cut across these slices to dice.

PEAR FAN
Leaving the stalk intact, peel, halve and core a pear. Cut slices along the length of the pear half and press down on the slices to fan them out.

PREVENTING DISCOLORATION
Using a pastry brush, paint the juice of a lemon, lime or orange all over the fruit's flesh as soon as it is exposed.

"COOKING" APPLES AND PEARS

When it comes to cooking, not all varieties of apples and pears are equal. For poaching, sautéing and being baked in tarts and pies, fruit should be tart, fairly acidic and able to maintain some firmness. Generally, apples and pears are classified either as "dessert" fruits – those that are eaten raw – and "cooking" fruits. The favoured varieties for using in desserts are set out below. Some of these are also eating varieties.

Apples
Granny Smith, Bramley, Gravenstein, Golden Grimes, Calville, Grenadier.
Pears
Anjou, Seckel, Bosc, Conference, Kieffer, Grieser Wildeman.

Basic techniques

PITTING CHERRIES

A cherry stoner is a small cup with a hollow base in which to place the cherry. A spike closes on to the fruit, piercing it and pushing out the stone.

Hold the fruit over a basin to catch the stones as they are released. To avoid damaging the fruit and losing juices, use your stoner with care. Hold and pierce the fruit gently.

STONING APRICOTS, PEACHES AND NECTARINES

Stone fruits such as apricots, peaches, nectarines and plums can all be stoned using the simple method shown here. When buying stone fruit, look for firm, but ripe flesh, avoiding hard specimens or those that are obviously over-ripe and squashy. The ease with which the stone can be extracted from stone fruits depends on both the ripeness of the fruit and the variety you use. The latter is particularly true of plums.

1 Cut around the fruit, following the natural indentation in the flesh. Make sure you cut right down to the stone.

2 Hold the fruit firmly and twist the two halves in opposite directions to free the flesh from the stone.

3 Lift off one half of the fruit and remove the stone from the other half.

SKINNING PEACHES AND NECTARINES

Peaches and nectarines are skinned by blanching briefly in boiling water. Use freshly boiling water and blanch only a few at a time. If too many are placed in the pot they will become soft and slightly cooked.

1 Score a cross on the base of the fruit and stand on a slotted spoon. Immerse in boiling water for roughly 10–20 seconds, then transfer immediately to iced water.

2 The edges of the skin where you scored the cross shape should be curling slightly. Starting here, peel back the skin. It should come away from the fruit easily.

PEELING AND PIPPING GRAPES

If using whole grapes in a dessert, bear in mind that the skin and pips taste bitter. To avoid this, remove the pips and peel of both black and green grapes using the methods shown below, which are easy to master.

PEELING
Peeling grapes is easy if you first blanch them in boiling water for a few seconds. The peel will then strip away easily with a sharp knife.

PIPPING
Pip grapes with an opened out, sterilized paper clip. Hook the pips with the paper clip, then pull them out through the stalk end.

102

WHOLE DATES

Whole dates look good, but for easy eating it is best to remove the stones first.

Hold the date in one hand and pull out the stone by the stalk. To help you get a good grip, use a knife tip as shown.

MANGOSTEEN

Use a paring knife to slice the fruit in half, cutting through the skin but not the flesh.

Scoop out the white segments of fruit with a small spoon. These segments contain stones which are inedible.

POMEGRANATE

Separate the seeds from the pith and membranes using your fingers.

Slice fruit in half. Pressing on the rounded base, invert one half over a sieve set over a bowl. Rub off the seeds.

STAR FRUIT

The sweetness of the fruit varies, so taste star fruit before adding to desserts.

Cut unpeeled fruit crosswise into slices with a small knife. Remove the central seeds before serving.

LYCHEES

The pearly white flesh of the lychee contains a long, brown and inedible seed.

Starting at the stalk end, cut through the brittle skin carefully with a small knife. It should peel off cleanly.

FIG FLOWERS

Fig flowers can be served plain, or with a filling piped into the centre.

Trim the stalk end of the fig with a small knife. Cut a deep cross shape in the top of the fig and open it out.

STRIGGING CURRANTS

Redcurrants and blackcurrants can be the simplest and most stunning ingredients: ensure perfection by picking or buying perfect fruit, each one ripe and just tender.

Use a fork to scrape the berries off the stalks as shown. The term 'strigging' derives from the word 'strigs', which is the 16th-century name for the stalks of berries. Hold the stalks down in a basin when strigging to avoid scattering currants.

HULLING AND HALVING STRAWBERRIES

Strawberries are the jewels in many desserts. Use whorls of whipped cream to crown glorious portions of this delicious summer fruit.

HULLING
Twist the leafy stalk end of the strawberry with your fingertips or a knife tip to remove the fibrous core.

HALVING
Leave the stalks as decoration and cut the fruit in half.

PEELING AND SLICING CITRUS FRUIT

Oranges, lemons, limes, grapefruit and kumquats, or any of the wide variety of sweet aromatic citrus fruit are the essence of many sweet dishes. Explaining a method of peeling citrus seems so fundamental as to be superfluous, but using the wrong technique results in unwanted pithy deposits that will ruin the flavour of the fruit.

1 Cut a slice off both ends of the fruit to remove the peel and pith at the top and bottom. Stand the fruit on a board and cut off the peel in wide strips, working from top to bottom. Remove all pith at the same time as the peel.

2 Turn the fruit sideways and cut it into slices of the required thickness. Remove and discard any pips that appear in the slices as you go.

3 If the fruit is intended for reassembly, stack the slices and secure them in place with a cocktail stick. Use a wooden cocktail stick, not plastic, if the fruit is to be coated in a hot caramel since plastic will melt.

SEGMENTING CITRUS FRUIT

Follow the instructions for peeling the fruit and removing all the pith. Then hold the fruit in one hand over a bowl so the juices that are produced as you cut can run into the bowl.

1 Cut in towards the middle of the fruit alongside one of the membranes that keeps the fruit segments separated. (Do not cut the membrane.) Cut on the other side of the segment in the same way, then ease it out, leaving the membrane in place.

2 Continue working around the fruit in the same way, cutting out segments from between the membranes, until all the fruit segments have been removed. As you cut each piece of fruit free, arrange it decoratively on a plate.

3 Finally, squeeze all the juice from the membranes over the fruit, then discard the membranes. As with the pith, the membranes are not sweet. They also have a chewy texture.

ZESTING CITRUS FRUIT

Citrus rind or zest is the coloured part of the peel which contains the essential oils that give the fruit its flavour and aroma. The bitter pith inside is not generally used. The rind can be grated off or removed using a zester.

USING A ZESTER
This small implement is scraped over the surface of the fruit to remove the zest in fine strands that are larger than those that are grated. Apply even pressure and use either long, slow strokes or short, quick ones depending on the length you require.

GRATING
Choose a grater blade that corresponds to the size and fineness of the zest that you require. Do not press too hard or you will remove a lot of pith with the zest.

JUICING FRUIT

Everyone has a favourite juicer, from snazzy electric attachments for food processors to classic fluted-dome glass dishes. A hand-held wooden juicer is useful for squeezing small amounts of juice from a lemon, but you may need a larger juicer for more substantial fruits.

Cut the fruit in half and hold one half over a basin. Squeeze out the juice by pushing the juicer firmly into the flesh and twisting it back and forth.

PREPARING RHUBARB

Rhubarb is not technically a fruit, but it is primarily used in sweet cookery and generally cooked as fruit. It should not be eaten raw in any significant quantity because it contains natural toxins, but the odd piece dipped in sugar does no harm. Raw rhubarb has a tart flavour. When preparing rhubarb, discard the leaves, as they are poisonous. Young, early rhubarb which has tender skin, needs little preparation other than washing and trimming.

1 Old stalks of rhubarb tend to have tough, stringy outer peel. Use a peeler or fine-bladed knife to cut off the skin. Slice the rhubarb into neat, regular pieces so they cook evenly.

2 Slice the rhubarb crosswise on the diagonal into neat chunks using a chef's knife. The rhubarb is now ready for cooking. Poach or pan-fry, then braise it in a glaze to use in pies.

VANDYKING MELON

Cutting fruit in half using a zigzag technique is known as vandyke cutting. The flesh can be removed from the shells which can then be used as decorative dessert containers. Make short, angled cuts into the centre of the fruit using a narrow-bladed, sharp knife, working in a zigzag pattern around the middle. Separate the two halves. The melon can be served as it is, or the flesh can be scooped out and used to make another dessert such as a sorbet, which is served in the melon shell.

1 Using the 'equator' of the melon to guide you, mark a zigzag line in the skin of each melon with the tip of a knife. Now cut the zigzags. Insert the knife to the centre of the fruit with each cut.

2 Gently pull the melon halves apart. Scoop out the seeds and fibrous flesh using a small spoon and discard them. The melon is now ready to serve or fill.

MAKING MELON BALLS

The flesh from a melon can be shaped into small scoops to form a decoration, or to become part of a fruit salad.

Halve a melon and remove the seeds. Use a teaspoon or melon baller. Press one edge into the flesh and twist your wrist to scoop out the shape.

TYPES OF DESSERT MELON

Cantaloupe
A popular choice, with scented, sweet, salmon-orange flesh.
Honeydew
Turns from green to yellow and sweetens when ripe.
Galia
Less sweet than other varieties, with pale green, firm flesh.

CUTTING PINEAPPLE FROM THE SHELL

Bear in mind when selecting fruit that sweet and juicy pineapples tend to have a hint of deep gold colour in the skin. There are two methods of preparing a pineapple shell as a container. The first is to halve the fruit lengthways, cutting straight through the leaves and body of the fruit, then to scoop out the flesh. The method here shows how to leave the whole shell intact, ideal for miniature pineapples, which can then be offered as containers for individual portions.

1 Lay the pineapple on its side on a cutting board. Take a large, sharp knife and cut off the leafy top. If you are intending to fill the empty fruit shell, reserve the top to act as a 'lid'.

2 Use a sharp pointed knife to cut between the fruit and the skin, working evenly all the way down the length of the fruit and around. Leave some flesh on the shell so it is fairly thick and sturdy.

3 Turn the fruit over and cut off the base so that the shell will stand neatly and evenly. This also allows you to release the flesh from the shell easily.

4 Push a fork into the fruit and, holding the shell firmly in one hand, pull out the fruit on the fork. The flesh can be cored and diced, then replaced in the shell and served.

PEELING PINEAPPLE

The important point to remember when peeling pineapple is to gouge out all the spiky spines that are extremely unpleasant to eat due to their tough texture. Unfortunately, there is no quick way of doing this without losing much of the fruit.

1 Trim the ends off the fruit, then stand it on a board and cut off the peel in wide vertical strips from top to bottom. Cut the peel off thickly enough to take the worst of the spines with it.

2 Use the point of a small sharp knife to gouge out the remaining spines, one by one. Cut only as deeply as you feel is necessary each time, cutting out a little more if some of the spine remains.

MAKING PINEAPPLE RINGS

REMOVING THE CORE
When you have removed the skin from a pineapple, cut slices across the length of the fruit. Lay each disc flat, then cut out the core or stamp it out with a cutter.

COOKING RINGS
Grill or sauté the rings with flavourings. A sprinkling of coconut, rum, orange juice or cinnamon, pieces of clove, star anise or lime zest are all delicious with pineapple.

PEELING AND SLICING MANGO

The best way to slice peeled mango is to remove the flesh from the stone in neat slices. The fruit should be just ripe. Soft fruit is difficult to hold, resulting in untidy slices.

PEELING
Peel the fruit using a knife. Work lengthways along the fruit, keeping the shape.

SLICING
Hold the fruit firmly, starting with the flat 'face' of the flesh in the palm of your hand. Cut off long, slim wedge-shaped slices. You should achieve a number of neat slices from the flat of the stone and a few misshapen slices from the narrow sides of the stone.

BLANCHING AND SKINNING NUTS

The skin of almond and pistachio nuts is bitter and can ruin the delicate flavour of the nuts if left on. The simplest method of skinning nuts is to blanch them in hot water. The skin is loosened by the process, so you can remove it easily while the nuts are still warm.

1 Cover nuts with boiling water and allow them to stand for 10–15 minutes until the water has cooled to tepid.

2 Take a nut and hold it between your thumb and index finger. Pinch the skin to encourage it to slip off.

TOASTING AND SKINNING NUTS

Nuts that are best toasted rather than blanched before skinning, such as hazelnuts and Brazil nuts, can be either toasted in the oven or dry-fried on top of the stove. Dry-fry in a non-stick frying pan and stir over a low heat for 2–4 minutes until lightly toasted on all sides.

1 Place the nuts on a baking sheet and toast at 175°C for 10 minutes. Agitate the sheet occasionally.

2 Steam the nuts for a few minutes by wrapping them in a tea towel, then rub them to remove the skins.

SHREDDING AND CHOPPING NUTS

Although it is easy to buy most nuts ready chopped, flaked and shredded, you may find a dish that calls for a specific treatment of a certain nut. Nuts will taste fresher and retain more moisture if they are cut just before use.

SHREDDING
Place a nut on a cutting board, flat-side down, and cut it lengthwise into shreds.

FLAKING
Place the thin side of a nut on a cutting board, support one side and cut into thin flakes.

CHOPPING
Once shredded, work a blade backwards and forwards over the nuts on a board.

MAKING A SYRUP

Syrup is fundamental to many areas of sweet cookery and confections and in the preparation of desserts. A syrup can provide a light sweetening to fruit juice or may end up as the ultimate pulled sugar decoration to finish a fabulous gateau. Whatever its eventual destination, a syrup begins as sugar dissolved in liquid. A heavy syrup is one with a high proportion of sugar to liquid. A light syrup has less sugar, is therefore less sweet in taste and has a thinner texture. The two golden rules are firstly to dissolve the sugar in the liquid over a fairly low heat, stirring gently without boiling and avoiding splashing the insides of the pan as far as possible. Secondly, when the sugar has dissolved completely, stop stirring and bring the syrup to the boil. Do not stir once it is boiling.

1 Stir the sugar and water gently over a low heat until the sugar has dissolved completely.

2 Bring to the boil. Dissolve any syrup that is drying into crystals on the inside of the pan by brushing cold water down from the rim.

SUGAR THERMOMETER

Sugar can be boiled to different 'stages' which are used in varying ways. Temperature is the guide to the different boiling stages. The temperature at which the syrup boils gives an indication of the sugar concentration, or the 'stage' the syrup has reached: soft-ball, hard-ball, soft-crack or hard-crack (see right). Heat the thermometer in hot water before use and replace in hot water after use (rinsing off hot syrup in cold water could break a thermometer). Do not allow the thermometer to touch the base of the pan as this is hotter so the reading will be false.

SYRUPS

Light Syrup: allow 250 g sugar to 500 ml water, or similar proportions. Use for fruit salads and poaching fruit.
Medium Syrup: use 250 g sugar to 250 ml water. Use for preserving fruit. This will keep for a period of days.
Heavy Syrup: use 250 g sugar to 225 ml water.

BOILING STAGES FOR SYRUPS

When boiling a heavy syrup for any length of time, the water evaporates and the sugar becomes concentrated. The syrup thickens and flows less quickly. The changing concentration of sugar gives the syrup exciting characteristics which can be put to many uses. Cooled syrup can be malleable or, if boiled long enough, brittle. Before it sets, the syrup can be worked in various ways, to part-crystallize the sugar and form a paste or to be spun into exciting decorations, for instance.

SOFT-BALL (116–118°C)
A little blob of syrup holds its shape and is soft. Syrup boiled to this stage is used for Italian Meringue and buttercream icing.

HARD-BALL (125°C)
The syrup forms a firm, but pliable, ball and has a chewy texture. Syrup is boiled to this stage when making marzipan and fondant icing.

SOFT-CRACK (134°C)
The syrup becomes brittle, but it can still be pressed into a soft and pliable texture. This stage is mainly used in confectionery.

HARD-CRACK (145ºC)
The syrup is very brittle and crisp and is used for glazing fruit and for pulled and spun sugar. Beyond this, it rapidly changes into caramel.

THE CRYSTAL PROBLEM

When boiling heavy syrups, it is vital that the sugar remains dissolved in solution. If any sugar crystals form, they will lead to more in a chain reaction and the syrup will rapidly become a crunchy mass. Stirring after the syrup boils causes crystals to form. Syrup splashed on to the inside of the pan will also form crystals, so stir very gently during the first stage. Brush the inside of the pan with cold water if there are any splashes – this stops the syrup from forming crystals.

CARAMEL

If the syrup boils beyond the hard-crack stage, it becomes caramel, changing colour, turning pale gold and rapidly darkening. The colour is a good guide to flavour: very pale caramels have a light taste, a rich, golden caramel has a warm, deep flavour and a very dark caramel has a nutty taste with a hint of bitterness. The change from pale to dark is rapid; equally, if the caramel is not quickly prevented from cooking it will turn very dark, taste bitter and soon burn. Use the caramel immediately as it sets quickly. Alternatively, to make a pouring caramel, remove the pan from the heat. Protect your hand and forearm with a thick oven glove and hold the pan away from you, then pour in just a little boiling water from a kettle. Tilt the pan away from you as the caramel spits and bubbles violently when the water is added. When it has calmed down, the caramel is thinned slightly, is still full-flavoured and coloured and will not harden.

1 Boil the syrup until it changes colour, then continue boiling without stirring until the caramel achieves the required richness. This is a dark, deliciously rich caramel.

2 Remove from the heat as soon as the required depth of colour is achieved and place the pan in a bowl of iced water. This cools the pan immediately and prevents the caramel from darkening or burning.

PRALINE

This is caramel with nuts added before it sets. Lightly toasted blanched almonds are the classic nuts, but pecans, cashews, skinned pistachios or chopped brazils can be added. Walnuts, however, may taste bitter. When the praline is cold it can be crushed with a rolling pin or ground in a food processor.

1 Add the nuts to the caramel and remove from the heat immediately.

2 Pour on to a greased baking sheet or a tray lined with non-stick baking parchment. Quickly spread the mixture into a thin and even layer with a greased palette knife.

NOUGATINE

This nut mixture is malleable due to added glucose. Make a caramel with 100 ml water, 1 kg sugar and 400 g glucose. Add 500 g blanched almonds (see page 107), toasted and flaked or coarsely chopped.

1 Turn out the mixture on to an oiled surface and allow to cool slightly. Then roll it out with a rolling pin to a thickness of roughly 5 mm.

2 When the nougatine has cooled until it is just warm it can be cut into shapes. Leave these to set until firm.

CHOPPING AND GRATING

Chill chocolate lightly before chopping or grating and make sure your hands are not hot. Use the coarse blade on a grater. Alternatively, a small mouli grater, or rotating drum-type grater can be used successfully. Chopping is difficult: the chocolate must be cool, but not too hard. Use a large chef's knife and a classic 'rocking' technique to avoid making a mess.

CHOPPING
Break the chocolate into small pieces then chill lightly. Place the chilled chocolate on a chilled chopping board and, holding the knife tip down with your fingers, lift then bring down the handle to finely chop the chocolate.

GRATING
Rub chilled chocolate against the face of your grater which has the widest holes. If chocolate warms, it will smear on the grater, so chill it lightly and work with cool hands.

MELTING CHOCOLATE

Unlike cooking chocolate, eating chocolate does not need to be tempered. Melt it with care. The merest drop of water causes the chocolate to separate and become firm, grainy and unusable. Overheating has the same effect. Use a heatproof bowl that sits on top of a saucepan, not down inside it. This prevents any water or steam from entering the bowl.

Heat some water until barely simmering, then reduce the heat so that it cools a little. Leave the pan over a low heat or remove it from the hob before placing a bowl filled with pieces of chocolate on top. Make sure the pieces are broken into small, roughly equal sizes so the chocolate melts quickly in a smooth and even consistency.

TYPES OF CHOCOLATE

Eating Chocolate
Glossy, hard, smooth and sold as confectionery, this varies widely in quality. Allow the cocoa butter content to be your guide.
Couverture
This is not an 'eating' chocolate. It is dull in appearance. Temper it before use so it sets to a hard and glossy finish.
Baker's Chocolate
This is a superior form of the common 'cooking' chocolate. Not particularly flavourful, it is used mainly for decorative purposes.

TEMPERING CHOCOLATE

If the fats within chocolate are not well mixed, they may, once melted and cooled, form grey streaks on the surface. Temper chocolate to avoid this. The process of heating, mixing and cooling causes the fats to be thoroughly blended, after which the chocolate can be melted and used. The result will set to a glossy, streak-free and crisp finish. Chef's work with couverture and always temper chocolate before use to ensure a high-quality finish.

1 Melt the chocolate in a bowl over a saucepan of hot, not simmering, water. Stir until it is smooth and at a temperature of 45°C.

2 As soon as the chocolate reaches the required temperature, cool it down by standing the bowl in a bowl of ice. Stir until the temperature drops to 25°C, then return to the heat.

3 Warm the chocolate again over hot water until it reaches 32°C. This is the working temperature for the tempered chocolate and it is now ready for use.

GANACHE

300 g plain chocolate
150 ml double cream

Chop the chocolate into even pieces and melt in a bowl over hot water. Remove the bowl from the heat and set aside. Heat the cream until hot, but not simmering, and pour it into the chocolate.

Stir the cream and the chocolate together until they are evenly combined. Continue stirring until the mixture has cooled and is smooth and glossy in texture.

At this stage, the ganache can be used as a coating for desserts or it can be whipped with a whisk until paler in colour and of a good consistency for piping.

MAKING CHOCOLATE GANACHE

Ganache is a versatile mixture of chocolate and cream. It tastes smooth and luscious and can be used as a coating or filling for gateaux or pastries. It can also be used as an 'ingredient' in complex desserts. When cooled but not set, ganache can be whipped to a light and airy consistency, forming a rich chocolate cream that can be piped or used in a wide variety of ways. Ganache can be flavoured with spirits and liqueurs, such as brandy or Crème de Cacao.

ADD THE CREAM
The cream should be just hot. If too hot it may cause the chocolate to seize and become grainy in texture.

STIRRING TOGETHER
Make sure that the chocolate and cream are thoroughly mixed. Use a wooden spoon.

BEAT THE MIXTURE
Thorough beating will cause the mixture to cool to a glossy finish.

BASIC CHOCOLATE SHAPES

When preparing chocolate shapes, use non-stick baking parchment laid on a board or baking sheet. Once the chocolate is evenly spread, cover it with a second sheet of parchment, then invert both sheets so that the new sheet is on the bottom. Leave to set and then peel off the top sheet of paper. This will leave the smooth surface of the chocolate uppermost. The chocolate should be cut or shaped before it is set hard and brittle. A wide variety of cutting and shaping techniques (see pages 198–203), can be used.

MAKING CUPS

Use paper cases – sweet cases, petits fours cases and cake or muffin cases for larger cups. If the paper cases are slightly floppy, use them double thick.

1 Ladle the melted chocolate on to non-stick baking parchment – tempered couverture sets to the ideal crisp texture and high gloss for chocolate decorations.

2 Use a large palette knife, spatula or cake icing rule to spread out the chocolate to a thickness of roughly 2 mm. Paddle the palette knife back and forth for an even result.

3 Stamp out shapes with a cutter or knife. Dip the implement in hot water and dry it between each cut. Place the shapes on a sheet of parchment and leave to set.

Paint a thin, even coating of melted chocolate inside the paper case and leave to set. When the chocolate is just firm, paint on a second layer. Add a third layer, if required.

USING ICING

Icings and glazes are used to add moisture, flavour and decoration to many desserts. Although certain flavours are traditional, such as apricot and chocolate, it is more the consistency of the icing that denotes its use. Smooth, spreadable glacé icing, for example, lends itself to cake covering, whereas thick fondant icing is ideal for coating fruit and drizzling on to pastries. Unlike other icings that are best used as they are made, fondant is best after a day or two and can be stored wrapped in polythene in an airtight container for up to 2 weeks.

GLACE ICING

175 g sugar
1–2 tbsp warm water
or other liquid

Sift the icing sugar into a bowl then add a little liquid. Do not add all the liquid in one go.

Gradually stir the liquid, whether water, fruit juice or liqueur, into the sugar using a spoon or whisk. It will seem stiff at first, but the consistency will thin rapidly and become a pouring texture.

A little lemon or lime juice can be added to the basic icing to contrast with its sweetness.

MAKING GLACE ICING

Use the icing promptly as a thin skin begins to form quickly. Ideally the mixture should set to a glossy, soft, but crisp-skinned finish.

SIFTING SUGAR
To ensure a smooth mixture, sift the sugar into a bowl, working hard lumps through with a spoon.

MAKING THE PASTE
Add only a small amount of liquid at a time, so that you can control the consistency of the icing.

FONDANT ICING

250 g sugar
150 ml water
1 tbsp liquid glucose

Make a syrup using the sugar, water and glucose. Boil to the soft-ball stage (see page 108). Brush a marble slab with cold water and pour the syrup on to it. Cool for 1 minute, until it begins to thicken. Use a palette knife or metal scraper to work the syrup, scraping and folding it over repeatedly until it is a thick, opaque paste. When the sugar cools and crystallizes it forms a white, crunchy mixture. Work the mixture with the fingers, kneading small chunks of it into a smooth paste. Wrap in polythene to store.

Ideally, fondant should be allowed to mature for 1 day after making before it is heated and used as a coating. To use the fondant, heat small pieces in a bowl over hot, not boiling, water until they melt.

CHOCOLATE ICING

150 g sugar
150 ml water
300 g chocolate pistoles

Make a syrup using the sugar and the water. Add the chocolate pistoles and whisk over moderate heat until the chocolate has melted and the mixture is smooth.

Heat to 110°C, or just below the soft-ball stage, known as the "thread" stage (see right). To test the stage, either use your fingers, dipped in iced water or make use of a sugar thermometer (see page 108).

When the chocolate sugar syrup has reached the correct consistency, remove the pan from the heat, knock out the air by tapping the pan on the work surface, then use immediately. Makes enough icing to cover a 25-cm cake.

MAKING CHOCOLATE ICING

Using a boiled syrup as a base for chocolate icing gives a rich, glossy result. The icing can also be served as a hot dessert sauce. High-quality plain chocolate is essential.

MELTING THE PISTOLES
Add pistoles to hot sugar syrup, stirring continuously until melted to avoid seizing (becoming thick and lumpy).

TESTING FOR "THREAD" STAGE
Dip your fingers in iced water, then chocolate, and pull apart. The mixture should stretch in a thread between your fingers.

KNOCKING OUT THE AIR
Stand the pan on a teatowel and tap the pan slightly to knock out any trapped air bubbles. If left in the mixture, they will eventually break on the surface of the icing once applied to a cake and spoil its smooth appearance.

COATING WITH ICING

Glaze your cake with a jam glaze (see below) before icing to add moisture and produce a smooth result. Allow to cool, then stand on a wire rack over a tray to catch drips of icing.

1 Ladle the warm icing on to the centre of the cake, forming an even puddle in the middle. Pour on more than is necessary to coat the cake. Work quickly and with a steady hand for good results.

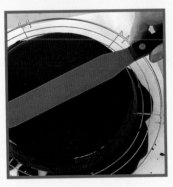

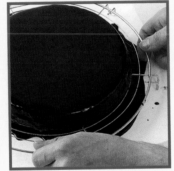

2 Use a warm palette knife to smooth out the icing. Use the minimum of strokes, allowing excess to flow off the cake on to the parchment.

3 Without disturbing the cake, tap the rack gently to ensure the icing is even and free of air bubbles. Leave to set for 5–10 minutes.

APRICOT NAPPAGE

100 g apricot jam (minimum)
50 ml water
(to every 100 g jam)

Melt the jam in a small saucepan – it will diminish in quantity by the time is it sieved, so heat more than you need. Sieve the jam into a small, clean pan to remove pieces of fruit. Add water and heat, stirring continuously. Bring to a full rolling boil and remove from the heat. Cool slightly and use as required, as a glaze or a coating under icing.

GLAZES

All jams can be melted, boiled and used as a glaze for cakes and gâteaux.

APPLYING A GLAZE
Brush the glaze generously over the cut surface of a sponge before icing.

PUREES AND COULIS

There are many uses for fruit purées, from simple sauces to soufflés. How to purée fruit depends on its texture. Soft fruit such as berries and bananas can be blended immediately. Hard fruits, such as apples, should be sautéed first. With berries, use a proportion of fully ripe fruit for sweetness (25 per cent), some that is only just ripe, for colour and to balance flavour (again, about 25 per cent). The rest should be ripe, not over-ripe. Add a squeeze of lemon to enhance weak fruit purées.

1 Use a blender or food processor to produce a smooth purée with speed. Take care not to over-process the mixture or it can become quite frothy.

2 Remove any seeds, fibres or traces of skin by pushing the mixture through a fine metal sieve. The purée is now ready to use.

USING A MOULI
Place the fruit in the hopper of the Mouli and turn the handle. This will force the flesh and juice through the Mouli into the bowl below but will trap skin and seeds in the hopper.

MAKING A COULIS
A coulis makes an excellent dessert sauce. It is simply a thickened purée. Stir icing sugar to taste into the purée. Sharpen the coulis with a squeeze of lemon juice or flavour with a little liqueur.

SAUCES

A sweet sauce may be an essential feature of a dessert or it can be an optional element that completely changes the image of a dish. Served individually or paired to create a marriage of tastes and colours, sauces can create a complex cornucopia of flavours around a simple main recipe. A sweet milk sauce may be thickened with cornflour, enriched with unsalted butter and cream, then flavoured with spirits or with chocolate. This type of sauce may be served with hot puddings, such as Christmas pudding instead of brandy butter. Rum or Grand Marnier may be added instead of brandy.

BUTTERSCOTCH SAUCE

85 g unsalted butter
175 g dark soft brown sugar
2 tbsp golden syrup
85 ml double cream

Melt the butter, sugar and golden syrup over low heat. Stir in the double cream and heat until boiling. Remove from the heat immediately.

CORNFLOUR SAUCE

2 tbsp cornflour
2 tbsp sugar
500 ml milk
30 g unsalted butter
½ tsp natural vanilla extract
100 ml single cream.

Blend the cornflour with the sugar and a little of the milk to a smooth paste. Heat the remaining milk, then pour it into the cornflour paste, stirring well. Pour the sauce back into the pan and bring to the boil, still stirring. Simmer gently for 1 minute. Beat in the unsalted butter and natural vanilla extract. Remove from the heat and stir in the cream. Serve immediately.

CHOCOLATE CREAM SAUCE

250 ml whipping cream
250 g dark plain chocolate or high-quality white chocolate

Heat the whipping cream in a small saucepan until hot, but not boiling. Remove from the heat and add the chocolate, broken into squares. Stir until the chocolate has melted and combined with the cream. Serve warm or cold.

MAKING SABAYON SAUCE

This pale, foamy sauce is based on custard, with egg yolks thickening wine. The sauce is whisked continuously to give the characteristic light texture. Fruit juice may be used instead of the wine.

SABAYON SAUCE

6 egg yolks
90 g caster sugar
150 ml sweet white wine
1 tbsp Madeira or sherry

Place the egg yolks and caster sugar in a heatproof bowl over a saucepan of hot, not boiling, water. Whisk the mixture until pale and foamy.

Gradually pour in the sweet white wine, whisking the mixture continuously.

When all the wine has been whisked in, continue whisking until the sauce becomes very pale, thick and light. Whisk in the Madeira or sherry and serve immediately.

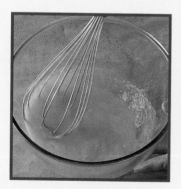

WHISKING YOLKS AND SUGAR
Do not whisk the eggs and sugar over too high a heat or the eggs will begin to cook and become lumpy.

THICKENING THE SAUCE
Constant whisking as the wine is added will add air to the sauce and cause it to start thickening.

WHISKING TO A RIBBON
When the sabayon is ready the whisk will leave a trail like a ribbon in the sauce behind it.

CHOCOLATE SAUCE

60 g sugar
4 tbsp water
225 g dark plain chocolate
½ tsp natural vanilla extract
30 g unsalted butter

Use high-quality bitter plain chocolate for this syrup-based sauce. Heat the sugar with the water until the sugar dissolves. Bring to a full rolling boil, then remove from the heat. Break the dark plain chocolate into squares and stir into the syrup until completely dissolved. Beat in the natural vanilla extract and the unsalted butter. Serve warm or cold.

WHITE CHOCOLATE SAUCE

60 g sugar
4 tbsp water
350 g high-quality white chocolate
100 ml single cream

Heat the sugar and water until the sugar dissolves. Bring to a full rolling boil, then remove from the heat. Stir in the high-quality white chocolate until it dissolves, then stir in the cream. Serve at once.

COFFEE SAUCE

60 g roasted coffee beans
500 ml milk
2 tbsp cornflour
2 tbsp sugar
45–60 g raisins
4 tbsp white rum

Before making the sauce, heat the roasted coffee beans in the milk until just boiling, then set aside until completely cold. Blend a little milk with the cornflour and sugar, then heat the remainder until very hot but not boiling. Strain the milk, discarding the coffee beans, and continue as above. A little rum or coffee liqueur may be added; soak the raisins in the white rum for 30 minutes (or longer) and add to the sauce.

BRANDY BUTTER

175 g unsalted butter
90 g icing sugar
4 tbsp brandy

Cream the butter and the icing sugar together until pale and soft. Gradually beat in the brandy and then chill until firm.

MELBA SAUCE

250 g raspberries
3 tbsp icing sugar
1–2 tbsp raspberry liqueur

Purée the raspberries and rub the purée through a sieve to remove seeds. Sweeten with icing sugar to taste and stir in the raspberry liqueur, if desired. Chill lightly before serving.

COCONUT MILK SAUCE

250 ml milk
250 ml canned coconut milk
6 egg yolks
150 g caster sugar
100 ml single cream

Pour the milk and coconut milk into a saucepan and heat gently. Bring slowly to the boil. Beat together the egg yolks and sugar until the mixture is pale and thick. Pour the heated milk into the eggs, stirring constantly, then pour this into the same saucepan and stir over a low heat until it begins to thicken. Remove from the heat and stir in the single cream. Strain the sauce before serving.

FLAMBEEING

Any high-proof alcohol such as brandy, rum, a fortified wine like Madeira, or a fruit-based liqueur can be used to flambée. Fruits, such as grapes or cherries, are best suited to flambéeing and the burning alcohol acts as a simple sauce.

1 In a pan separate from that for the fruit, warm the alcohol, ignite it away from the heat and pour it over the fruit. This will stop the fruit from burning as the alcohol is lit.

2 While the alcohol is still alight, baste the fruit evenly, coating all the fruit in the alcohol while taking care that none of the fruit burns. For safety, use a long-handled metal spoon.

CUSTARDS AND CREAMS

Many of the most delicious fillings and ice creams begin as simple dairy ingredients which are transformed into sublime custards or luxurious creams. When making these classic custards, controlling the temperature is essential for perfect results.

CREME CHANTILLY

250 ml double cream
30–40 g icing sugar
¼ tsp natural vanilla extract (optional)

Whip the double cream with the icing sugar until the cream stands in soft peaks. Flavour with the vanilla extract, if desired. Use or serve at once.

CREME ANGLAISE

1 vanilla pod
500 ml milk
6 egg yolks
150 g caster sugar
100 ml single cream

Split the vanilla pod and place in a saucepan. Pour in the milk and bring slowly to the boil. Beat the egg yolks with the sugar until pale and thick. Remove the vanilla pod and pour the milk into the eggs, stirring continuously. Pour the custard back into the saucepan and stir over a low heat until the mixture begins to thicken and coats the back of a spoon. Do not allow to overheat or boil, or the eggs will curdle. Remove from the heat and stir in the single cream. Strain the custard. Makes roughly 650 ml.

CREME PATISSIERE

500 ml milk
½ vanilla pod
5 egg yolks
125 g caster sugar
25 g plain flour
25 g cornflour

Heat the milk and vanilla pod gently until just boiling. Remove from the heat and cool slightly. Beat the egg yolks with the sugar until pale and thick, then stir in the flour and cornflour. Remove the vanilla pod and gradually stir the milk into the egg and flour mixture. Pour the custard back into the saucepan and heat gently, beating continuously until the mixture thickens and boils. Boil for 1 minute, stirring continuously. Pour into a large bowl or shallow dish and cover with clingfilm or baking parchment. Set aside to cool. Beat until smooth before using.

CREME CHIBOUSTE

250 ml milk
4 eggs, separated
240 g caster sugar
20 g cornflour
3 leaves gelatine
6 tbsp water
1 tsp natural vanilla extract

Use the milk, egg yolks, 40 g caster sugar and the cornflour to make a Crème Pâtissière. Cover with clingfilm, then leave to cool until just warm.

Soak leaf gelatine in water, or dissolve powdered gelatine in 2 tbsp of the water.

Use the remaining sugar and water and the egg whites to make an Italian Meringue (see page 68). Beat the vanilla extract into the Crème Pâtissière and stir in the dissolved gelatine, then fold in the meringue. Use as required or chill until set.

WHIPPING THE CREAM
Crème Chantilly is a simple, sweetened whipped cream. For quick results, whip the cream and sugar with an electric whisk to maximize the air whisked into it.

COATING THE SPOON
Keep the heat low and stir the custard continuously. If the sauce becomes too hot or cooks for too long, the egg will set and separate from the milk. This, in turn, will cause the custard to curdle. Stirring in single cream stops the cooking process and enriches the custard. When the custard coats the back of a spoon, remove the pan from the heat and stir in the cream. Strain the custard and serve.

BREAKING UP LUMPS
Crème Pâtissière is thickened with flour and cornflour. To avoid a lumpy mixture, vigorous mixing is essential throughout cooking. Do not be alarmed if lumps form, just beat hard and they will break up as the custard thickens and comes to the boil. The cold custard can be enriched by folding in whipped cream.

ADDING MERINGUE
This is a lighter version of Crème Pâtissière, with a cooked meringue folded in to the custard once it has cooled. Gelatine is used to set the mixture.

CREME AU BEURRE

160 g sugar
85 ml water
1 egg
2 egg yolks
250 g softened unsalted butter
¼–½ tsp natural vanilla

Prepare a syrup boiled to the soft-ball stage using the sugar and water (see page 108). In an electric mixer, beat the egg and egg yolks until well combined. With the mixer running, gradually pour in the boiled syrup in a thin, steady stream down the inside of the bowl. Continue beating until the mixture has cooled into a thick, pale custard.

Finally, add the butter gradually in small knobs, ensuring each is thoroughly combined with the custard before adding the next. Beat in the vanilla extract and use as required.

TESTING THE SYRUP
French buttercream or Crème au Beurre is used as a filling for pastries and gateaux. It is based on a custard made of egg, egg yolks and boiled syrup creamed with butter. To test the syrup, dip your fingers into iced water and take a tiny pinch of sugar syrup, returning your fingers to the water immediately. The drop of sugar syrup should hold its shape, but be soft when pressed.

BUTTERCREAM

100 g sifted icing sugar
100 g unsalted butter
1 tbsp lemon juice
½ tsp natural vanilla extract

Mix together the sifted icing sugar and butter until smooth. Beat in the lemon juice and vanilla extract and serve. Alternatively, flavour with liqueurs, citrus rind, coffee essence or cocoa to taste.

MAKING BUTTERCREAM

A simple, British-style buttercream may be used to sandwich layers of sponge for gâteaux or tiny pieces of sponge as a base for petits fours.

CREAMING THE BUTTERCREAM
Cream equal quantities of unsalted butter and icing sugar until very soft, pale and fluffy.

USING A PIPING BAG

Professional chefs fill a piping bag whilst holding it in one hand, as shown here. Another method is to pull the sides of the bag over the rim of a jug to act as a support.

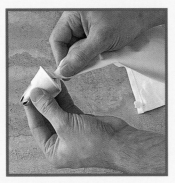  

1 Fit the nozzle inside the bag and twist the bag above it to seal the nozzle.

2 Make a collar by folding the top of the bag over your hand and spoon in the filling.

3 When full, clear any pockets of air by twisting the top of the bag until the filling is visible in the nozzle.

FATLESS WHISKED SPONGE

4 eggs
120 g caster sugar
120 g plain flour, sifted with
a pinch of salt

Grease and flour a 20 cm deep, round cake tin. Preheat the oven to 170°C.

Place the eggs in a heatproof bowl and add the sugar. Stand the bowl over a saucepan of hot, not quite boiling, water and whisk until the mixture is pale and thick. Remove the bowl from over the pan and continue whisking until the mixture is cool.

Sift the flour and fold it into the mixture using a large metal spoon or spatula. Using a figure-of-eight action, lift the mixture over the flour to incorporate it without knocking out any of the air.

Pour into the prepared tin and bake at 170°C for about 25 minutes. The sponge should be risen and pale golden. When cooked, it will feel firm but springy. Serves 6–8.

MAKING A WHISKED SPONGE

To make the perfect whisked sponge the water in your saucepan should be simmering, not bubbling, as this will be too hot and will cause the mixture to cook. A large balloon whisk is the chef's choice of utensil, but an electric whisk can be quicker and easier.

1 Use eggs and caster sugar at room temperature. Place in a heatproof bowl and whisk slightly to mix the ingredients.

2 Stand the bowl over the pan of hot water and whisk until the mixture is pale and thick and holds a trail in a clear ribbon.

3 Remove the bowl from the pan and continue whisking until the mixture has cooled.

4 Fold in the sifted flour. Use a spatula or a large metal spoon to incorporate the flour, adding it in two or three separate batches.

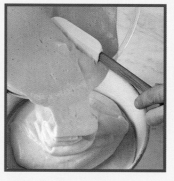

5 Pour the mixture into the prepared tin and allow the mixture to settle by itself. If filling a tin with corners, it may be necessary to coax the mixture into the corners using the point of a knife or metal skewer.

6 Transfer the cooked sponge to a wire rack to cool. To avoid indenting the sponge with wire marks from the wire rack, cover the rack with a clean teatowel.

TIN SIZES AND COOKING TIMES

The basic 4 egg mixture for a whisked sponge can be used to make one 20 cm round cake. Alternatively, prepare:

Deep Square
Use a 17 cm deep square tin and bake as in the basic recipe.
Round Sandwich Cake
Use two 20 cm round shallow tins and bake at 180°C for 20–25 minutes.
Swiss Roll
Use a 3 egg mixture for a rolled sponge. Bake in a lined, greased 23 x 33 cm Swiss roll tin. Bake at 200°C for 4–5 minutes.
French Madeleines
The 4 egg mixture can be used to make about 24 madeleines. Grease and flour the classic fluted tins and bake the cakes at 200°C for 5–7 minutes.

FLAVOURING WHISKED SPONGE

CHOCOLATE
Add 2–3 tbsp cocoa, sifting it with the flour.

COFFEE
Dissolve 2 tbsp instant coffee in 2 tbsp boiling water. Add to the eggs and sugar.

VANILLA
Add 1 tsp natural vanilla extract to the eggs and sugar.

CITRUS
Add the grated rind of 1 orange, lemon or lime to the eggs and sugar.

ROSE/ORANGE FLOWER WATER
Add 1 tsp of either to eggs and sugar.

CARDAMOM
Remove the seeds from 6 green cardamoms and grind them to a powder in a mortar using a pestle. Fold into the mixture with the flour.

ENRICHING A SPONGE

Melted butter can be used to enrich sponges. Melt 20 g unsalted butter and allow it to cool; if it is too hot, it will cook the mixture. Prepare the whisked sponge following the recipe and steps on the opposite page. As soon as the butter is incorporated, pour the mixture into the tin and cook immediately.

ADDING THE BUTTER
Trickle the melted butter evenly over the surface of the mixture. Then, working quickly, but without actually stirring the mixture, fold in the butter using a spatula or metal spoon. Use a figure-of-eight action to incorporate the butter into the mixture.

MAKING SPONGE FINGERS

Although these resemble a crisp whisked sponge when cooked, the mixture is made by enriching a meringue rather than following the basic whisked sponge method. Applying two coats of sifted icing sugar to the piped mixture before baking results in the characteristic sugar crust.

1 Take care to pipe all the biscuits to the same length, either to fit a particular charlotte tin or to roughly 10 cm long, as here. Allow space between them for the mixture to spread as it bakes. Alternatively, pipe the fingers so that they touch to make a continuous strip of fingers.

2 Dust the piped fingers with icing sugar. Leave the biscuits to stand, until the sugar has dissolved, then dust them generously again.

3 Holding the baking parchment in place, tilt the baking sheet to tip off any excess sugar which may burn during baking.

SPONGE FINGERS

3 eggs, separated
100 g caster sugar
75 g plain flour
icing sugar, to dust

Grease a baking sheet and line it with baking parchment. Whisk the egg whites until they stand in soft peaks. Gradually whisk in half the caster sugar, and continue whisking until the mixture is stiff and glossy.

In a clean bowl, whisk the egg yolks with the remaining sugar until pale and thick. Using a metal spoon or spatula, fold the egg yolk mixture into the meringue. Sift the flour, then fold it into the mixture.

Spoon the mixture into a piping bag fitted with a plain 2 cm nozzle. Pipe 10 cm long fingers on to a prepared baking sheet, leaving 5 cm between the fingers to allow space for the mixture to spread.

Bake at 180°C for about 10 minutes, until golden brown and firm to the touch. Transfer the biscuits to a wire rack to cool. Dust with icing sugar. Makes 10–12.

ROLLING A SPONGE

The sponge for a Swiss roll is baked in a shallow tin of a rectangular shape, then turned out, coated on one side with a filling and rolled up. Follow the whisked sponge technique on the opposite page, using 4 eggs, 125 g sugar and 75 g plain flour. Bake the mixture in a 22 x 33 cm Swiss roll tin at 190–200°C for roughly 4–5 minutes.

1 Lift the sponge from the tin to a rack on the lining paper. Dust a parchment sheet with sugar and place the sponge on it, crust-side down. Peel off lining paper.

2 Transfer it, still on the parchment, to a teatowel. Spread with filling. Fold over 2 cm of sponge along one long edge. Using the aid of the parchment, begin to roll.

3 To tighten the roll without damaging the sponge, push a palette knife under the sponge in the parchment. Pull the paper away from the knife.

MAKING PUFF PASTRY

While cooking, puff pastry rises into thin, crisp layers that are light and buttery. It is used to cover or enclose desserts, as a base for tarts, or assembled in layers with a filling. There are three stages to preparing puff pastry: making the basic dough or detrempe, *the elastic texture of which allows for the next stage; working in the butter; rolling and folding the enriched dough incorporates the butter fully.*

1 Melt and cool 75 g butter. Sift the flour and salt on to a marble slab or into a bowl. Make a well in the middle and pour in the water and melted butter. Begin mixing the dough with your fingers.

2 Use a plastic scraper to gather the ingredients, or continue mixing them with your fingers. Sprinkle in a little extra water, if needed, for a moist dough. Too much water will make it sticky.

3 Work the dough into a smooth ball, then place on floured baking parchment and cut a cross on the top. Wrap the parchment around the dough and chill the parcel for 30 minutes.

INCORPORATING BUTTER

Do not attempt to speed up the process by shortening the chilling times. If the dough is not rested and chilled, the butter will melt and seep out. Shape the butter into a 2 cm-thick oblong and chill. The proportion of butter is important: too little and the dough is heavy, too much and it is greasy. Some pastry chefs weigh the basic dough and incorporate exactly half its weight in butter.

1 Lightly flour your work surface and roll out the dough, leaving a thick area in the middle. Roll out four sections in a cross shape.

2 Place the butter in the middle and fold the extended sections of dough over to enclose it completely. Stretch the dough over the butter, if necessary.

3 Dust the dough and rolling pin lightly with flour, then press the dough to seal in the butter. Roll the parcel into a rectangle, wrap and chill for 30 minutes.

PERFECT PUFF PASTRY

One of the most common mistakes in making puff pastry is to try and rush the process. Good results are achieved only with patience. Allow a day for the process so that the pastry can be prepared with care and kept well chilled. Keep all ingredients and equipment (including your hands) cool as you work.

Strong plain flour contains a high proportion of gluten which strengthens the dough, making it elastic. As the dough cooks, the butter melts and the strong dough forms fine layers which trap air and puff up in the high oven temperature.

Chill the pastry after rolling, folding and turning, and before the final shaping. Chill the shaped final item before cooking. Cook puff pastry at a high temperature, 200–220°C, to ensure that it puffs, becomes crisp and browns well.

PUFF PASTRY

375 g unsalted butter
500 g strong plain flour
2 tsp salt
250 ml iced water

Melt and cool 75 g unsalted butter. Mix the flour and salt in a bowl or on a marble slab and make a well in the middle. Pour the water and melted butter into the well, then work in the flour to make a soft dough. Work together into a smooth, slightly elastic ball. Cover and rest for 30 minutes.

Flatten the remaining butter into a square of approximately 2 cm in thickness. Roll out the dough in a cross shape, with a slightly mounded centre that is large enough for the butter. Place the butter in the middle, fold over the sections of dough and flatten with a rolling pin.

Roll, fold and turn the dough six times, chilling for 30 minutes between each rolling so that the dough rests. Chill before using as required. Makes 1.25 kg.

ROLLING AND FOLDING

The correct way to roll and fold the dough is to keep the edges straight and aligned whilst folding the dough like a letter. This ensures that the pastry rises with an even puff and the layers are consistent throughout.

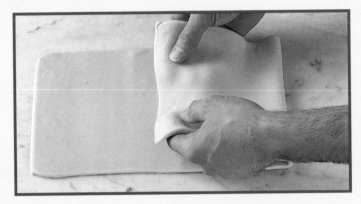

1 Roll out the dough into a long rectangle. Think of the dough as three square sections: fold the lower third section over the middle section.

2 Next, fold the top third down over the middle to the bottom edge.

3 The end result is a square of dough, three layers thick with aligning edges.

TURNING AND RESTING

Wrap the dough in clingfilm or floured baking parchment and chill for 30 minutes each time it has been rolled, folded and turned. This process should be repeated six times in all. This will produce light and flaky layers.

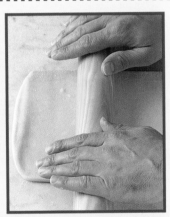

1 Turn the square of dough through a quarter so the top fold is now on the left and the original right edge of the square is now on the top.

2 Press the edges of the dough to seal them, then roll it out into a rectangle as before.

3 Fold the dough as before. Press marks in the dough as a reminder of the number of times it has been folded, rolled and turned. Chill.

CUTTING BASIC SHAPES

To ensure that puff pastry rises evenly, make sure that it is kept to an even thickness when rolled out.

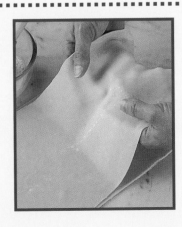

1 Roll the pastry to the desired thickness and lay it on a cool, clean surface. Brush with egg wash (see page 123).

2 Chill or freeze the pastry for 30 minutes, then cut it to the size you require with a greased pastry cutter.

SHORT PASTRIES

Short pastries have a crumbly, slightly crisp, texture. Rich pastries contain a lot of fat, so are very short, with a fine crumb texture and melt-in-the-mouth quality. A small amount of water or liquid is used to bind the pastry, ensuring it does not fall apart. This gives it a certain crispness, acquired also by baking at a fairly high temperature. Make sure you work in a cool environment when making short pastries and use chilled ingredients. Handle the pastry lightly and as little as possible. Heavy handling results in heavy, or tough, pastry.

PATE SABLE

150 g unsalted butter
90 g icing sugar
1 small egg, beaten
250 g plain flour

Cream the butter and icing sugar until soft and pale, then stir in the egg. Sift the flour, then stir it into the mixture to make a smooth dough. Wrap in clingfilm and chill for about 30 minutes.

PATE SABLE
A rich biscuit-like crust, Pâte Sablé is sweeter than Pâte Sucrée. It may be used for flans and tarts, or for making plain dessert biscuits.

PATE SUCREE

200 g plain flour
100 g unsalted butter
40 g caster sugar
2 egg yolks
¼ tsp natural vanilla extract

Sift the flour into a bowl and rub in the butter. Stir in the sugar. Use a fork to lightly whisk the egg yolks and vanilla, then add them to the dry ingredients and mix to form a short dough. Press together lightly and chill for 30 minutes.

PATE SUCREE
This lightly sweetened pastry is enriched with additional egg yolk and flavoured with vanilla. Use for flans, tarts and all sweet pastries.

PATE BRISEE

200 g plain flour
½ tsp salt
100 g unsalted butter
1 egg, lightly beaten
approximately 2 tsp water

Sift the flour and salt into a bowl, then rub in the butter. Mix in the egg and enough water to bind the ingredients to a firm dough. Roll into a smooth ball to remove from the bowl and wrap and chill for 30 minutes before use.

PATE BRISEE
A plain short pastry, this is the French equivalent of the classic Short Crust Pastry and is widely used for fruit tarts and baked dumplings.

MIXING METHODS

Whether mixing by hand or with a machine there are techniques and practices that make mixing pastry easier.

On a cool marble slab, make a mound of the flour, creating a well in the middle. Cut the fat into chunks and place them in the well with the eggs and sugar. Work the ingredients into the flour, pinching and kneading with your fingers. This technique is useful for rich pastries with a high proportion of fat to flour.

A food processor is ideal for blending fat with flour, but do not process more than the capacity suggested by the manufacturer. Process the mixture for short bursts to avoid overprocessing it, or it will become a soft paste which is extremely short and difficult to handle.

MAKING SHORT PASTRY

1 Sift the flour into a bowl. If you are using salt, sift this in with the flour.

2 Rub the fat into the flour until it is incorporated evenly, when the mixture looks similar to breadcrumbs.

3 Make a well in the middle and add egg or sprinkle water over the dry mixture.

4 Use a small palette knife or round-bladed knife to mix in the liquid.

5 When the pastry begins to form clumps, press it gently together with a cupped hand to form a smooth ball.

LINING A FLAN TIN

It is important that you do not stretch the dough when rolling it out and fitting it into the tin or the baked pastry will shrink. Chill the shell for at least 30 minutes before baking to help it to keep its shape.

1 Roll out the dough to a circle that is 5 cm larger than the tin. Wrap the dough loosely around a rolling pin to help you transfer it and then unroll it over the tin.

2 Press the dough over the bottom of the tin and into the seam using a small ball of excess dough that is pinched from the overhanging edge of the pastry.

3 Cut off the rest of the excess dough by rolling the rolling pin over the top of the tin, pressing down firmly with your hand.

EGG WASH

A mixture of egg yolk and water is brushed over bread or pastry before baking to give a rich, golden colour and a glossy glaze. Egg wash can also be used to seal pastry before baking, for example, for pie lids and turnovers.

BLENDING TOOL

A wire, handheld pastry blender may be used to break the fat into the flour. The blender is made of sharp metal wires attached to a handle. By moving the blender up and down through the mixture the fat is cut into the flour.

Mix 1 egg yolk with 1 tbsp water and a pinch of salt. Whisk with a fork until combined. Brush the egg wash over bread or pastry with a pastry brush just before baking.

SHORT PASTRY VARIATIONS

CHOCOLATE
Add 2 tbsp cocoa, sifting it with the flour or 60 g finely grated plain bitter chocolate for a mottled result.

CITRUS
Add the finely grated rind of I orange, lemon or lime to sweetened pastry dough.

TOASTED NUT
Add 60 g finely chopped, toasted almonds or hazelnuts to Pâte Sablé or Pâte Sucrée.

FLAVOURING SHORTCAKE

NUTS
Add 60 g finely chopped, blanched almonds, walnuts or pecan nuts with the sugar.

CINNAMON
Stir in I tsp ground cinnamon with the sugar.

GINGER
Stir in 2 tbsp finely chopped, candied ginger and the grated rind of I lime with the sugar. Fill with mascarpone cheese and exotic fruit.

SHORTCAKE

Shortcake is not a pastry, but it is prepared by the same basic technique used for short pastries. The result is rather like a firm, rich, fine-crumbed scone; softer than a pastry or biscuit. Filled with whipped cream and strawberries, shortcake is a classic British dessert. Individual shortcakes can be layered with a variety of cream fillings and fruit. The basic dough can also be used as a base for baked cheesecake.

SHORTCAKE

90 g unsalted butter
250 g self-raising flour
60 g caster sugar
I egg, beaten
I tbsp milk

Filling
150 ml double cream, whipped
350 g soft fruit
icing sugar to dredge

Rub the butter into the flour until the mixture resembles fine breadcrumbs. Stir in the sugar, then mix in the egg and milk to make a soft dough. Knead the dough into a smooth ball and roll out into a 23 cm circle.

Place on a greased baking tray and bake at 190°C for about 20 minutes, until risen and lightly browned. Cool on a wire rack. Split and fill with whipped cream and soft fruit. Dredge with icing sugar.

MAKING CHOUX PASTE

Although it is grouped with pastries, choux is quite different from them in terms of preparation techniques. However, the result is a crisp, risen mixture which forms a moist, airy cavity that can be filled in a variety of ways. Like other pastries, choux is used as a casing – most commonly for cream and fruit fillings.

Once the paste is ready to use it can be piped or spooned into shapes.

The cooking time for choux depends on the size and shape of the pastries. Very small items (cocktail-sized buns or small lattice shapes, for example) can be baked at 220°C for the entire cooking period. Bake larger items at 220°C for 10 minutes, then reduce the oven temperature to 190°C and cook for a further 15–20 minutes, or until the pastry is crisp and golden in colour. Reducing the temperature in this way ensures that the insides are cooked by the time the outsides are golden brown.

CHOUX PASTE

150 g plain flour
1 tsp salt
15 g sugar
100 g unsalted butter
250 ml water or 125 ml water and 125 ml milk
4 eggs, beaten

Sift the flour and salt together, then stir in the sugar. Heat the butter and water, or water and milk, in a large saucepan over a low heat until the butter melts. As soon as the butter melts, increase the heat and bring quickly to a full boil.

Tip in the flour mixture, remove from the heat and stir. The mixture should form a smooth paste which leaves the side of the pan clean. Do not beat the paste at this stage or it will become oily. Set aside to cool for about 15 minutes.

When the paste has cooled slightly, the eggs can be incorporated – if they are added too soon, they will cook. Gradually pour in the beaten egg, beating in each addition. Beat hard when all the egg has been added until the paste is smooth and glossy.

PREPARING CHOUX PASTE

There are two stages to preparing the paste. First, water, butter and flour are combined, then eggs are beaten in. Water and butter are heated gently until the butter melts, then brought to the boil. If the mixture heats too quickly and the water boils before the butter melts, liquid is lost by evaporation. Add the flour to the boiling liquid at once and stir immediately to form the cooked ball of paste, before you add the eggs.

1 Heat the butter and water gently until the butter melts. Increase the heat to maximum and bring the mixture to a full rolling boil.

2 Tip in all the flour, then remove from the heat and stir. A smooth paste will form which comes away from the pan in a clean ball. Allow to cool for about 15 minutes.

3 Once the dough has become smooth, return it to the heat until it is dry and forms a ball. It should pull away from the side of the pan as you stir it.

4 Remove from the heat and beat in the eggs gradually, incorporating as much air as possible.

5 Continue beating until the paste is smooth and very glossy. The paste is now ready to use.

DEEP-FRYING CHOUX

Place oil in a pan to a depth of 7.5 cm and heat to 190°C. Fill a piping bag fitted with a plain 1.5-cm nozzle with choux paste. Hold the bag over the hot oil and squeeze it to extrude a piece of dough, roughly 3 cm in length. Cut off the dough close to the nozzle, using a chef's knife, so the dough falls directly into the oil. Deep-fry for 3–5 minutes until puffed and golden. Remove with a slotted spoon and drain on paper towels. Serve warm.

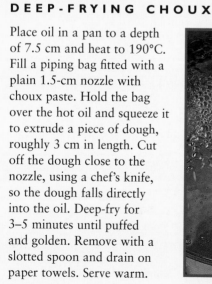

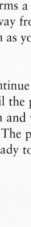
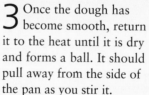

USING BATTERS

Batters are used for many desserts – fine pancakes, crisp fritters or baked fruit puddings. The ingredients vary according to the type of batter and its use, but the following basic techniques ensure smooth, light results. Plain or self-raising flour may be used: plain for pancakes, fritters and pudding batters; self-raising for waffles and dropped pancakes. To avoid lumps, the liquid – water, milk or eggs – must be incorporated gradually. The technique of beating also incorporates air, which lightens the batter, making baked puddings rise when cooked. For perfectly flat, fine pancakes, the batter should stand for 30 minutes or longer before cooking. During standing, the flour grains expand and absorb liquid, so the batter becomes slightly thicker. Extra water may be added before cooking if the batter is too thick.

FRITTER BATTER

300 g plain flour
2 tbsp potato flour or starch
a pinch of salt
2 eggs
1 tbsp sunflower oil
250 ml light beer or lager
4 egg whites
40 g caster sugar

Sift the flour, potato flour or starch and salt into a bowl. Make a well in the middle. Add the eggs, sunflower oil and a little of the beer and gradually work into the flour mixture. Beat well, pouring in more beer as needed. Beat until smooth.

Whisk the egg whites until stiff, then whisk in the sugar to make a smooth, glossy meringue. Beat about a quarter of the meringue into the batter. Then use a metal spoon to fold in the remaining meringue. Use immediately.

MAKING FRITTER BATTER

MIXING THE EGGS AND MILK
Sift the flour into a bowl and mix in other dry ingredients. Make a well in the middle and into this, add the eggs then a small quantity of the measured liquid, such as milk. Stir the ingredients together gently, gradually making a paste that is thick, not smooth.

BEATING TO A SMOOTH BATTER
Add more liquid to make a fairly thick paste. Beat until smooth, making sure all lumps are broken down before adding the additional liquid a little at a time. Gradually add the remaining liquid, beating until smooth after each addition. Use a spatula to scrape any thicker mixture down from the side of the bowl occasionally. This ensures that when all the liquid is added the batter is completely smooth.

MAKING A SMOOTH BATTER

The smoother the batter the more light and even the end result will be. If lumps occur as you mix the flour and eggs you can save your batter in the following ways.

ELECTRIC MIXER
Pour your batter mixture into an electric blender and blend for 1 minute until the batter is smooth and lump-free.

SIEVE
Rest a sieve over a bowl and pour the batter mixture into the sieve. Press any lumps in the batter through the sieve with the back of a spoon.

MAKING LIGHT FRITTER BATTER

Some thick batters, for example fritter batters that are used to coat other items, are lightened by adding beer or by folding in whisked egg whites.

ADDING LIQUID
Make a smooth, thick batter, beating in beer with the egg yolks. The batter should be thick, with a dropping, not pouring, consistency.

ADDING EGG WHITES
Whisk the egg whites until stiff. Stir about a quarter of the whites into the batter. Then fold in the remaining whites and use the batter immediately.

SHAPING BASIC BISCUITS

The basic biscuit dough (given below) can be rolled and stamped out or it can be formed into a long cylinder, chilled and cut into slices.

ROLLING A CYLINDER
Roll the dough into a rope, then wrap it in clingfilm and roll it again before chilling to ensure it has a good shape. Once chilled, use a sharp knife to cut slices off the roll. Here, 50 g raisins are added to the dough before it is rolled into shape and chilled.

STAMPED SHAPES
Roll out the dough and stamp out shapes using a floured cutter. Reroll the trimmings once only to avoid waste. Sprinkle with demerara sugar before baking.

BASIC BISCUIT DOUGH

125 g unsalted butter
150 g caster sugar
2 egg yolks
225 g plain flour
1 tsp vanilla extract (optional)

Cream the butter and sugar together until pale and very soft. Beat in the egg yolks, then stir in the flour and vanilla to make a soft dough. Knead the dough lightly, then chill it for about 15 minutes. Preheat the oven to 180°C and grease two baking sheets.

Roll out the dough on a lightly floured surface and stamp out biscuits using shaped cutters, or roll into a log, chill and slice. Place on the baking sheets and bake for about 15 minutes, until pale golden. Transfer to a wire rack to cool. Makes 12–15.

MAKING BRANDY SNAPS

For success when shaping these lacy biscuits, they should stand briefly when removed from the oven until firm enough to stay in one piece when lifted off the sheets, yet malleable enough to shape. If they harden before you have time to remove them all from the sheets, simply place them back in the oven for about 30 seconds, which is long enough to soften them again.

PLACING THE PASTE
Place teaspoonfuls of the biscuit paste well apart on to greased baking sheets, pressing the mixture out slightly into 3 cm circles.

LEAVE TO SET
Once baked, allow the biscuits to stand for a few seconds on the baking sheet, until the mixture has set sufficiently for it to be lifted off without breaking.

BRANDY SNAPS

115 g unsalted butter
115 g demerara sugar
2 tbsp golden syrup
115 g plain flour
1 tsp ground ginger
1 tsp brandy

Preheat the oven to 180°C and grease two baking sheets. Melt the butter, sugar and the syrup together in a small saucepan. Remove the pan from the heat and stir in the flour, ginger and brandy.

Place teaspoonfuls of the mixture well apart on the baking sheets – the mixture spreads widely, so you will only get about four biscuits on each sheet. Bake for 7–10 minutes, until the mixture is well spread, lacy and golden brown.

While the biscuits are baking, grease several wooden or mixing spoon handles. Leave the biscuits on the sheets for a few seconds, until they are just firm enough to stay together when lifted. Slide a palette knife under a biscuit, then wrap it around a spoon handle. Allow to set for a few seconds, then slide on to a wire rack to cool. Repeat with the remaining biscuits. Makes 20.

SHAPING THE BISCUITS
Wrap the biscuits around greased wooden spoon handles and leave until set, then slide off and place on a wire rack to cool.

TUILES

3 egg whites
100 g icing sugar
100 g plain flour
60 g unsalted butter, melted
½ tsp natural vanilla extract
(optional)

To make the basic stencil paste, whisk the egg whites and icing sugar until smooth. Add the flour, whisking lightly until just combined. Stir in the melted butter and vanilla extract until the mixture is smooth. Cover and refrigerate for 30 minutes.

Preheat the oven to 200°C and grease two baking sheets.

Place teaspoonfuls of the mixture well apart on the baking sheets, spreading out each spoonful with a wet fork to make a 5 cm circle. Bake for 5–8 minutes, until the biscuits are pale golden around the edge.

While the biscuits are baking, grease a rolling pin. Allow the biscuits to cool for a few seconds on the baking sheet, until the mixture is just firm so that it will hold its form, then use a palette knife to slide them off. Curl the biscuits over the rolling pin, leaving them on it until they are just set. Makes 18 tuiles.

MAKING TUILES

Tuile biscuits are made from a basic stencil paste . They can be shaped in a variety of ways (see pages 210–211), but the classic shape for this crisp dessert accompaniment is the slightly curled disc shown here. To obtain this, the cooked and still-warm biscuits are curled into shape over a greased rolling pin, as shown below. Lacy brandy snaps can also be shaped using the same method. The centre of a larger biscuit can be weighted down over an open mould to make attractive containers for desserts – Tulipes. Tuile biscuits can also be crushed and sprinkled on to desserts for a contrasting texture.

1 If large tuiles are required, use a tablespoon of stencil paste for each biscuit instead of a teaspoon and spread it out into a 10 cm circle.

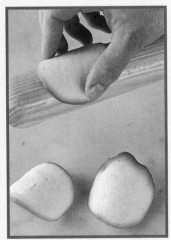

2 Shape the warm biscuits by immediately wrapping them around a greased rolling pin after baking. Cool on a wire rack.

MAKING SHORTBREAD

Shortbread is a classic accompaniment for desserts, particularly fruit salads and ice creams. Here the basic recipe is shaped into finger biscuits. The dough can be cut into any shape. Try squares, diamonds, triangles or stamped shapes such as hearts or circles.

FILLING THE TIN
Press the dough firmly into the prepared tin. Use your fingers for this and try to make sure that the dough is spread evenly across the tin.

CUTTING THE DOUGH
Cut the cooked dough immediately after baking. Sprinkle with caster sugar. Leave to rest in the tin.

SHORTBREAD

115 g unsalted butter
55 g caster sugar
115 g plain flour
caster sugar from sprinkling

Preheat the oven to 170°C and butter a 31 x 21 cm shallow tin. Cream the butter and sugar together until pale and very soft. Stir in the flour.

Turn the mixture into the tin and press it out evenly using your fingertips. If you intend to cut the dough into shapes, such as fingers, mark the shapes before baking.

Bake for about 35 minutes, until pale golden. Cut the cooked shortbread immediately, using the marks you made prior to cooking as guides. Sprinkle with caster sugar as soon as the dough is removed from the oven and leave to cool in the tin for about 15 minutes, or until the dough has set. Then lift out the biscuits and transfer them to a wire rack and leave to cool. Makes 18–20.

COOLING THE BISCUITS
As soon as the dough is firm, use a palette knife to remove the biscuits and carefully transfer them to a wire rack to cool completely.

FRUIT JELLIES AND GELATINE

When using gelatine in desserts it is important to bear in mind that an enzyme in some raw fruit and fruit juices breaks down the protein in gelatine and reduces its setting qualities. The gelatine may set initially, but then, on standing for 24 hours, the mixture softens. Raw pineapple and papaya and unheated lemon juice all have this effect. Heating destroys the enzyme, so in pasteurized juices and canned fruits, the enzyme has been destroyed, eliminating the setting problem.

FRUIT JELLY

150 ml water
150 g sugar
15 g gelatine
500 ml fresh fruit juice
3 tbsp liqueur or spirit
500 g fruits

Make a sugar syrup from the water and sugar and add the prepared gelatine to it.

With the sugar syrup still warm, add the fruit juice and the liqueur or spirit and allow to cool.

Ladle the liquid jelly over a layer of fruits in the base of a mould and chill until set. Repeat until the mould is full.

ADDING GELATINE
When preparing jellied desserts with raw fruit or juices, either heat them, increase the gelatine slightly, or make sure the desserts are served soon after setting.

ADDING JUICES AND ALCOHOL
It is important to add the flavoured liquids while the jelly is still warm so that the flavours mix evenly throughout the jelly.

USING GELATINE

Whichever type of gelatine you use, ensure that it is properly soaked before dissolving it. This is vital if you want to avoid uneven dissolving and setting. Add a little of the mixture you wish to set to the dissolved gelatine to dilute it. Never add chilled liquids or mixtures to gelatine. The cold will set it into strings. Stir the diluted, dissolved gelatine into the main batch of mixture at room temperature. Boiling gelatine for any length of time reduces its setting properties. As a general rule, 3 leaves (7 g), 2 ¼ tsp powder (7 g) or 1 sachet (7 g) sets 600 ml liquid.

SOAKING LEAF GELATINE
Soak the leaves in cold water for about 5 minutes. The leaves will not dissolve, but become limp and soft. Remove from the water and gently squeeze out excess moisture, then place in a clean heatproof bowl with the measured liquid in which they are to be dissolved.

SPONGING POWDERED GELATINE
Put 4 tbsp cold water (or other liquid) in a small heatproof bowl. Sprinkle gelatine evenly over the water but do not stir. If the gelatine is stirred it will form lumps. Leave to stand for about 5 minutes until the gelatine has absorbed the water and swollen. It will look spongy, hence the term 'to sponge'.

DISSOLVING GELATINE
Set the bowl with the gelatine and the dissolving liquid over a pan of simmering water and heat, stirring occasionally, until the gelatine completely dissolves, leaving clear liquid.

AGAR-AGAR

This vegetarian alternative to gelatine is prepared from seaweed extract. It sets at a higher temperature than gelatine, with a differnt consistency – mixtures set with agar-agar are less 'wobbly' and do not melt quickly in the mouth. Follow packet instructions.

Few professional chefs cook with the vegetarian gelatine substitutes. Desserts, in particular, lend themselves to other setting agents such as chocolate or butter, which chefs recommend in favour of agar-agar. Cocoa butter is one of the best vegetarian gelatine substitutes and can be incorporated into many recipes. It has a rather strong flavour, but very little is needed to aid setting and so the taste can usually be masked by the dessert's own flavour.

CAKES &
GATEAUX

GATEAUX
·
INDIVIDUAL GATEAUX
·
CLASSIC CAKES
·
SPONGE PUDDINGS
·
YEASTED CAKES

GATEAUX

The adaptability of gâteaux allows for a variety of flavours to be brought together into beautiful cakes for every occasion. These uncomplicated techniques are easy to master and demystify the assembly process.

CUTTING LAYERS

For a perfect finish, layers for gâteaux must be cut evenly. Make sure the knife you use is long and serrated and that you cut using a sawing action.

ALIGNMENT
Cut a vertical notch in the side of the cake and use this as a guide to align the layers during reassembly.

CUTTING FREEHAND
Cut horizontally towards the centre, then around the cake to ensure that layers are cut evenly all around.

USING GUIDES
Place two mixing spoons (or pieces of smooth dowelling) that are of the same size on either side of the cake, parallel to one another. Cut across the cake with the knife resting on these.

COMPLEMENTARY AND CONTRASTING LAYERS

Layering sponges of different flavours can create attractive and delicious results. If you are combining two flavours, separate your cake mixture into halves, flavour each of these and bake them in two sandwich tins of the same size. Most importantly, choose two flavours that complement each other. Try the suggestions here or devise your own favourite combinations.

- *Chocolate and plain sponges: brush the plain sponge with rum syrup. Fill the layers with chocolate Ganache or a coffee, chestnut or fruit mousse.*
- *Chocolate and coffee sponge: fill with a cream flavoured with mocha or chocolate.*
- *Angel Food Cake: fill with chocolate Ganache, fruit and Crème Chantilly or coffee mousse.*

IMBIBING AND FILLING

Moisten and flavour sponge layers before assembly with a liqueur, fortified wine or spirit. Apply fillings in proportion to the size of the layers for expert results. Spread thin layers of sponge thinly and use finely cut fruit. Thick layers require a deeper filling. Reserve some filling for the coating.

IMBIBING
As you assemble the layers, brush them with rum or brandy. You may prefer to use a light syrup flavoured with a touch of liqueur.

FILLING
Flavoured cream mixed with finely diced fruit is ideal for thin layers. Luscious cream with whole berries works well in thick sponge layers.

COATING THE SIDE AND TOP

When assembling and filling, make sure you position the base of the cake as the top layer, as this has the flatter surface. Then turn your attention to coating the sides and top. Use some of the filling reserved from the assembly process for this. Here, a coating of chopped nuts on the side of the cake provides textural contrast.

1 Spread a thin, even layer of filling around the side of the cake using a palette knife.

2 Press on the coating gently with the palette knife. Experts simply roll the sides of the gateau over it.

3 Spread the topping, taking care not to disturb the edge of the coating around the side.

ANGEL FOOD CAKE

12 egg whites
(approximately 350 ml)
1½ tsp cream of tartar
280 g caster sugar
85 g plain flour, sifted
25 g cornflour, sifted
1 tsp natural vanilla extract

Whisk the egg whites until frothy, add the cream of tartar and continue until they are stiff. Whisk in the sugar gradually to make a meringue.

Sift the plain flour and cornflour together (sifting them twice ensures the cake is light). Fold them into the meringue. Lastly fold in the vanilla extract.

Turn the mixture into an ungreased 21 cm Angel Food Cake tin or loose-bottomed tin and bake at 175°C for 40–45 minutes until the cake has risen and is golden and springy to the touch. Invert the tin, placing a rack under an ordinary tin without feet. Leave to cool completely. Serves 10–12.

Fill Angel Food Cake with American Frosting. Make this as for Italian Meringue (see page 68), using 150 g caster sugar and 1 egg white. Add ¼ tsp vanilla extract.

MAKING ANGEL FOOD CAKE

This classic American sponge is made with egg whites, without using any yolks, so is very light in texture. Cooling the cake upside down in the tin helps to retain its shape and avoids shrinkage. American frosting is used as a filling and coating. For a less sweet result use Crème Chantilly (see page 116) flavoured with a few drops of rose or orange flower water.

FOLDING
Use a spoon or spatula to fold in the sifted flours. Do not overmix, as the air will be knocked out of the mixture. Add the vanilla extract in the same way.

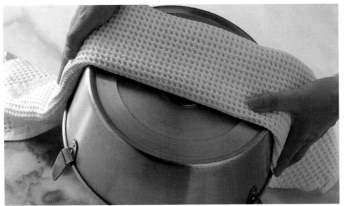

COOLING
Invert the tin on to its feet and leave the cake to cool. If the tin has no feet, invert it on to a wire rack.

UNMOULDING
Once it has cooled, unmould the cake. Loosen it from the side with a knife, if necessary.

Chocolate Nut Dome

A smooth layer of rich chocolate glaze blankets a dome of pistachio cream and cherry-studded chocolate mousse, sitting on a pistachio sponge base. Once chilled, the dark chocolate glaze layer is beautifully contrasted with fine, delicate white chocolate shapes.

PREPARATION PLAN

▶ Prepare the pistachio sponge and pistachio cream.

▶ Make the chocolate glaze and line the mould.

▶ Prepare the chocolate mousse.

For the pistachio dacquoise

2 egg whites
20 g (1 tbsp) caster sugar
45 g ground almonds
50 g icing sugar
10 g (2 tsp) pistachio paste

• • •

For the pistachio burnt cream

125 ml double cream
75 ml milk
40 g pistachio paste (50 g pistachios puréed with 1 tbsp sunflower oil)
25 g sugar
3 egg yolks

• • •

For the chocolate glaze

300 ml whipping cream
50 g sugar
250 g chocolate
50 g butter

• • •

For the chocolate mousse

75 g syrup, made from 40 g sugar and 40 ml water
3 small egg yolks (60 g)
160 g chocolate
300 ml whipping cream

• • •

100 g Griotte cherries in alcohol
White chocolate

Prepare a circular pistachio dacquoise. Whisk the egg whites until standing in peaks, then fold in the sieved ground almonds, caster sugar and icing sugar. Mix the pistachio paste with a little of the mixture to soften, then fold in the remainder. Spread on to a baking tray lined with baking parchment and bake at 180°C for 15 minutes.

Make the pistachio burnt cream. Warm the cream and milk then add the pistachio paste. Whisk the egg yolks with the sugar until smooth, then pour on the warmed milk and cream. Strain through a fine sieve and pour into a baking dish. Bake for 30 minutes at 100°C. Set aside to cool.

Prepare the chocolate glaze. Warm the cream with the sugar, pour over the chopped chocolate and stir in the butter until all the chocolate has melted and the glaze is smooth. Pour the glaze into a 16 cm diameter dome mould and tip the mould to evenly coat it. Tip out excess and repeat until the mould is coated in a substantial layer of the glaze. Leave to set.

Prepare the chocolate mousse. Cook the syrup to 120°C. Meanwhile whisk the egg yolks until pale and tripled in volume. Pour the hot syrup on to the egg yolks whilst whisking them and continue to whisk until cool. Melt the chocolate, heat to 35°C then add to the yolk and syrup mixture. Fold in to incorporate, then quickly fold in the whipped cream. When cool, fill a piping bag and pipe a spiral of mousse from the bottom to the top of the mould following the shape of the dome and smooth with the back of a spoon. Reserving the liquid, drain the Griotte cherries and press some into the mousse.

Spoon in a layer of pistachio burnt cream, pipe a layer of chocolate mousse then add more cherries.

Cut a disc of sponge slightly smaller than the circumference of the dome mould and imbibe with the alcohol you drained from the cherries. Place the disc on top of the last mousse layer and press gently into the mould. Chill in the freezer until firm.

Unmould the dessert and place it on a rack. Ladle chocolate glaze over the entire cake to give it a smooth, glossy finish, and chill.

Melt and temper white chocolate and spread over acetate. Place more acetate on top and mould to the required shape. Freeze until firm. Discard the acetate and place the white chocolate decorations around the cake, affixing them with melted white chocolate.

ASSEMBLING MOUSSE-FILLED GATEAUX

For a perfect finish, assemble a mousse-filled gâteau in a mould until set. This technique can also be used for other gâteaux. Here, an Angel Food Cake (see page 131) is layered with a mousse made from peach purée (see page 113 – make 1½ times the quantity) and assembled in the same 23 cm loose-bottomed tin in which the sponge was cooked.

1 Assemble the layers of cake and mousse in the tin. Begin and end with cake and press each layer gently before adding mousse. Chill until set.

2 Place a serving platter on top of the tin and invert both platter and tin simultaneously. Hold the tin in place with your thumbs to stop it from sliding.

3 Wrap a warmed teatowel around the side of the tin for 2 minutes. This helps to release any mousse that may be stuck to the inside of the tin.

4 Use a warm palette knife to smooth the mousse around the sides of the cake in a thin coating, applying more mousse if necessary.

The crispness of the icing makes a strong contrast with the darkness of the chocolate slabs and lattice. Cherry clusters add a touch of brightness.

ASSEMBLING SQUARE AND OBLONG GATEAUX

Layers of Whisked Sponge are moistened with Kirsch for this strawberry and white chocolate gâteau. Special attention is paid to the neatness of corners. Replace the base of a loose-bottomed tin with a cake card. Once layered, wrap a warm teatowel around the tin, stand the base on a jar and gently slide the sides of the tin downwards to release the gâteau.

Bake a Whisked Sponge (see page 118) in a 20 cm square tin. Assemble the cut layers in an 18 cm tin, using 250 g fruit for the mousse filling (see page 65 – make double the quantity).

CHEQUERED GATEAUX

Precise cutting is the key to a neat chequered pattern. Make sure the filling is well-flavoured and easy to spread. Here, chocolate and vanilla sponges are filled with coffee-flavoured Crème Chantilly (see page 116). Make a Whisked Sponge mixture (see page 118). Flavour half by folding in ½ tsp vanilla extract. Fold 10 g sifted cocoa into the second half. Bake each sponge in a 20 cm sandwich tin for 15 minutes at 170°C. Cool and slice each into two layers.

1 Use 15, 10 and 5 cm metal rings or cutters to stamp out circles from each layer. Position the cutters precisely in the centre to ensure that the rings are cut evenly.

2 Assemble alternate rings of chocolate and vanilla on a 20 cm cake card. Apply a thin layer of filling inside each piece before adding the next. Apply filling over the top of the assembled layer.

3 Assemble the next layer of alternate rings. Start with a contrasting ring, so vanilla and chocolate alternate both vertically and horizontally. Repeat with the remaining layers.

LOAF-SHAPED GATEAUX

Use a 20 x 30 cm tin. For a chequered loaf, make a vertical dividing wall with double-thick foil leaving two compartments in the tin measuring 20 x 15 cm. Divide Whisked Sponge mixture into two and flavour. Bake at 170°C for 15 minutes.

LOAF
Bake two loaf shapes and slice each into two horizontal layers. Sandwich these layers with thin layers of a soft filling, such as a flavoured cream or Crème Chantilly.

CHEQUERBOARD
Slice each sponge into two horizontal layers, then trim each layer into six 20 cm long strips. Assemble in a chequered arrangement as shown above.

*Chocolate and vanilla gâteau with coffee cream piping and chocolate fingers. Buttercream icing complements **plain and pistachio chequers**.*

135

INDIVIDUAL GATEAUX

Individual cakes are easy to serve, a factor that attracts many – the way they look is another. The recipes and decorative approaches here are intended as an inspirational starting point for your own ideas.

FOLDING SPONGES

Thin circles of light almond sponge can be folded and filled to make individual portions, to be served either cold or hot. When hot, almond sponge has a flexible consistency that is ideal for folding. It should be folded promptly, before it cools.

1 Line two baking trays with parchment. Drop 3 dessertspoons of almond sponge mixture in a circle to one side of a tray, flattening the middle slightly with the back of the spoon. Do not spread the mixture – as it bakes, it will spread by itself. Place two portions, well spaced, on each baking tray.

2 Slide a broad palette knife under the sponge to free it, then turn it over on to a wire rack. Fold it in half immediately, creating a generously curled fold. Hold the sponge in position gently for a few seconds until set in shape. Once cool, fill with whipped cream and fruit. Dust with icing sugar.

ALMOND SPONGE

40 g ground almonds
40 g icing sugar
3 eggs
Few drops of natural vanilla extract
Few drops of orange flower water
30 g caster sugar
50 g plain flour, sifted
25 g unsalted butter, melted

Mix the almonds and icing sugar in a bowl. Add 1 egg. Separate the remaining eggs and add the yolks to the almond mixture. Beat until pale and thick. Stir in the vanilla and orange flavourings. Whisk the egg whites until stiff. Sprinkle the caster sugar over the whites and whisk until stiff and glossy. Fold a third of this into the almond mixture, then fold in half the flour. Fold in half the remaining meringue, the rest of the flour, then the remaining meringue. Pour the melted butter around the edge of the mixture and fold it in. Place on a baking tray (see step 1) and bake at 220°C for 6–8 minutes, until risen, set and pale golden. Makes 6.

SERVING HOT FOLDED SPONGES

Thin some warmed apricot or raspberry jam or a little redcurrant jelly with liqueur or spirit. When you remove the hot sponges from the oven, spread them with warm jam immediately before folding. Transfer the sponges on to a warm plate and slide fresh fruit into them. Serve with a dusting of icing sugar.

CUTTING AND ASSEMBLING SPONGE SHAPES

The clean lines of sponge shapes that have been cut with a knife or shaped cutters allow for emphasised decoration. Cut and assemble shapes in a way that allows you to display your decorative filling. If you prefer, layer shapes and coat them to hide the filling. Here, a thin whisked sponge is baked as for Swiss roll in a 22 x 33 cm tin (see page 138), using three eggs.

CUTTING
Cut shapes from thin layers of sponge using a sharp serrated knife, or preferably, shaped cutters, which produce clean lines.

ASSEMBLING
Your imagination is the limit with layering – try a variety of ensembles. Decorations should be proportional – cut fruit finely, and use a finely serrated nozzle for piping.

COATING
Once shapes are layered with filling, they can be coated, as here, with cream, chopped nuts and coconuts, using a palette knife. Fine cocoa powder also works well.

FANNING SPONGE LAYERS

As an alternative to the classic miniature gâteaux, try a more contemporary arrangement. Overlap sponges on a plate in the shape of a fan, using three or four sponges per portion. Between these, add the filling. Using a variety of fillings makes for quite an attractively coloured arrangement.

MAKING A ROLLED SPONGE

Professional chefs refine the popular Swiss roll (rolled while hot from the narrow end) by rolling thin sponge from the wide end when cool. This produces a neat dessert roulade which allows for a good proportion of filling to sponge. For a 22 x 33 cm Whisked Sponge, use 3 eggs, 90 g caster sugar and 40 g each of cornflour and plain flour. Follow the method on page 108. Dust the completed roll with caster or icing sugar or apply a coating.

1 Lift the sponge and the lining paper from the tin and place on a wire rack to cool.

2 Transfer crust side down to parchment paper dusted with caster sugar. Peel off the lining paper.

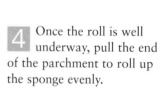

3 Spread the chosen filling evenly over the sponge. Fold approximately 2 cm of the wide end over tightly to start the roll.

4 Once the roll is well underway, pull the end of the parchment to roll up the sponge evenly.

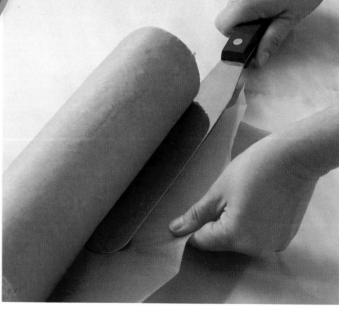

5 Take the end of parchment you pulled to roll the sponge and tuck it in along the inside of the roll. Hold it down with a palette knife and pull the parchment to tighten the roll.

FILLINGS AND COATINGS FOR ROULADES

- *Sweetened whipped cream combined with fruit or flavoured with liqueur.*
- *Crème au Beurre (see page 117) or Crème Patissière (see page 116).*
- *Mousse (see pages 63–65): fruit mousse for plain sponge; dark or white chocolate mousse for chocolate sponge.*

Set to a creamy consistency. Use also as a coating and decoration.
- *Coat thinly with cream or mousse, then with chopped nuts, crushed biscuits, grated chocolate, toasted desiccated coconut or crushed praline. Place coating on parchment and roll roulade over it.*

CHOCOLATE CHESTNUT ROULADE

Prepare the chocolate roulade sponge. Make a rich chestnut mousse from 250 g sweetened chestnut purée, 1 tbsp whisky, 3 tbsp light syrup, 1½ tsp gelatine and 300 ml double cream. Follow the method for Simple Fruit Mousse (see page 65).

CHOCOLATE ROULADE SPONGE

5 eggs, separated
140 g caster sugar
60 g plain flour
20 g cornflour
40 g cocoa powder

Beat the egg yolks with 100 g sugar in a bowl over hot water until pale and thick. Whisk the whites into a meringue with the remaining sugar, also in a bowl over hot water. Fold the meringue into the yolk mixture.

Sift the plain flour, cornflour and cocoa powder together, then fold these dry ingredients into the mixture. Spread the mixture on a baking tray lined with parchment to a neat 38 x 28 cm oblong, 5 mm thick. Bake at 180°C for 10 minutes, then transfer to a wire rack to cool.

1 Moisten the sponge by brushing it with light syrup (see page 108) flavoured with whisky, spread with two-thirds of the mousse and roll up.

2 Using the remaining mousse, coat the roulade, spreading it evenly along the length with a palette knife.

3 Dust with cocoa and decorate with marron glacé (glacé chestnuts).

CLASSIC CAKES

Some cakes never lose their appeal, no matter how old the recipe or how good the competition. For these classic cakes, select the best ingredients, use light mixtures and make fillings that are not too sweet.

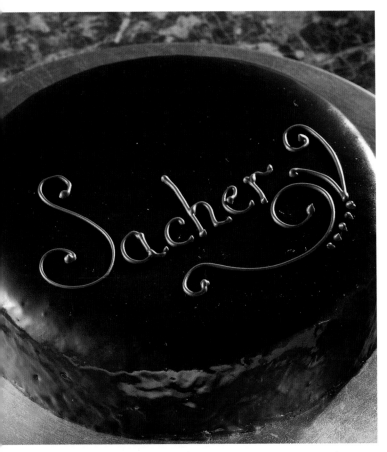

MAKING SACHERTORTE

The plush richness of Sachertorte is due to the addition of butter and melted chocolate, but for many mixtures, the egg yolks are creamed with sugar. Traditionally, flour or other dry ingredients and meringue are folded in in alternating batches. This results in a light, moist sponge.

1 Prepare the meringue and set it aside. Beat the yolks into the creamed butter and sugar gradually, then fold in the cooled melted chocolate.

2 Fold roughly one third of the meringue and half the sifted cornflour into the creamed mixture. In batches, fold in half the remaining meringue, the cornflour, then the rest of the meringue.

SACHERTORTE

150 g dark plain chocolate
250 g unsalted butter, softened
200 g caster sugar
5 eggs, separated
100 g cornflour, sifted

Grease and flour a 20 cm round cake tin. Melt the plain chocolate in a bowl over a pan of hot, but not simmering, water, then set aside and allow to cool. Cream the butter with half of the caster sugar until the mixture is pale and soft, then beat in the egg yolks gradually.

Whisk the egg whites until they stand in soft peaks, then gradually whisk in the remaining sugar to make a soft meringue.

Fold the melted and cooled chocolate into the creamed mixture. Then fold in the meringue and cornflour in two or three alternating batches.

Turn the mixture into the tin and spread evenly. Bake at 160°C for 40–45 minutes. Leave to cool in the tin for 5 minutes, then turn out on to a wire rack and leave to cool.

COATING AND ICING SACHERTORTE

Once baked, cooled and sliced into two layers, the next step is decoration.

Sandwich the layers together with redcurrant jelly. Coat the entire cake with melted jelly and pour Chocolate Icing (see page 112) over. Spread quickly with a warm palette knife, then tap the rack on the worktop to settle the icing in a smooth, even layer. Leave to set.

NUT TORTE

Finely ground nuts replace flour in an Austrian-style torte. The result is moist, close-textured and rich. The cooked torte will feel slightly soft in the middle, but becomes firm on cooling.

Stir the chocolate and nuts into the creamed mixture, (see above) then gradually fold in the meringue.

TIPSY CAKE

Create the basic mixture for Tipsy cake with 150 g unsalted butter, 150 g caster sugar, 3 eggs and 225 g self-raising flour. Cream the butter and sugar until pale and soft, then beat in the eggs, adding small amounts of flour until it is all used. Turn the mixture into the prepared mould (see below).

1 Make sure the ring mould is buttered thickly before turning the mixture into it. Bake at 160°C for approximately 35 minutes, until firm to the touch. Cool on a wire rack.

2 Make a syrup (see page 108) with 150 ml very strong black coffee and 50 g sugar, then stir in 2 tbsp brandy or rum. Spoon this over the baked cake to soak it evenly before decorating.

CHOCOLATE NUT TORTE

225 g unsalted butter, softened
150 g soft brown sugar
4 eggs, separated
200 g plain bitter chocolate, grated and chilled
200 g hazelnuts, finely ground
25 g ground almonds
50 g caster sugar

Grease and line a 23 cm round tin. Cream the butter and sugar until soft and light, then beat in the egg yolks. Stir in the chocolate and nuts.

Whisk the egg whites until they stand in soft peaks, then gradually whisk in the caster sugar to make a meringue. Fold this into the nut mixture. Turn into the tin and bake at 150°C for about 60 minutes.

Fill this sweet cake with plain whipped cream to balance the sweetness. Strawberries may be added to the cream.

Tipsy Cake is decorated with a coating and piped swirls of Crème Chantilly and chocolate-coated coffee beans. Chocolate Nut Torte is coated with ganache and hazelnuts, with white chocolate in a loose lattice pattern.

Pain de Gênes

The mainstay of this traditional dessert is its dense but moist almond sponge – the "bread". It is always cooked in a round mould and here, topped with white chocolate mousse and decorated with fruit, nuts and white chocolate curls, it makes a grand finale to a special occasion.

For the almond sponge cake

75 g icing sugar
175 g finely ground almonds
Vanilla essence
1 whole egg
4 egg yolks
4 egg whites
50 g sugar
90 g flour
45 g melted butter

• • •

For the white chocolate mousse

300 ml whipping cream
150 g white chocolate

• • •

150 g white chocolate
250 g raspberries
50 g redcurrants
Sliced, toasted almonds

Butter a 22 cm cake tin and sprinkle liberally with the sliced toasted almonds, making sure that the tin is thoroughly lined with nuts so that the finished cake will have an even coating. Shake the excess nuts out of the tin and set aside.

Prepare the almond sponge. Sieve the icing sugar and the ground almonds into a bowl. This ensures that the sponge mixture is free of lumps and also incorporates air into it. Add the vanilla essence and then beat in the whole egg and the egg yolks. Keep beating the mixture until fluffy and thoroughly mixed.

Make a Swiss Meringue (see page 68). Whisk the egg whites and sugar together in a bowl that is resting over just simmering water. Turn the bowl as you whisk for an even consistency. Keep whisking until the mixture stands in firm peaks. Fold the meringue into the sponge mixture. Add the flour and finally fold in the melted butter. Transfer to the prepared almond-lined cake tin and bake at 170°C for roughly 30 minutes, until risen and golden brown.

Meanwhile, make the white chocolate mousse. Melt the white chocolate in a large bowl over simmering water. Gently heat 30 ml of the whipping cream in a saucepan over a low heat and add this to the melted chocolate. Mix the chocolate and cream together well and allow to cool. Semi-whip the remaining cream and fold it into the chocolate base until evenly mixed.

Remove the sponge from the tin and place it on a wire rack. When it is cool, cut it horizontally in half with a serrated knife. To make an even cut, use two wooden spoons laid on either side of the sponge to act as cutting guides (see page 130). Spread the lower disc of sponge with the white chocolate mousse and place the upper disc on the mousse layer. Using a large plain nozzle, pipe a little more mousse around the edge of the top of the cake.

Melt 150 g white chocolate in a bowl over gently simmering water. Pour the chocolate on to a smooth surface such as marble or a laminate surface and spread it thinly using a palette knife. Work the white chocolate over the surface several times until it is smooth and even. Allow the chocolate to cool a little then cut it into 2.5 cm squares. Test a corner of the chocolate first – it is cool enough to cut when the knife cuts it cleanly rather than dragging. Allow to cool a little more then, using a spatula, begin to scrape the squares off the surface. Scrape them diagonally, starting at one corner of a square and keeping the pressure steady. This encourages the chocolate squares to curl. Keep the white chocolate curls cool until ready to use.

Place the white chocolate curls carefully on top of the piped chocolate mousse, so as not to disturb the piping. Decorate the centre of the top of the cake, within the mousse edging, with fresh fruit, a mixture of raspberries and redcurrants. Add a few sliced, toasted almonds for a contrast in look, flavour and texture. To finish, sprinkle the whole of the top of the cake with icing sugar, tapped from a small sieve.

SPONGE PUDDINGS

Sponge puddings, both steamed and baked, are an understandably enduring British tradition. There are many variations on the basic recipe, but in all cases they should be served hot, freshly cooked.

STEAMED SPONGE PUDDING

100 g unsalted butter
100 g caster sugar
½ tsp natural
vanilla extract
2 eggs
175 g self-raising flour
250 g jam or other preserve

Grease a 1.1 litre pudding basin with butter. Prepare a piece of greaseproof paper and double-thick foil to cover the basin, making a pleat in the middle. Allow plenty of extra foil for folding on to the basin edge. Prepare a steamer over a pan of boiling water.

Cream the butter with the caster sugar and vanilla until pale and soft. Beat in the eggs, adding a little flour to prevent the mixture from curdling.

Fold in the remaining flour. Place the jam in the bottom of the basin and spoon in the mixture. Spread it lightly, then cover with the pleated paper and foil (tie them on with string), sealing the basin well with foil – this keeps the steam out, maintaining a moist environment to prevent a crust from forming on the pudding. If the pudding rises during cooking, the pleats in the paper and foil give it space to do so.

Steam the pudding for about 1¾ –2 hours. Top up the pan with boiled water as necessary. Turn out the pudding and serve with Crè;;me Anglaise (see page 116). Serves 6.

SERVING SPONGE PUDDINGS

Steamed sponge pudding is traditionally served with a hot custard, such as Crème Anglaise (see page 116). However, it may be accompanied by a fruit coulis (see page 113), with cream or fromage frais, with syrup (see page 108), or topped with praline, grated chocolate, or a warm fruit preserve.

STEAMING SPONGE PUDDINGS

The texture of a steamed sponge differs from that of a baked sponge in that it is slightly more moist, soft and heavy. Covering the pudding mixture with greaseproof paper and foil (which can be buttered on the side that faces the pudding) ensures that the pudding does not become waterlogged and allows it to rise.

1 Mix high-quality apricot jam or some such topping with 1 tbsp dry sherry and some chopped ready-to-eat dried fruit, such as apricots. Place them in the bottom of the basin.

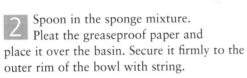

2 Spoon in the sponge mixture. Pleat the greaseproof paper and place it over the basin. Secure it firmly to the outer rim of the bowl with string.

3 Cover with pleated foil (to keep out steam). Secure it to the outer rim. Cook the pudding in a steamer over boiling water.

4 Remove the pudding. This is easier if you tie a piece of string around the foil before steaming, leaving a loop to act as a handle.

PUDDING BASIN

A traditional pudding basin is ideal for steaming sponge puddings. The rim (around which floured muslin was originally tied) can be used to tie the string handle. The base is slightly flat so the pudding can be topped.

5 Remove the paper and foil, cover with a plate and invert, then lift the basin off the pudding. Serve the steamed sponge pudding immediately with Crème Anglaise.

145

The versatile Almond Sponge mixture (see page 136) makes a light, hot dessert when steamed or baked. Make either individual portions, or, for a large pudding, use a 900 ml pudding basin and steam for 1 hour.

PREPARING THE MOULD
Grease six 175 ml individual pudding basins or moulds with a brush. Grease them up to the rims so the cooked pudding does not stick.

INDIVIDUAL SPONGE PUDDINGS

Prepare a half quantity of the basic sponge pudding mixture (see page 144) and flavour it with the finely grated rind of 1 lemon instead of vanilla.

1 Coat the base of four ramekins with a light caramel (see page 109) and arrange pieces of fruit in the base; here neat slices of orange are used.

2 Spoon in the sponge mixture and bake at 190°C for 15 minutes, until risen and firm. Invert on to plates and decorate with shreds of candied lemon rind.

STEAMED PUDDINGS
Divide the mixture between the prepared moulds. Cover as for a large sponge pudding (see previous page) and steam the puddings for 30 minutes.

BAKED PUDDINGS
Alternatively, bake the puddings, uncovered, at 180°C for 12–15 minutes, until risen and firm to the touch.

LEMON PUDDINGS

Add to the Almond Sponge mixture (see page 136) the grated rind of 1 lemon. Place 2 tbsp high-quality lemon curd in the base of six 175 ml moulds before adding the sponge mixture. Steam the puddings for 30 minutes and serve them with hot Crème Anglaise (see page 116).

CHOCOLATE SPONGE PUDDINGS

Make 1 quantity of Steamed Sponge Pudding mixture (see page 144), using 125 g self-raising flour sifted with 30 g cocoa. Divide the mixture between six 175 ml individual moulds, cover and steam for 40 minutes. Serve hot with warm, freshly made chocolate sauce (see page 115).

YEASTED CAKES

Cakes made with yeasted batters, such as the traditional savarin and babas desserts, are wonderfully soft, with a characteristic flavour. Preparing the batter is easily mastered.

PREPARING YEASTED BATTER

Aim for an elastic consistency. The batter will look sticky to begin with, but as it is worked it will become smooth and glossy, and can be formed into a ball.

1 Beat the liquid mixture into the dry ingredients until smooth. Holding your fingers together, slap the batter against the bowl with your hand.

2 Cover and leave to rise, then beat in softened butter by the same method. Continue beating until the batter is elastic in texture.

RUM BABAS

Delicious Rum Babas may be served hot, fresh from the oven, or once cooled, saturated with syrup and decorated with whipped cream.

1 Follow the recipe for the yeasted batter, adding 75 g sultanas with the butter. Bake the mixture in eight 95 ml moulds or individual ring tins.

2 Soak the babas by spooning over them 300 ml syrup (see page 108). Cool as for savarin (see overleaf). Decorate with piped whipped cream.

YEASTED BATTER

250 g strong plain flour
1 tsp salt
1 tsp caster sugar
3 eggs, beaten
80 ml milk
20 g fresh yeast
50 g unsalted butter

Sift the flour, salt and sugar into a bowl. Make a well in the middle of the dry ingredients and pour the eggs into it. Warm the milk until tepid. Crumble the yeast into a small bowl and gradually stir the milk into the yeast. Add this to the eggs.

Stir the dry ingredients into the liquid ingredients gradually to make a stiff batter. Using the palm of your hand, beat the batter with a slapping action until it is smooth. Cover and leave in a warm place until doubled in volume.

Cream the butter until very soft, then beat it into the batter as before and continue beating for about 5 minutes, until the batter is elastic in texture.

Brush the mould with melted butter. Chill, then brush with a second coat of melted butter. Turn into the buttered mould to fill it by about a third. Cover and leave to rise to the rim of the mould. Then bake at 190°C for 25–30 minutes.

Exotic Fruit Savarin

A new interpretation of the Brillat-Savarin creation, a French favourite for over 150 years, the traditional ring-shaped cake is here filled with whipped cream and exotic fruit set in syrup and topped with a spice-filled spun sugar ball.

PREPARATION PLAN

- Preheat the oven to 170°C.
- Prepare and bake the sponge.
- Make the syrup and soak the fruit.
- Whip the cream and fill the cake.
- Make the sugar decoration.

For the savarin sponge
250 g flour
20 g yeast
5 g salt
10 g sugar
3 eggs
50 g melted butter

• • •

For the fruits
1 mango
2 kiwis
1 papaya
1 large pineapple

• • •

For the syrup
200 ml water
200 g sugar
1 cinnamon stick
Peel of 1 orange and
½ lemon
4 whole cloves
1 vanilla pod
1 sprig of mint

• • •

For the spun sugar
250 g sugar
500 ml water

• • •

Apricot jam
Whipped cream
Cinnamon
Star anise
Vanilla

1 Prepare the savarin dough. Sift the flour into a bowl and then add the yeast, salt and sugar. Pour the eggs, making sure you add only a little at a time, into the dry ingredients, mixing the whole time with a wooden spoon until the mixture is smooth. Add the melted butter and mix well. Half-fill a buttered savarin mould and set aside in a warm place to allow the dough to rise until it has doubled in size. Place the dough in a 170°C oven and bake for 40 minutes until golden brown.

2 Prepare the mango, kiwis and papaya. Take a sharp knife and score along the length of the mango and papaya then strip the skin away. It may be easiest to remove the kiwi skin with your fingers rather than a knife. Cut the flesh of the fruits into 1 cm cubes.

3 Prepare the pineapple. Remove the outer rind and core. Trim off the ends, stand on a board and cut away the peel in strips from top to bottom, thickly enough to take off the worst of the spines. Gouge out the remaining spines with a knife tip, remove the core and discard. Cut the flesh into 1 cm cubes.

4 Make the syrup. Bring the water and sugar to the boil then add the flavourings. Chop the citrus peel and steep in the syrup for 15 minutes. Pour the warm syrup over the fruits, cover and marinate.

5 Drain the syrup from the fruit and set aside. Dip the sponge into the syrup, then brush the sponge with warmed apricot jam to give it shine and place on the serving dish. Fill a piping bag with whipped cream and pipe it into the centre of the sponge. Arrange the marinated fruits on the cream.

6 For the spun sugar ball, make a sugar syrup and cook to hard crack stage (see page 108). Arrest the cooking by plunging the base of the pan into cold water. Holding two forks back to back, dip them into the syrup. As the syrup begins to flow off the tines of the forks, flick them rapidly back and forth over the handle of a saucepan. The strands of sugar will drape over the saucepan handle and set (see page 209).

7 Very gently, gather up the sugar strands and mould into a ball. Clean several pieces of cinnamon, star anise and vanilla and gently insert them into the sugar ball. Place the ball on top of the exotic fruits and serve. The decorative ball should not be eaten.

SAVARIN

This ring-shaped cake, named after the famous French gastronome Jean-Anthelme Brillat-Savarin, is generally flavoured with rum and sugar and served with Crème Chantilly and fruit. The recipe is over 150 years old.

1 Follow the yeasted batter recipe (see page 147). Turn the batter into a prepared 23 cm mould, cover with lightly oiled polythene or clingfilm and leave to rise to the rim. Bake at 190°C for about 25–30 minutes.

VARYING SAVARIN OR BABAS

Any combination of fresh fruit may be used for savarin. Pineapple and mango go well with the spiced syrup shown here. Lightly poached cherries and apricots work wonderfully with a kirsch-flavoured syrup.

SYRUP

Flavour the syrup with the seeds from 3 green cardamoms, 2 bay leaves and the pared rind of 1 orange as well as lemon rind and rum. Strain after standing.

COCOA

Cocoa powder may be dissolved in the syrup and Crème de Cacao or brandy can be added.

KIRSCH

Kirsch may be added to the syrup instead of rum.

COFFEE

Use strong black coffee to make syrup for babas.

Fill the central ring of savarin with fruit. Here, scooped passion fruit is scattered over star fruit slices, papaya and pineapple chunks, peeled lychees and whole cherries and physalis.

2 Bring 500 ml water, 5 tbsp rum, 200 g sugar and the pared rind of 1 lemon to the boil, then leave to stand for about 10 minutes. Soak the cooked savarin in the mould thoroughly with this syrup, then allow it to cool and unmould. (Or turn the savarin out on to a wire rack and place over a tray or dish. Brush the syrup over to soak the savarin, then leave to cool.)

3 Place the savarin on a serving platter and brush with Apricot Nappage (see page 113).

4 Finish the Savarin by filling with Crème Chantilly (see page 116) and topping with fresh fruit.

PASTRIES

PIES, TARTS & FLANS
·
SABLE & SHORTCAKE
·
PUFF PASTRY DESSERTS
·
STRUDEL & FILO PASTRIES
·
CHOUX PASTE

PIES, TARTS & FLANS

French tarts and flans are renowned worldwide for their short pastry, creamy fillings and glorious glazed fruit toppings. These straightforward techniques need only a light touch and a little time to perfect.

LINING A FLAN TIN

Add 1–2 tsp cold water to Pâte Sucrée before rolling it out to line a flan tin. Avoid rolling it too thinly, as it will fall apart. Roll out the pastry so that it is larger than the size of the tin, fold it in half over the rolling pin and move it to the tin (ensuring it does not stretch), unrolling it loosely on top. If the pastry is slightly too small in places, press it gently to the correct size with your fingers. For the fruit and almond cream pie here, use a 900 ml metal flan or tart tin. Serves 4–6.

1 Support the pastry with one hand. Press it gently into the tin with a knuckle on the other hand. Work quickly to stop the edge breaking where it overhangs the rim.

2 Gently press the pastry on to the inside edge of the tin. If there is any excess pastry, ease it over the rim of the tin to leave an overhang.

3 To remove any excess pastry, roll the rolling pin over the rim to remove it. Chill the pastry for at least 30 minutes before proceeding.

BAKING AN EMPTY SHELL AND BAKING BLIND

Some fillings require quick cooking, so the pastry shell is part-baked (baked blind) before being filled and returned to the oven. If the filling requires no cooking, the pastry must be fully baked before being filled. Cook the pastry shell for 15–25 minutes at 200°C until pale golden.

BAKING BLIND

The weight of ceramic baking beans holds the pastry shell in place during cooking so that it maintains its shape. Any ordinary dried beans can be used instead.

1 Prick the base of the pastry shell evenly all over with a fork.

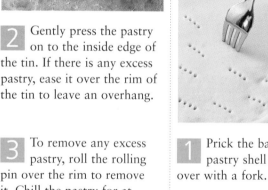

2 Line the pastry with foil or parchment and fill up to the rim with ceramic baking beans or dried beans. Bake for 10–15 minutes at 200°C, until the pastry has set and is partly cooked.

FILLING A COOKED FLAN

Crème Pâtissière (see page 116) is the classic base for a glazed fruit flan, but here, Almond Cream is used.

1 Apply a thin glaze of either melted chocolate (dark or white) to the base of the pastry shell to prevent it from softening. Leave to set.

2 Half-fill the flan with almond cream, then top with fruit, either fresh or glazed. A 250 g combination of whole red and green grapes, halved strawberries and sliced kiwi fruit – all uncooked – are used here.

GLAZING SOFT FRUIT

Brush uncooked fruit with Apricot Nappage (see page 113) or melted redcurrant jelly. Alternatively, light caramel (see page 109) may be drizzled over the fruit to three-quarters coat it.

ALMOND CREAM

120 g caster sugar
4 tbsp water
2 eggs, separated
120 g toasted ground almonds
4 tsp rum
½ tsp natural vanilla extract

Make a syrup using 60 g caster sugar and 2 tbsp water, then boil to the soft-ball stage (see page 108). Meanwhile, lightly beat the egg yolks. Gradually pour in the syrup, beating continuously, until the mixture is pale and creamy.

Fold in the ground almonds, rum and vanilla extract.

Boil a second syrup to soft ball stage using the remaining sugar and water. Whisk the egg whites until stiff, then pour in the syrup gradually, whisking continuously to make a stiff, glossy meringue. Fold the meringue into the almond mixture. Use the almond cream at once to fill a flan or tartlets.

CREAMY FILLINGS AND ADDITIONAL TOPPINGS

■ **Fillings**
Pipe Crème Chantilly (see page 116) into tartlets. Try a vanilla or fruit mousse (see page 65), or white chocolate mousse (see page 64).

■ **Toppings**
Melted chocolate (dark or white) may be drizzled across the fruit. Italian Meringue may be piped on top. Glaze under the grill until golden.

ALSATIAN PLUM TART

Combine custard with flambéed plums, pears, apples or berries in this open tart. Use Pâte Sucrée (see page 122) for the pastry, baked blind in a 23.5 cm flan tin at 170ºC for 15 minutes.

1 Halve and stone 400 g plums and fry them briefly in 30 g unsalted butter. Add 2 tbsp plum brandy or liqueur and ignite the alcohol. Once the flame has died, arrange the plums and their juices in the pastry case.

2 Beat 2 eggs with 60 g sugar. Stir in 60 ml each of milk and single cream and pour this over the plums. Bake the flan for 10 minutes at 170°C, then sprinkle with 50 g slivered almonds and cook for a further 5 minutes.

TARTE TATIN

This classic up-turned, caramelized apple tart has been popular since its first appearance at the turn of the 20th Century. Use good quality eating apples for a perfect tarte Tatin.

1 Melt 50 g unsalted butter in a shallow pan, then add 100 g sugar and 1 tbsp water. Add 1.2 kg peeled, cored and halved Golden Delicious apples and cook until golden underneath. Cool slightly.

2 Place the apples in a 23 cm flameproof tin. Cover with Pâte Brisée (see page 122) and bake at 220°C for 20 minutes. Nudge the pastry rim to loosen it and invert on to a platter. Serve warm with crème fraîche.

FRENCH APPLE TART

In this simple open tart, the fruit is baked with the pastry. Use 4–5 Granny Smith's or well-flavoured dessert apples. Once peeled and cut into slim, even slices, toss the apples in lemon juice to prevent discolouration. Use Pâte Sucrée (see page 122) for this recipe, but not baked blind.

1 Overlap the apple slices attractively in the pastry case (use a 23.5 cm flan tin). Then brush the flan with 75 g melted butter.

2 Sprinkle with 100 g caster sugar and bake at 190°C for about 45 minutes, until the apples are tender and browned.

MAKING FRUIT TARTLETS

1 quantity Pâte Sucrée can be baked in patty tins to make 12–14 fruit tartlets.

Prick the pastry before baking at 180°C for 10 minutes. Cool on a wire rack. Fill the cases with Crème Pâtissière or Crème Chantilly, top with fruit and glaze with Apricot Nappage (see page 113).

Tartlets filled with redcurrants and pineapple combined with kiwi (left); mango, blueberries and red- currants (middle); whitecurrants, raspberries and apricots (right).

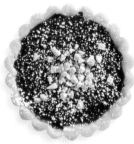

CHOCOLATE PRALINE CREAM

100 ml double cream
3 drops natural vanilla extract
110 g dark plain chocolate, finely chopped
50 g praline (see page 109)
20 g unsalted butter, softened

Heat the cream with the vanilla to just below boiling, then pour it over the chocolate in a bowl. Stir until smooth. When cool, add the praline and butter. Stir until thoroughly combined and cool, stirring occasionally.

MAKING CHOCOLATE TARTS

To make chocolate praline tarts, spoon the chocolate praline cream into pastry cases cooked in individual tart tins. Chill until set. Top with chopped toasted almonds and hazelnuts and dust with icing sugar.

MAKING CUSTARD TARTS

Custard tarts are quick and simple to make so are perfect last-minute dessert treats, especially if served with poached fruit. Use Pâte Sucrée (see page 122) to line 12 standard sized patty tins. Prick the bases and chill well. For the custard, make a half quantity as for Crème Caramel (see page 46), adding 2 tsp plain flour to the eggs.

1 Fill the tarts to just below their pastry rims with custard and bake at 180°C for about 20 minutes, until set and pale golden.

2 Serve warm or cold. If serving warm, slice poached pear (see page 14) and drizzle with chocolate sauce (see page 115).

Tarte Tatin

Made famous by the Tatin sisters of Lamotte-Beuvron, the classic recipe was for a single apple tart, cooked under a lid of pastry, but served inverted with the pastry underneath and the fruit on top. Our individual servings are sweetened with caramelized nuts and ice cream.

PREPARATION PLAN

- ▶ Make the pastry.
- ▶ Prepare the apples and caramel.
- ▶ Preheat the oven to 190°C.
- ▶ Assemble the tart and cook.
- ▶ Invert and serve.

For the pastry
200 g plain flour
A pinch of salt
100 g butter
30 g sugar
1 egg
1 tbsp water

• • •

For the filling
1 kg apples (Golden Delicious)

• • •

For the caramel
115 g sugar
1 tbsp water
60 g butter
½ vanilla pod

• • •

50 g pecan nuts
50 g pine kernels
50 g pistachios
Vanilla ice cream

1 Prepare the pastry. Sift the flour and salt into a bowl, then rub in the butter. Stir in the sugar. Lightly beat the egg then mix it and enough water into the dry ingredients to bind them. Wrap the dough in clingfilm and refrigerate for 30 minutes.

2 Meanwhile, prepare the apples. Peel and core the apples then cut each one into 6 segments. Take your time when cutting the segments, making them as equal in size as you can to create a perfect, uniform look to your finished desserts.

3 To make the caramel, melt the sugar, water and butter. Split the ½ vanilla pod and scrape out the seeds. Add this to the caramel ingredients and cook them all to a light caramel. Add the apple segments and cook for 2 or 3 minutes, then add the nuts and pine kernels to the caramel, keeping them separate from the apples so that they flavour the caramel but are easy to remove at the next stage. Cook for approximately 5 minutes.

4 Roll out the dough into a circle about 3 mm thick. Using the bottom of one of your moulds or pans as a guide, cut out 4 discs. Bake them in a preheated oven at 190°C for 7–10 minutes until pale golden.

5 Remove the nuts from the caramel mixture and overlap the apple slices in the individual moulds, using most of the syrup. Cover the top of each with a disc of pastry. Bake for 10–15 minutes at 170°C.

6 Let the tarts cool down and turn each one upside down on to a serving plate. Place a quenelle of vanilla ice cream in the centre of the fruit and spoon around some of the caramel and nuts from the pan.

LINZERTORTE

Pastry

100 g ground almonds
100 g icing sugar
2 tsp ground cinnamon
5 tsp water
560 g unsalted butter, softened
600 g plain flour

Raspberry Jam

500 g raspberries
450 g sugar
50 g glucose
35 g pectin

Mix the almonds, icing sugar, cinnamon and water into the softened butter. Mix in the flour without overworking the dough. Wrap in clingfilm and chill for 30 minutes.

For the jam, cook the berries with 225 g sugar until reduced and pulpy. Mix the remaining sugar and pectin and add to cooked the fruit. Bring to a rolling boil, remove from heat and allow to cool.

Line a 23 cm flan tin with half the pastry. Fill with the cooled jam. Top with a closely woven lattice of pastry, brush with egg wash and bake at 180°C for 45 minutes, until pale golden. Dust with caster sugar and return to the oven for 5 minutes. Leave to cool.

APPLYING A LATTICE TOPPING

A lattice topping can be used on a flan or plate tart for an attractive edible finish. Here the lattice is applied to the classic Linzertorte.

1 Roll out the pastry for the lattice into an oblong of the same length as the diameter of the tart. Cut it into 1.5 cm wide strips.

2 Lay a row of strips equidistantly in one direction across the tart.

3 Weave the lattice in the opposite direction, lifting alternate pastry strips to begin each row.

4 When the lattice is complete, dampen the pastry edge, press the strips in place, then trim their ends.

FRUIT PIES AND PLATE TARTS

In Britain, a pie has a single crust top and a tart has a double crust (the exception is the double-crust pie). A tart also differs from a pie in that it is baked in a shallow dish or deep plate, known as a tart plate. A pie is always deeper than a tart.

For pies with no pastry base lining the dish, attach a pastry strip to the rim, as with the deep fruit pie shown here (right). Treat this as if it were the edge of a pastry base that is lining the dish and press the top crust on to it to secure it well on to the pie.

MAKING A FRUIT PIE

Pâte Brisée is used to make the deep fruit pie here. So that the pastry lid is sealed to prevent fruit juices from escaping, a strip of pastry is pressed on to the rim of the pie dish.

1 Roll out the pastry to about 5 cm larger than the 900 ml oval pie dish. Cut a 2 cm strip from the edge. Dampen the rim of the dish and press on the pastry strip.

2 Fill with 675 g prepared fruit – fresh apricots, rhubarb, plums, or an apricot and raspberry mix as here. Layer the fruit with caster sugar as you go.

3 Dampen the pastry rim with water, then cover the pie with the pastry lid. Trim off excess pastry, holding the dish up in one hand and cutting from below with downward strokes, with the knife pointing outwards at a slight angle.

4 To scallop the pastry edge, press sections of it outwards with your knuckle. At the same time, tap it inwards gently at regular intervals with the blunt side of a knife blade.

5 Press out the sections further with the tip of your index finger and pull the knife taps further in with the blunt edge of a knife. Small scallops such as these are classic edges for sweet pies. Cut a hole or slits in the top pastry layer and brush the layer with milk. Bake at 180°C for 30–35 minutes.

Apple and Pear Tart

A sweet pastry case is filled to overflowing with a mélange of caramelized fruit pieces and nuts. This delicious filling is held in place by a nut-flaked nougat ring with a hole in the centre into which slices of fresh fruit are decoratively placed.

PREPARATION PLAN

- ▶ Preheat the oven to 170°C.
- ▶ Bake the pastry.
- ▶ Prepare the filling.
- ▶ Create the nougat ring.
- ▶ Add the decoration.

For the sweet pastry
100 g butter
200 g flour
1 tsp salt
40 g sugar
1 egg
¼ tsp vanilla essence

■ ■ ■

For the fruit and nut filling
2 dessert apples
2 dessert pears
50 g butter
50 g sugar
1 tbsp honey
50 g almonds
50 g pistachios
50 g pine nuts

■ ■ ■

For the nougat
150 g sugar
50 g glucose
50 ml water
50 g flaked almonds

■ ■ ■

Apple and pear slices

First prepare the sweet pastry. Rub the butter into the flour with your fingertips until it resembles fine breadcrumbs, then mix in the salt, sugar and finally the egg and vanilla essence. Knead the dough until it is smooth, then refrigerate for 30 minutes. Roll it out and use it to line a 24 cm tart tin. Line the pastry with foil or parchment, fill with ceramic baking beans and bake blind (see page 152) for 10–15 minutes.

Prepare the filling. Peel the apples and pears and cut the flesh into 1 cm cubes. Make a caramel by cooking the sugar with the butter and the honey. Add the apples and pears and cook for 5 minutes before stirring in the nuts (reserve some of the nuts

for later use). Cook a little further until all the ingredients are thoroughly coated with the honey caramel. Remove from the heat and spoon the filling into the pastry case. Smooth the filling out into an even layer on the pastry.

To prepare the nougat, cook the sugar, glucose and water to a light caramel (see page 109). Stir in the almonds and pour the mixture on to an oiled baking tray. Allow the nougat to cool, then chill until set. Place the hardened nougat in a food processor and process into a powder. Cut a circle the size of your tart tin out of a sheet of card and place on to a lined baking sheet. Sprinkle the powdered nougat evenly in the template and add the reserved flaked almonds, pistachios and pine nuts. Place in the oven and cook at 170°C for about 5 minutes until just coloured. Remove from the oven and carefully cut a smaller circle out of the middle of the nougat disc with a pastry cutter. Leave to cool.

Place the nougat ring on top of the tart, ensuring you position it so they sit neatly together and fill the middle of the nougat ring with slices of apple and pear. Serve warm or cold.

What's in a Name?

Though almost any type of apples and pears can be used, if necessary, for cooking, certain varieties of dessert fruit are juicier and sweeter and, if making a special dish, are worth the extra time it takes to locate them. Dessert apples are usually smaller, with a darker, more mottled skin than other apples and are extremely fragrant with an aromatic flavour. Varieties include James Grieve, Starking, Sturmer Pippin, Cox's Orange Pippin, Blenheim Orange and Russet. There are fewer dessert pears but Williams, Conference and Comice are good choices.

SABLE & SHORTCAKE

Although not technically pastries, these alternatives are prepared with pastry-making techniques. Shortcake is a classic cheesecake base. Firmer Pâte Sablé is softer than shortbread and may be used for tarts or flans.

MAKING CLASSIC SHORTCAKE

Rich, soft and crumbly shortcake is traditionally filled with whipped cream and strawberries in Britain.

1 Prepare the shortcake (see page 123) and slice it into two horizontal layers. Cut the top layer into six triangular wedges and dredge these thickly with icing sugar.

2 Spread the base layer with Crème Chantilly (see page 116) and 300 g strawberries and blueberries on the cream. Arrange the wedges on top as shown.

ASSEMBLING SABLE CIRCLES

Make 1 quantity Pâte Sablé (see page 122), adding 1 tsp ground cinnamon with the flour. Roll out the pastry to 2–3 mm thick and cut out 24 circles, each 8 cm in diameter. Bake on a greased baking tray at 170°C for about 15 minutes, until pale golden. Cool on a wire rack.

1 Take eight sablé discs and arrange the fruit on top of each; here 260 g lightly poached apricots are used.

Serve with a syrup flavoured with lavender.

2 Top eight more discs of Pâte Sablé with piped rosettes of Almond Cream (see page 49) or Crème Chantilly (see page 116).

3 Marble plain and white chocolate (50 g each). Cut into circles around a disc. Attach with melted chocolate and assemble 3-tiered towers.

PUFF PASTRY DESSERTS

The appeal of puff pastry lies in the crisp, flaky thinness of the layers. This versatile pastry can be used for a broad variety of desserts – for ensembles that are large or small, elaborate or simple and served hot or cold.

MAKING MILLEFEUILLE

For this simple puff pastry dessert, thin layers of pastry are sandwiched together, traditionally with jam and cream. Here, raspberry jam is used and high-quality lemon curd is mixed with whipped cream. Millefeuille may be round or cut in a ring and assembled on a Pâte Sucrée base. Rectangles of pastry are also often used, as here.

1 Make a half quantity of puff pastry (see page 120). Roll it out to the size of a rectangular baking sheet, prick all over and chill for at least 40 minutes.

2 Bake the pastry for 15–20 minutes at 220°C until puffed and golden. Cool on wire racks, then cut into quarters. Trim the edges using a card template for neatness.

3 Whip 150 ml double cream until it stands in soft peaks, then fold in 200 g lemon curd. Pipe lemon cream rosettes on one of the pieces of pastry and place 220 g raspberries between the rosettes. Repeat on a second piece of pastry, then take the third piece and spread it liberally with raspberry jam.

4 Take the last piece of pastry and dredge the top thickly with icing sugar. Use a hot metal skewer to brand a pattern in the sugar. Now assemble the dessert as shown (right).

*Decorate the top of the **Millefeuille** with raspberries and strips of candied lemon peel.*

ROLLING PALMIERS

These sweet, crispy swirls illustrate a very simple method of using puff pastry. They may be served as a decorative accompaniment to ice cream or fruit desserts, or they can form the base for a plated sweet.

1 Roll out a half quantity of puff pastry (see page 120) to 30 x 15 cm. Sprinkle with caster sugar. Fold the ends over the middle, roll out to 24 x 24 cm and trim.

2 Brush with melted butter and fold in two opposite edges to meet in the middle. Brush again and fold in half along the meeting point for a long rectangle.

3 Cut the pastry into a series of strips, each 1 cm wide. There should be enough pastry to cut 16 strips. Place them on a greased baking tray.

PALMIERS WITH ICE CREAM AND POACHED APRICOTS

Use a Vanilla Ice Cream (see page 36) or make a simple yogurt ice cream by churning and freezing 425 g plain yogurt with 80 g icing sugar, 5 tbsp single cream and 1 tbsp honey. Freeze scoops of ice cream. Assemble the palmier pairs with ice cream and serve with poached apricots (see page 14) and a lightly sweetened raspberry coulis (see page 113). Decorate with mint.

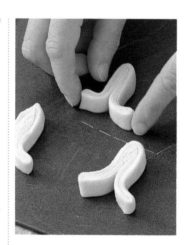

4 Fan out the unattached end of each strip, then bake them at 200°C for 10 minutes. Turn over and bake for a further 10 minutes. Cool on a wire rack.

FILLINGS FOR PALMIER PAIRS

- *Whipped cream decorated with whole raspberries or sliced strawberries.*
- *Sprinkle a little cinnamon over the pastry with the sugar and serve spiced*

palmiers with grilled chunks of pineapple and crème fraîche.
- *Blackberries and sliced pears poached in red wine syrup, with Greek-style yogurt.*

MAKING TURNOVERS

Turnovers are a delicious combination of fruit and pastry. Use a well-flavoured filling, such as the thick apple purée spiced with cinnamon here. For the pastry, roll out 225 g (a two-thirds quantity) of puff pastry and cut half a dozen 8½ cm diameter circles with a serrated cutter.

1 Roll out the pastry circles to elongate them very slightly into oval shapes.

2 Brush the pastry edges with egg wash and place the filling neatly on one side. Fold the pastry over and press down the edges to seal.

3 Place the turnovers on a greased baking tray and brush with egg wash.

FILLINGS FOR TURNOVERS

- Fruit purées (see page 113) should be simmered until thick and well flavoured, not watery. Sweeten the purée once it has been reduced.
- Cut lightly poached fruit, such as pears, apricot halves (fresh or dried), prunes or peaches, into neat pieces that sit well inside the pastry.
- Mix 100 g finely ground almonds with 50 g icing sugar. Bind the mixture with a little kirsch and use this as a filling with ready-to-eat dried fruit, such as apricots, mango, pineapple or prunes.

MAKING FEUILLETES

Fill these diamond-shaped pastry containers with cream and fruit for a simple dessert.

1 Roll out pastry as for turnovers above, but cut squares. Fold in half to form a triangle and cut a 1 cm border, leaving 1 cm uncut at two opposite corners.

4 Score a pattern on the pastry without cutting through it. Sprinkle with caster sugar and bake at 220°C for 10 minutes, then at 190°C for 10–15 minutes. Dust with sugar and serve hot with Crème Anglaise, or cool on a wire rack and serve with ice cream and poached fruit.

2 Unfold the pastry and brush the inner edges with egg wash. Lift up the loose corners, cross the border strips and press in place. Bake as for turnovers.

MAKING JALOUSIE

Jalousie – a filled pastry with a slatted top – is usually served with a filling of mincemeat or jam, puréed or poached fruit, or a sweetened paste of ground almonds moistened with egg or liqueur. Using these techniques, slices of Jalousie can be made large or small, depending on your requirements. Here, a half quantity of puff pastry (see page 120) is used.

1 Roll out and trim two 30 x 15 cm pieces of pastry. Set one aside and fold the other lengthways in half. Cut slats along the fold. Leave the outside edge uncut.

2 Spread the base with apricot jam, chopped dried apricots macerated in brandy and flaked almonds, leaving a 1 cm border around the edge. Brush the edge with egg wash.

3 Lay the slatted pastry over the filling to one side and unfold it to cover the filling completely. Seal the edges well, brush with egg wash and bake at 220°C for 10 minutes, then at 190°C or 10–15 minutes. Glaze thinly with Apricot Nappage while still hot and serve warm or leave to cool.

A TRANCHE

A tranche is a long, narrow pastry case that, once cooked, is filled with a cream filling and fresh or poached fruit, such as the fresh figs, raspberries, blueberries and apricots, here. Brush fresh fruit with glaze – here, Apricot Nappage (see page 113).

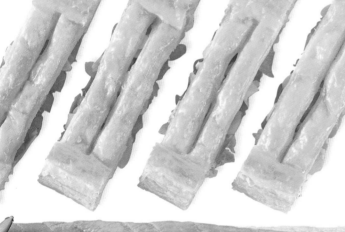

1 Make a half quantity of puff pastry (see page 120) and roll it out to 30 x 15 cm. Cut a 1.5 cm border all around and lift out the middle. Roll the middle to 30 x 15 cm, trim the edges and place on a baking tray.

2 Brush the edge with egg wash and lay the border on top. Lightly score it with a sharp knife and brush with eggwash. Prick the centre all over. Bake at 220°C for 10 minutes, then at 190°C for 10–15 minutes, then fill.

STRUDEL & FILO PASTRIES

Strudel and filo pastries are rolled into paper-fine sheets which are layered
before cooking, resulting in the fine, light pastry that is famous in **Austria**.
They must not be allowed to dry out or they crack and break.

MAKING STRUDEL

*For the strudel dough, sift
300 g strong plain flour with
1 tsp salt. Mix in 40 ml
vegetable oil with 200 ml
warm water.*

1 Knead the dough until
smooth, throwing it
down to make it stretchy.
Cover with a damp tea towel
and set aside in a cool place
for 2 hours. Roll it out on a
floured surface. Cover with a
damp tea-towel and allow to
rest for 15 minutes.

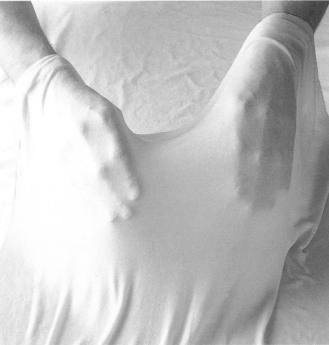

2 Working on a floured
sheet, stretch the dough
over the backs of your hands,
working from the centre
outwards. When ready, you
should be able to see your
hands through the dough.

3 Brush with 75 g butter.
Add the filling. Draw
one edge of the sheet up over
the strudel and roll up the
dough and filling together,
keeping the pressure even.
Bake on a buttered tray at
190°C for 30–40 minutes.

STRUDEL FILLINGS

■ **Apple**
*Sweat 500 g cooking
apples, peeled, cored and
chopped in 75 g unsalted
melted butter. Cool slightly,
then mix with 150 g brown
sugar, 100 g raisins, 100 g
walnuts, toasted and
chopped, 1 tsp cinnamon
and 50 g cake crumbs.*

■ **Cherry**
*Mix 500 g cherries, 100 g
chopped walnuts, 150 g
brown sugar, 50 g cake
crumbs, the grated rind of
1 lemon, 1 tsp cinnamon.*

LITTLE FILO PASTRIES

Filo pastries can have very sweet fillings, such as a sweet and spicy paste of dried dates or highly sweetened ground nut mixtures. A lightly sweetened paste of ground almonds or chopped fresh, poached or dried fruit may be used. Grated chocolate goes well with ground hazelnuts in a paste flavoured with brandy. Bake at 180°C for about 30 minutes and cool on a wire rack.

CIGAR

Cut an 8 cm wide strip of filo and brush with butter. Place the filling at one end, fold the short edge over the filling and roll up, brushing the pastry with butter as you go.

TRIANGLE

Cut an 8 cm wide strip of filo and brush with butter. Place some filling in a corner at one end and fold filo over the filling in a triangular shape. Fold the triangle repeatedly along the length of the strip and brush with butter.

LAYERING FILO IN BAKLAVA

Baklava is a traditional Middle-Eastern sweet in which filo is layered with finely chopped nuts and honey or syrup. Use walnuts or pistachio nuts and add a sprinkling of ground cinnamon to each layer.

2 Sprinkle with nuts and cinnamon and continue layering pairs of filo sheets with filling. Add three sheets of filo on top, brushing each with butter.

1 Prepare 450 g filo and melt 100 g butter. Grease an ovenproof dish and place a sheet of filo in the base. Brush with melted butter and add another sheet.

3 Cut into diamond shapes and bake at 170°C for 1¾ hours, until golden. Meanwhile, make a light syrup (see page 108). Stir 100 g clear honey into 150 ml hot syrup and trickle this over the baklava as soon as it is removed from the oven. Leave to cool.

FILO FRUIT PIES

Filo is a light alternative to short or layered pastries and is ideal for covered tarts or fruit pies. Use a shallow dish such as a flan dish or tart plate, rather than a deep dish. The fruit may be fresh or lightly poached in syrup; here, apricots are used for a filo fruit pie. As with stretched strudel dough, sheets of filo dry and rapidly become unusable if they are left uncovered. Keep filo securely wrapped in clingfilm when not actually working with it. Always work on a dry, lightly floured surface, as any dampness will make the filo sticky and encourage it to break. Brush with melted unsalted butter to prevent cracking, give crisp results, seal edges or layers and enrich the pastry.

Rhubarb and strawberry pie *retains its moisture with a filo crust. Serve* **apricot pie** *in slices.*

1 Butter a 23 cm flan dish and line with filo, with the excess overhanging the rim. Use several sheets, brushing each one with butter.

2 Place the filling on to the filo layers. Here, 450 g poached, halved apricots are used.

MAKING A SHREDDED FILO TOPPING

Ribbons of filo can be used as a decorative topping for fruit pies, in the same way as a pie crust. The crisp, light filo complements the soft cooked fruit.

1 Line the dish with double-thick filo and brush with butter. Fill with the chosen filling and fold the excess lining pastry over the fruit. Brush with butter.

2 Roll up several sheets of filo and cut into 1 cm slices, then shake out into ribbons over the pie. Brush lightly with butter and bake until golden brown at 180°C for about 35 minutes.

3 Cover the fruit with filo and brush with butter. Fold the overhanging pastry over the top and brush with butter. Bake at 180°C for about 40 minutes.

169

CHOUX PASTE

Although often referred to as pastry, choux is actually a soft paste of a piping consistency. It rises during cooking into a crisp, light case with a slightly moist lining and hollow centre. It is one of the easiest of 'pastries' to prepare.

CHOUX BUNS

Choux buns make excellent cases for cream or chocolate. Use a piping bag fitted with a large plain nozzle to shape the paste on to a greased baking tray.

1 Pipe neat globes of choux (see page 124). Avoid forming a peak at the top of the shape by holding the nozzle down into the paste as you pipe. Allow plenty of space between the buns for rising, increasing this proportionally if you are piping larger buns.

2 If there are peaks on the buns, flatten them with a fork dipped in beaten egg. Brush the buns lightly with beaten egg. Bake at 220°C for 10 minutes, then at 180°C for a further 5–10 minutes for small buns or 15 minutes for large buns.

3 If you are not sure that the buns are cooked properly, make a small split in one bun to check if the inside looks cooked. Cool on a wire rack.

4 When cool, cut a small split in the base of each bun. Fill the buns by piping cream in through the split using a large, plain nozzle.

*Cut fruit thinly to fill **choux buns** and place on a bed of cream. Top with a caramel lattice. A glazed fruit topping looks attractive on a cream-filled bun. Complement a coffee mousse filling with a caramel topping.*

CHOUX FINGERS

Choux fingers are well-known as éclairs, both filled and topped with chocolate. Many different fillings can be used with this shape.

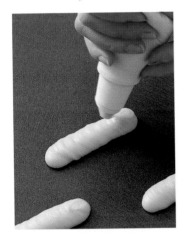

1 Pipe the choux paste with a plain nozzle, making each finger identical in length.

2 Bake and cool the fingers as for choux buns (see left). Split and fill – a flavoured mousse, here coffee-flavoured, is piped on to the base.

FILLINGS FOR CHOUX

- Whipped cream, Crème Chantilly (see page 116) or Crème Pâtissière (see page 116).
- A mousse, chocolate or fruit, set to a piping consistency.
- Fresh or poached fruit mixed with whipped cream.
- Coffee, chocolate or liqueur-flavoured creams.

TOPPINGS AND SAUCES

- Icing sugar, caramel, melted chocolate or glacé icing.
- Chocolate or butterscotch sauce or Crème Anglaise.
- Fruit coulis or a flavoured syrup such as vanilla or lemon balm.

CHOUX RINGS

Choux rings can be piped to any size, using either a plain or a decorative serrated nozzle. Give them a simple ice cream filling, or construct a more elaborate fruit and cream ensemble.

1 Mark out circles of your chosen size on a baking tray using a circular cutter dusted with flour. These form a template for your choux rings.

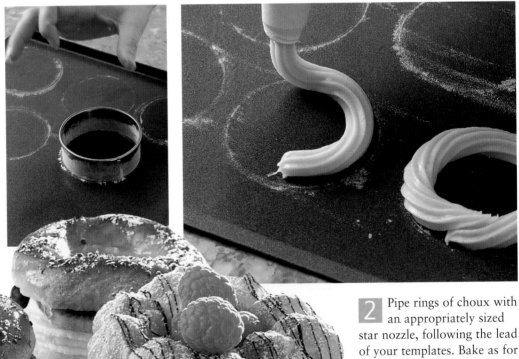

2 Pipe rings of choux with an appropriately sized star nozzle, following the lead of your templates. Bake as for choux buns (see left). Split, cool and fill.

*Fill **choux rings** with cream, kiwi slices and blueberries, or try piped rosettes of raspberry mousse with a fine drizzling of chocolate on top.*

171

DECORATIVE PIPED SHAPES

When piping decorative choux shapes, allow plenty of space between them for the choux to expand during cooking. Sprinkle chopped nuts on top before cooking if desired. Instead of filling the shapes, dust with icing sugar and use as a dessert base or topping.

SPIRALS

Draw 15 cm circles clearly on parchment to guide you. Turn it over and pipe spirals from the centres of the circles to the outlines.

*The filled choux shapes may be topped with piped whipped cream, caramel (see page 109), glacé icing (see page 112) or piped melted chocolate (see page 198). Cooled poached pineapple chunks and blueberries, with a drizzling of passion fruit and some vanilla ice cream make a superb filling for **choux lattice squares**.*

PARIS-BREST

This is a large ring of choux filled with Crème Pâtissière (see page 116) or whipped cream. It was designed to resemble a bicycle wheel by a pastry cook whose shop was on the route of the annual Paris to Brest bicycle race.

LATTICE SQUARES

Pipe a lattice of choux to form a 12–15 cm square. Brush with beaten egg and bake at 200°C for 15 minutes. Cool on a wire rack and serve in pairs with ice cream and poached fruit.

CHOUX SWANS

These delicate fancy pastry swans are filled with Crème Chantilly (see page 116) and fruit and can be served on a 'pond' of fruit sauce, individually or in pairs.

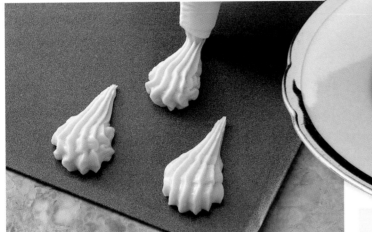

1 Using a large star nozzle, pipe 6 cm long teardrop shapes on to a buttered baking tray, allowing one per swan. Brush with egg wash and bake at 200°C for 15–20 minutes.

2 Fill a paper piping cone (see page 198) with choux paste mixture and cut a small hole in the tip of the cone. On a buttered baking tray pipe a small shape resembling the number '2'. Pipe more choux paste on to the upper tip of the '2' to make the swan's head and beak. Bake at 200°C until lightly browned.

3 When the teardrops are cooked, cut them through the middle lengthwise with a sharp knife. Remove one half of each teardrop and cut it in half again to form the wings.

4 Pipe Crème Chantilly on to the uncut teardrop halves with a large star nozzle and fit the choux wings into the cream with the wing tips pointing upwards. Fill the body of the bird with a little fruit and dust with icing sugar.

5 Fill a paper piping cone with melted chocolate and, holding the baked swan's neck in one hand, pipe a beak and eyes on to the head. Place the neck on to the cream-filled body, facing away from the points of the wings.

SAINT HONORE

This dessert combines a base of Pâte Sucrée with a choux pastry topping. The name has two possible sources. It may be that the variety of pastries used in this dessert has led to it taking the name of the Patron Saint of Pastry Chefs, Saint Honoré, or that the pastry chef, Chibouste, whose name is given to the cream, set up a bakery on the Rue Saint-Honoré in Paris.

SAINT HONORÉ

1 quantity Pâte Sucrée
(see page 122)
½ quantity Choux paste
(see page 124)
1 quantity Crème Chibouste
(see page 116)
1 quantity Caramel
(see page 109)
1 egg yolk
1 tbsp water

Make the Pâte Sucrée. Roll out a 20 cm circle and place on a baking tray. Prick all over and chill for 30 minutes.

Make the choux paste and pipe a broad spiral of it on to the Pâte Sucrée base. Brush with eggwash made from the egg yolk and water beaten together and bake at 200°C for 25–30 minutes.

Pipe small choux buns on a separate baking tray and bake them at 220°C for 10 minutes, then at 180°C for 5–10 minutes. Remove from the oven and cool on a wire rack. Do not split the buns open but allow them to cool completely while still intact.

Make the Crème Chibouste. When the choux buns are cool, make a small hole in the base of each bun and fill with cream.

Make a caramel. Dip the filled buns in the caramel and place on to an oiled work surface to harden.

Fit a piping bag with a Saint Honoré nozzle (see opposite) and fill with Crème Chibouste. Pipe approximately one third of the cream on to the pastry base and smooth the top with the back of a spoon. Pipe a criss-cross pattern of Crème Chibouste over the cream.

If necessary, reheat the caramel over a low heat. Dip the base of each bun into the caramel and place on the pastry border. Serve with a spun sugar ball (see page 209).

MAKING SAINT HONORE

The various components of the Saint Honoré can be prepared separately before you begin assembly, although the caramel will be at its best if prepared as you need it. If necessary, practise the criss-cross piping off the cake before you begin the decoration.

2 Pipe 12 to 14 petite choux buns. Keep the size of the buns as uniform as possible throughout.

EQUIPMENT

Saint Honoré nozzles are available in plastic or stainless steel. They have a characteristic slanting top and tapering opening. This produces a feather-like design with a narrow tip and thicker base.

1 The piped choux spiral on the Pâte Sucrée base rises and expands to take up space on the base. This helps to reduce the amount of Crème Chibouste needed for filling, stopping the cake from becoming too rich.

3 After filling, coat the top of the buns with caramel. Take care not to ruin the shape of the buns or squeeze out the Crème Chibouste filling.

4 The characteristic criss-cross pattern may take some time to perfect. Keep the narrow edge of the nozzle pointing upwards and apply steady pressure on the bag.

5 Dip the buns in caramel a second time to help stick them to the cake, seal the Crème Chibouste filling and form a sweet, crunchy shell.

CHOUX AND SABLE CASES

Choux can be used in combination with other pastries. For instance, a Pâte Sablé base can be piped with a choux border which will expand during cooking. This will enclose the filling and provide textural contrast to the Pâte Sablé base.

1 Cut out a Pâte Sablé shape, such as a heart, oval, diamond or flower, and place on a baking tray. Prick all over with a fork and chill for 30 minutes.

2 Pipe a line of choux around the edge of the shape, adding small stars of choux to neaten joins or to emphasise corners where necessary. Brush with beaten egg and bake at 200°C for about 20 minutes. Cool on a wire rack.

3 Fill the cooked case with your chosen filling. Here, Crème Chibouste (see page 116) is used, with fresh whole raspberries and slices of kiwi fruit.

Crème Chantilly mixed with grated plain chocolate makes a good bed for an apricot-glazed orange segment topping. Crème Chantilly and glazed fruit fill a plain choux border. Make individual portions in fruit shapes. Fill with poached fruit (here poached pear and apple) and top with fruit slices or a caramel lattice.

VARYING EDGES

Choux borders need not be simple piped lines. These star shapes rise sufficiently to retain the filling within the case and create a decorative effect. Experiment with different nozzle shapes for a variety of looks.

DEEP-FRIED CHOUX

Choux pastry makes superb fritters or beignets. These should be served freshly cooked, with a thin fruit coulis, flavoured syrup or dredged with caster sugar.

1 Flavour the choux paste with grated lemon or orange rind. Beat in currants and/or candied fruit.

2 Heat vegetable oil for deep frying to 190°C. Use two wet spoons to drop small walnut-sized portions of choux into the oil.

3 Fry until puffed, crisp and golden. Drain on a slotted spoon, then on absorbent paper. Toss in caster sugar mixed with a little cinnamon and serve immediately.

CHOUX ICE CREAM FRITTERS

Choux ice cream fritters have a delightful hot-cold contrast which relies on quick and skillful frying. Fill small choux buns with ice cream and freeze, then dip them in batter and deep fry rapidly in vegetable oil.

Cool the choux buns and fill them with a fruit or zesty flavoured ice cream. Place in the freezer for several hours to freeze the choux well. Prepare a basic fritter batter (see page 125) and heat vegetable oil for deep frying to 190°C. Dip the frozen choux buns in batter to coat them thinly, then deep fry them for a few seconds. Sprinkle them with caster sugar and serve immediately with a fruit coulis or maple syrup.

Chocolate Macarannade

This contemporary confection consists of a range of classical constituents. A fine macaroon-like paste of ground almonds, egg whites and sugar forms a nest into which is placed a dome of chocolate cream. Praline Chantilly cream forms the inner circle.

PREPARATION PLAN

- ▶ Pre-heat the oven to 180°C.
- ▶ Prepare and bake the macarannade base.
- ▶ Make and mould the chocolate cream.
- ▶ Prepare the chocolate glaze and praline Chantilly.

For the macarannade
75 g icing sugar, plus extra for dusting
60 g ground almonds
40 g flour
3 egg whites
75 g sugar

▪ ▪ ▪

For the chocolate cream
200 g chocolate
460 ml whipping cream

▪ ▪ ▪

For the chocolate glaze
250 g chocolate
300 ml whipping cream
50 g sugar
50 g butter

▪ ▪ ▪

For the praline Chantilly
230 ml whipping cream
35 g praline

▪ ▪ ▪

Toasted flaked almonds to decorate

1 First prepare the macarannade. Sieve the icing sugar, ground almonds and flour together in a bowl. In a separate bowl, whisk the egg whites until they form stiff peaks. Whisk in the sugar and continue to work it until the mixture is glossy. Fold in the dry ingredients, taking care not to knock out too much of the air in the egg mixture.

2 Using a plain nozzle, pipe the macarannade into a 18 cm circular cake tin. Begin by overlapping large globes of macarannade around the edge of the tin, then pipe a spiralled circle starting in the middle of the tin and working right up to the piped globes, so that they form a border for the spiral. Sprinkle the base of piped macarannade entirely with icing sugar and bake for 25 minutes at 180°C. Once cooked,

remove from the tin by loosening the edges and slipping it out, and cool on a wire rack. Trim the edges evenly and neatly with a sharp knife.

3 While the macarannade is cooking, prepare the chocolate cream. Roughly chop the chocolate and place in a saucepan. Gently melt the chocolate, then stir in 115 ml of the cream. Bring the chocolate and cream mixture to the boil, stirring continuously with a whisk to keep it smooth. Remove the chocolate cream from the heat, allow to cool, then softly whip the remaining cream and fold it in. Pour into a half-spherical mould and allow to set.

4 Next, prepare the chocolate glaze. Roughly chop the chocolate and place in a bowl. Gently warm the cream with the sugar in a saucepan. Pour this over the chopped chocolate and, as it begins to melt, gradually stir in the butter until all the chocolate has melted and the glaze is smooth. Set the glaze aside and allow to cool while you prepare the dome.

5 Carefully remove the chocolate cream dome from the half-spherical mould and place, dome-side up, on a wire rack. Place a tray under the wire rack to catch the excess glaze that pours off the dome. Pour the chocolate glaze over the dome and, once the dome is completely covered, lift the rack up a little and drop it down on to the work surface or tray to help settle the chocolate coating. Leave to set.

6 Finally, prepare the praline Chantilly. Place the praline in a blender and blend into a fine powder, pulsing the power for even results. Whip the cream until thickened. Add the praline powder and continue to whip until stiff peaks have formed.

7 Assemble the chocolate macarannade. Place the coated dome on to the cooled macarannade circle, directly on the centre. Using a piping bag with a star nozzle, pipe small globes of praline Chantilly between the macarannade border and chocolate cream dome. Decorate the dome with toasted flaked almonds.

FRUIT DUMPLINGS

Use Pâte Brisée (see page 122) for these tempting fruit dumplings (1 quantity makes 4 dumplings). Halve and core or stone your chosen fruit and prepare the filling. Here, nectarines are filled with marzipan. If using fruit that discolours, such as apples, brush with lemon juice.

1 Place a piece of marzipan into the stone hollow of the nectarine half and press it down to fill the hole.

2 Cut a 7 cm circle of Pâte Brisée. Place the flat side of the filled fruit on the pastry and press it neatly around the sides of the fruit. Brush with beaten egg.

3 Cut a larger circle of pastry to cover the fruit. Lay it over the fruit and press it neatly on to the pastry base. Do not overlap it in a thick wedge under the fruit.

4 Trim off excess pastry. Decorate with pastry leaves and brush with beaten egg. Bake at 190°C for about 40 minutes, until golden. Sprinkle with caster sugar.

ALTERNATIVE FRUIT

Fresh, poached, bottled or canned fruit can be used for dumplings. Try:
- *Bottled peaches in brandy syrup.*
- *Lightly poached pears.*
- *Halved and cored apples filled with brown sugar, ground cinnamon and and a mixture of raisins, sultanas and chopped apricots.*
- *Halved papaya (seeds removed), packed with rum-macerated sultanas. Cover flat side down.*

GRAINS

RICE DESSERTS
·
SEMOLINA

RICE DESSERTS

Rice is delicious in sweet dishes, which are referred to as milk puddings.
When cooked in milk, each grain of rice becomes succulently swollen,
with a tender and wonderfully creamy texture.

SIMMERED RICE PUDDING

Round-grain rice or pudding rice absorbs a large quantity of liquid whilst simmering. This results in a creamy pudding with tender grains.

Place 100 g pudding rice in a saucepan with a heavy base and add 600 ml milk and a vanilla pod. Bring to the boil, stirring constantly. Reduce the heat to the lowest setting and cover the pan. Cook gently for approximately 40 minutes, stirring often, until thick and creamy. Remove the vanilla pod and sweeten the cooked rice with caster sugar, adding 30–60 g according to taste. Serves 2–4.

FLAVOURINGS FOR RICE PUDDING

BAY LEAF

Crush a large bay leaf and stir it into the rice during cooking for a delicate, elusive herb flavour.

ROSE OR ORANGE FLOWER WATER

Add rose or orange flower water and decorate the pudding with crystallized rose petals.

CINNAMON

Add a cinnamon stick and a strip of orange peel to simmered or baked rice pudding.

LAVENDER

During cooking, add a small sprig of lavender, then serve the rice topped with exotic rose-petal jam or preserve (available from Eastern European delicatessens).

CRYSTALLIZED ANGELICA

Add chopped crystallized angelica to the rice in the final stages of cooking. Lemon rind and finely chopped crystallized citron peel may also be added – their flavours complement the angelica.

CREAMY SIMMERED RICE

Increase the creaminess of the pudding if required, using one of the two methods shown here. Make sure the cooked rice is at room temperature before adding cream.

POURING IN CREAM
Stir 150 ml double cream into the simmered rice just before serving. This thins the pudding in texture and enriches its flavour.

FOLDING IN WHIPPED CREAM
Whip double cream until it stands in soft peaks, then fold into the rice pudding before serving it either warm or cold.

SUMMER AMARETTO CONDE

A conde is a chilled dessert of creamy rice pudding served with fruit. Cool simmered rice and enrich it with whipped cream, then chill. The fruit may be poached, stewed, preserved in alcohol, or fresh and chilled, dressed with sieved, warmed apricot jam or redcurrant jelly.

1 Make a syrup using 200 ml water and 50 g sugar. Peel, stone and slice six peaches and poach them in the syrup until tender.

2 Transfer the peaches to a bowl. Boil the syrup until reduced and thickened, then pour it over the fruit. Leave to cool. Add 350 g fresh raspberries and chill.

3 Prepare the simmered rice pudding, then cool to room temperature. Whip 300 ml double cream with 4 tbsp Amaretto liqueur, then fold this into the pudding. Arrange alternating layers of fruit and rice pudding in 280–300 ml serving bowls or glasses. Serves 6.

Layer the rice and fruit in sundae glasses for an attractive presentation. End with a layer of rice and decorate with fruit.

BUBBLING RICE BRULEE

For fruits filled with rice, prepare the simmered rice (see page 182), cool and spoon into 6 poached, halved and hollowed pears. Chill well, sprinkle with sugar and caramelize. (Peaches also work well.) For rice brulée, spoon the mixture into 4 120 ml ramekins and chill for about 20 minutes. Sprinkle with sugar, caramelize, then cool and chill to allow the glaze to harden.

HOLLOWED POACHED FRUIT
Select large fruit. Slice and core them and trim the bases so they stand neatly. Poach until just tender. Scoop out some flesh from the hollow left by the core to enlarge it.

CARAMELIZING
Place the ramekins or the filled fruit halves under a pre-heated hot grill until the sugar caramelizes. Chill, or at least allow the glaze to cool before serving

Gâteaux de Riz

A moulded rice cake cooked with caramel and currants is a traditional French dessert. Here, the chef takes it to new heights by serving individual cakes on shortbread bases topped with strawberry slices and orange peel and served with apricot and caramel sauces.

PREPARATION PLAN

▶ Prepare the rice pudding.
▶ Make the caramel and coat the moulds
▶ Prepare and chill the dough for the shortbread.
▶ Preheat the oven to 170°C.

For the rice
125 g round rice
½ litre milk
1 vanilla pod
A pinch of salt
Orange zest
100 g sugar
2 egg yolks
50 ml double cream
25 g currants or sultanas

• • •

For the caramel
125 g sugar
50 ml water

• • •

For the shortbread
250 g flour
180 g butter
1 egg
A pinch of salt
125 g sugar
A pinch of baking powder

• • •

For the apricot sauce
125 g tinned apricots in syrup
½ vanilla pod
1 tsp caster sugar

• • •

**250 g strawberries
Orange zest**

1 Pour the rice into a saucepan of water and bring to the boil for 2 minutes. Heat the milk, vanilla, salt and orange zest in another saucepan over a low heat. Drain the water from the rice, transfer the rice into the warm milk mixture and bring to the boil. When the rice has absorbed the milk completely, add the sugar and bring back to the boil. Remove the rice from the heat and mix in the egg yolks and cream. Add the raisins and mix the whole mixture together very quickly. Leave to one side.

2 Make the caramel. Cook the sugar with the water until light blond colour. Pour about a quarter of the caramel into a dariole mould and turn the mould to coat the insides. Use a teatowel to protect your hands from the heat. Return excess caramel to the pan. Repeat with three more moulds.

3 Quarter-fill the caramel-coated moulds with rice cake mixture and bake in a bain marie or stand in a roasting tin with 5 cm of water in the bottom and place in the oven. Bake at 170°C for 15 minutes.

4 Meanwhile, prepare the shortbread. Rub the flour and butter together to a sand-like consistency. Add the egg and then the salt, sugar and baking powder and knead until the dough is smooth. Refrigerate the dough for at least half an hour.

5 Remove the dough from the refrigerator and roll out to approximately 1 cm thick. Cut out four circles, slightly larger in circumference than the base of one of your dariole moulds. Place the circles on a baking tray and bake in a 170°C oven for 15 minutes. Remove from the oven and allow to cool on a metal rack.

6 Take one of the shortbread circles and place on a clean, flat surface then carefully unmould one of the rice cakes. Place the rice cake on the shortbread with a palette knife. Repeat with the other shortbread circles and rice cakes. Finely slice the strawberries lengthwise and decorate the rice cakes with the slices. Add fine slithers of orange zest to the decoration.

7 Make the apricot sauce. Cut the vanilla pod in half lengthways, scrape out the seeds and crush them lightly with the sugar using the back of a teaspoon. Process or blend the apricots into a rich sauce then add the vanilla and sugar. Add syrup from the tin to adjust the consistency. Drizzle the sauce around the edges of a small plate and contrast it with similarly drizzled caramel. Place the strawberry-topped rice cake in the centre of the sauces. Repeat with the other cakes and serve.

ZESTY RICE DESSERTS

To present rice pudding with a bold dash of colour, serve in citrus fruit cups, with sweetened and grilled orange slices. Use 1 quantity of Simmered Rice Pudding (see page 182), adding the grated rind of 1 lemon, lime or orange.

Decorate the **filled citrus cups** with candied zest which helps to lighten the flavour of the rice pudding and complements the colours of the fruit shells. Allow one orange half, or two lime or lemon halves per portion.

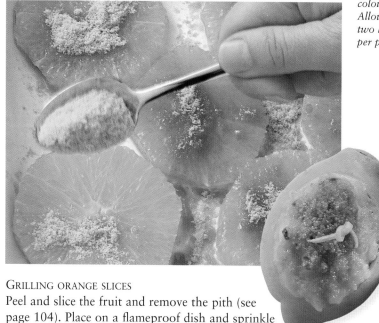

PREPARING AND FILLING
Scoop out the citrus fruit flesh and trim the bases so they stand well. Stir 225 g mascarpone into the chilled pudding. Use a small spoon to fill the cups with this mixture. (Roughly 8 orange cups, 8–10 lemon cups, or 16 lime cups are filled with this quantity.) Chill well.

GRILLING ORANGE SLICES
Peel and slice the fruit and remove the pith (see page 104). Place on a flameproof dish and sprinkle with soft brown sugar. Flash the slices under a hot grill to melt the sugar. Serve alongside the filled citrus cups.

EXOTIC RICE PUDDING

75 g blanched almonds
900 ml milk
6 green cardamoms
1 tbsp rose water
100 g basmati rice
50 g unsalted butter
50 g raisins or sultanas
50 g pistachio nuts
¼ tsp saffron strands
75 g caster sugar

Purée half the almonds in a blender with 150 ml milk. Pour the almond purée into a large, heavy-based saucepan and add the remaining milk.

Split the cardamoms and scrape the black seeds into a mortar. Use a pestle to grind them to a powder, then add this to the almond and milk mixture. Add the rose water, basmati rice and butter.

Bring to the boil, stirring, then reduce the heat. Uncover and simmer for about 45 minutes. Stir the pudding frequently to prevent it sticking to the base of the pan. Add the raisins or sultanas and continue to cook for a further 20–30 minutes, until the pudding is reduced and creamy.

Meanwhile, cut the remaining almonds into fine slivers and toast them lightly. Skin the pistachio nuts (see page 107) and cut them into slivers. Pound the saffron strands to a fine powder in a mortar with a pestle. Dissolve the saffron powder in 2 tbsp boiling water.

Stir the saffron liquid and sugar into the pudding until the sugar has dissolved. Add most of the toasted almonds and pistachios, then set aside to cool. Chill the pudding lightly before serving, sprinkled with the remaining toasted almonds and pistachios. Serves 6.

INDIAN-STYLE RICE PUDDING

Almonds, rose water, ground cardamom and basmati rice give this rich, sweet-spiced dessert its character. Chopped, dried apricots or mango, or mixed dried fruits make interesting substitutes for raisins and sultanas.

1 Simmer the ingredients over a low heat, stirring often, until the milk has evaporated and the rice is rich and creamy. Use a large, heavy-based pan so that the milk neither burns nor boils over. Add the dried fruit after 45 minutes of cooking.

2 Stir in the sugar towards the end of cooking. Add the saffron at this stage – if added too early, its flavour is lost. Once the pudding has chilled to room temperature, fold in whipped double cream if required, and sprinkle with slivers of nuts.

BAKED RICE PUDDING

The perfect baked rice pudding is creamy, with a fine golden crust. The secret of success lies in the slowness of the cooking. Traditionally, rice puddings were baked overnight in the relatively cool oven of a kitchen range.

The pudding should be cooked in an ovenproof dish, using 50 g pudding rice and 600 ml milk. Stir in a vanilla pod, a strip of pared lemon rind and 2 tbsp caster sugar. Sprinkle with nutmeg and dot with 30 g unsalted butter before baking. Bake the pudding at 150°C for about 2½ hours. Stir the pudding after it has cooked for 1 hour, then again after 2 hours – stirring in the skin helps to make the result nice and creamy. Do not stir the pudding during the final 30 minutes of cooking.

VARYING BAKED RICE PUDDING

- *For a creamier result, the pudding can be made with a rich combination of 300 ml milk and 300 ml single cream .*
- *For a richer texture and flavour, 1 whole egg, or 2 egg yolks, can be whisked lightly with 2 tbsp milk or 3 tbsp single cream, then stirred into the pudding for the final 30 minutes of cooking.*
- *For a flavourful mixture, add 50 g sultanas or 100 g ready-to-eat and roughly chopped dried peaches or apricots to the rice pudding. Sprinkle with 30 g almonds once you stir the pudding for the last time, 30 minutes before the end of cooking.*

BAKED RICE WITH SPICED FRUIT

Fruit compotes and poached fruit (see pages 14–15) are classic accompaniments for baked rice pudding, offering both complementary flavours and contrasting textures. The fruit should be hot and served alongside the baked rice. The spiced exotic fruit shown here is colourful and offers a contemporary treatment.

2 Stir in 50 g sugar, 50 g sliced, crystallized ginger, 2 peeled and sliced mangos and 2 peeled and sliced guavas. Simmer the mixture gently for 5 minutes.

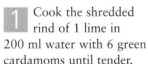
1 Cook the shredded rind of 1 lime in 200 ml water with 6 green cardamoms until tender.

3 Remove the fruit with a draining spoon and boil the syrup until reduced and thickened. Replace the fruit and turn it in the syrup. Serve the fruit compote with individual portions of baked rice pudding.

COCONUT RICE WITH CARAMEL-COATED FRUIT

Cooked rice pudding can be baked in a mould and served as a gâteau. A classic example is Gâteau de Riz (see page 184), for which cooked rice is moulded and baked. Dried or candied fruits may be added and the rice can be baked in a caramel-coated mould. Here, coconut milk replaces dairy milk and the cooked rice is set in a coconut-coated mould – the result is entirely different to traditional rice puddings.

1 Cook 200 g pudding rice in 1–2 litres coconut milk. Line the base of a charlotte mould with non-stick parchment. Brush the mould with melted unsalted butter and coat with lightly toasted fine desiccated coconut, including the base.

2 Beat 2 eggs and 6 yolks with 200 ml double cream and stir into the coconut rice. Spoon this into the mould, taking care not to disturb the base lining or the coconut coating. Bake at 160°C for 45 minutes. Allow to cool, then chill.

3 Prepare caramel-coated fruit (see box, page 212) to accompany the pudding. Use a knife to loosen the pudding from the mould. Keep the knife as close as possible to the mould to preserve the coconut coating on the side of the pudding.

4 Cover the pudding in its mould with a platter or tall stand. Invert both mould and stand, then remove the mould very gently. Press on additional toasted coconut if necessary.

*Serve **coconut rice pudding** straight after preparation with the caramel-coated fruits piled on top of and around it. Strawberries, physalis, kiwi fruit, pineapple, grapes and apricots are all suitable. Include a visually appealing variety.*

SEMOLINA

Hard, coarsely ground grains of wheat are known as semolina, which can be used to make superb desserts. The most essential technique is to make sure you stir the mixture continuously as it cooks for a smooth result.

MAKING SMOOTH SEMOLINA

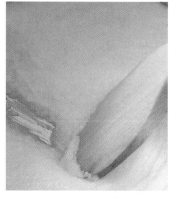

1 When the milk has boiled, remove the pan from the heat and add the semolina in a thin, steady stream, stirring continuously.

2 Once the sugar is added, stir until the mixture boils and thickens. Cook gently for 20 minutes, stirring frequently, until creamy.

SIMPLE SEMOLINA PUDDING

600 ml milk
1 vanilla pod
50 g semolina
50 g caster sugar

Heat the milk and vanilla in a large saucepan over a low heat until almost boiling. Remove from the heat, cover and allow to infuse for 30 minutes.

Reheat the milk, then remove the vanilla pod. Bring to the boil, remove from the heat and add the semolina gradually, stirring continuously. Stir in the sugar and return to the heat. Bring to the boil, stirring continuously.

Reduce the heat to the lowest setting and simmer gently for 20 minutes, stirring often to prevent it from burning on the bottom of the pan. Serve with poached fruit, a fruit compote or chocolate sauce. Serves 4–6.

CHILLED CHOCOLATE SEMOLINA

Semolina can be set in a mould and served cold. This luscious, lightly spiced chocolate dish is superb with nutmeg-seasoned strawberries. Prepare the semolina, infusing the milk with a long cinnamon stick. Use 75 g sugar.

1 Break 225 g plain chocolate into squares. Remove the semolina from the heat and stir in the chocolate until melted.

2 Stir in 4 tbsp rum and 225 g mascarpone. Run a 1 litre loaf tin under cold water and turn the semolina into it. Cover with clingfilm. Cool and chill for several hours until set. Unmould the semolina and serve with spiced strawberries and mascarpone cheese.

CHOCOLATE FRITTERS

Frying semolina produces a nutty flavour and crisp texture. For these fritters, make a half quantity of the Simple Semolina Pudding (see previous page) and flavour it with a few drops of oil of bitter almonds. Allow to cool, then chill.

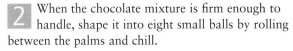

3 Divide the semolina into eight portions and shape one portion neatly around each chocolate ball. Roll the semolina in ground almonds first to stop it sticking to your fingers.

1 Melt 100 g plain chocolate and cool slightly, then stir it into 100 g mascarpone cheese. Allow to cool, then chill.

2 When the chocolate mixture is firm enough to handle, shape it into eight small balls by rolling between the palms and chill.

*Lightly sweetened apricot coulis (see page 113) is delicious drizzled over and around **chocolate fritters**.*

FLAVOURING SEMOLINA

CINNAMON
. . . .
Add a cinnamon stick and the grated rind of 1 orange in place of the vanilla when heating the milk.

RUM
. . . .
Stir in raisins macerated in rum a few minutes before the end of cooking and top the pudding with lightly toasted pecan nuts.

CARDAMOM AND FRUIT
. . . .
Spice the heating milk with the ground seeds of 4 green cardamoms in place of vanilla. Add diced ready-to-eat dried mango and fresh or canned pineapple a few minutes before the end of cooking. Serve topped with pistachios or toasted almond slivers.

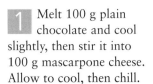

4 Chop 100 g blanched almonds finely so they resemble breadcrumbs. Mix with 100 g fresh white breadcrumbs. Roll the fritters in beaten egg and coat in the almond and breadcrumb mixture. Chill for at least 30 minutes. Deep-fry the fritters until crisp and golden. Roll in caster sugar and serve immediately.

SEMOLINA FRITTERS

Cooked, cooled semolina can be shaped, coated in egg and breadcrumbs and fried until crisp, then served with a fruit sauce, warm honey or maple syrup. It can also be flavoured and moulded around a fruit filling, coated in flour, egg and breadcrumbs, then deep-fried until crisp and golden.

Petits Fours

MINIATURE DESSERTS
·
FRUIT PETITS FOURS
·
MINIATURE ICES

MINIATURE DESSERTS

Petits fours are an art form in themselves. Serve these tiny cakes, pastries and confectionery with coffee, or arrange a good selection on individual plates for a fabulous finale.

MINI MERINGUES

Tiny meringue shapes can be piped with a cake decorating nozzle, cooked, then filled. Use French Meringue (see page 68). Dry them out in the oven at 120°C for 40 minutes.

MERINGUE NESTS
Pipe a circle, then the sides for a nest and cook as above. Fill with cream and fruit, or chestnut purée mixed with icing sugar, brandy and finely grated chocolate. Decorate with piped white chocolate.

MERINGUE SWIRLS
Swirls of meringue piped with a small nozzle can be used to sandwich a delicious filling, such as chocolate ganache or cream mixed with chopped pistachios. The swirls can be part-dipped in chocolate before sandwiching.

MINI MILLEFEUILLE

Thinly roll out 1 quantity puff pastry (see page 120) and stamp out 16 circles using a 4.5 cm cutter. Prick the pastry all over and bake at 220°C for about 5 minutes, until golden. Cool on a wire rack. Cut them in half, add a filling and possibly a topping to create a delicious bite-sized treat.

FINISHING TOUCHES
Sandwich with warmed blackcurrant, raspberry or apricot preserve and cream. Dredge with icing sugar and brand with a pattern using a hot metal skewer. If desired, top with a raspberry and tiny chocolate leaf or crystallized mint sprig before serving.

MAKING MINIATURE DESSERTS

Most of your favourite desserts can be made in miniature form. Try tiny salads of minutely diced fruit in biscuit cups, or sorbets piped on to chocolate discs, or bite-size pastries and gâteaux cut from a plain Swiss roll using cocktail cutters.

- *When baking small items or drying out meringues in the oven, remember that the cooking times will be greatly reduced. Depending on your oven you may also have to reduce the cooking temperature.*
- *Work methodically for perfect results, using a 'conveyer belt' approach, completing an entire batch of the petits fours to each stage. This is much easier than finishing individual items separately. It also encourages results that are consistent.*

HAZELNUT PASTRIES

Mix 100 g ground hazelnuts, 1 tbsp each of icing sugar and chocolate liqueur and 60 g grated plain chocolate for the filling (makes 60). Bake for 10–12 minutes at 190°C. Heat clear honey to boiling point and brush over the cooked pastries.

CINNAMON DATE PASTRIES

For the filling, stone and finely chop 100 g medjool dates. Mix with 2 tbsp ground almonds, 1 tsp icing sugar and ½ tsp ground cinnamon. Moisten with 2 tsp brandy. Makes 26.

BUNDLES
For 30 chocolate hazelnut bundles, use 1 quantity filo pastry. Cut out 9 cm squares of pastry. Place some filling in the middle of each bundle and wrap it up. Gather the edges of the pastry and pinch together to seal.

TRIANGLES
Cut 30 strips of filo that are 5 x 15 cm, for triangular pastries. Place some filling at one end and roll over an edge to form a triangle. Fold this triangle repeatedly over the filling along the entire length of the pastry strip.

ROLLING
Cut 3 x 10 cm filo strips. Fold in the long edges, brush the length with butter, place the filling at one end and roll up. Brush again and bake at 180°C for 10 minutes. Cool and dust with icing sugar.

RED FRUIT TARTLETS

20 of these tasty red fruit tartlets can be made with a half quantity Pâte Sucrée (see page 122). Fill with almond cream and bake. Using a small spoon, add a little strawberry jam to each of the tartlets (use 50 g). Top with fruit. Place half a strawberry, 1 raspberry and 1 wild strawberry on top of each tartlet. Select good quality fruit for an attractive finish.

1 Roll the pastry to 2 mm thick. Cut appropriately sized circles using a cutter.

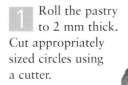

2 Use the pastry circles to line tartlet moulds that are 2 cm deep and measure 3.5 cm at the base, 4.5 cm at the rim. Part-fill each one with a half quantity almond cream (see page 49) and bake at 170°C for about 25 minutes. Remove from the moulds and cool completely before filling and garnishing.

SYLLABUB CUPS

Coat the insides of 24 petits fours cases with 250 g melted chocolate. Build up a thick coating by brushing on several layers, allowing one layer to dry before applying the next.

1 Remove the paper cases when the chocolate cups are firmly set.

2 Pipe half quantity of syllabub (see page 54) into cups. Chill until serving.

COFFEE BRANDY SNAPS

1 Make 28 brandy snaps (see page 126), curling them around wooden spoon handles to shape them. Allow the biscuits to set into shape before filling.

2 Whip 180 ml double cream with 1 tbsp each of icing sugar, coffee essence and coffee liqueur. Pipe this mixture into the biscuits before serving.

FLORENTINES

For 28 of these ideal dessert accompaniments, add 60 g finely chopped raisins, glacé cherries and candied peel to the basic brandy snap mixture (see page 126). Bake as per brandy snaps (see page 126). Once slightly set, move to wire racks to cool before decorating with chocolate.

Coat the smoothest side of each biscuit with melted chocolate (use 180 g) and, using a fork, mark wavy lines into the chocolate. Leave to set.

CHOCOLATE AND CINNAMON BISCUITS

For chocolate dough, mix 325 g butter with 20 g icing sugar until smooth. Add 1 egg yolk, 400 g flour and 35 g sieved cocoa powder. Knead the dough until smooth, wrap and chill before use or freeze until ready to use. For cinnamon dough, rub 280 g butter into 400 g flour until the mixture resembles fine breadcrumbs. Stir in 125 g icing sugar, ½ tsp each of vanilla essence and cinnamon. Knead until smooth, then shape. (Makes 96.)

1 Roll the cinnamon dough into a rope, roughly 3 cm in diameter and chill. Roll out the chocolate dough to 13 mm thick and shape around the cinnamon rope. Chill before proceeding.

2 Cut into discs using a sharp knife, dipping it in hot water and wiping it dry between each cut. Place the discs on buttered baking trays and bake at 160°C for approximately 15 minutes.

FRUIT PETITS FOURS

Fruit petits fours make the most of the natural beauty of fruit – a variety, served together, certainly creates an appealing presentation. Coatings provide additional sweetness and also enhance the look.

DIPPING AND COATING FRUIT

Fruits, individually dipped in a sweet coating, make simple and delicious petits fours. Try small, neat pieces of fruit, whole or cut, such as physalis, mandarin segments, cherries and strawberries. Coatings such as caramel, chocolate and fondant allow for a range of colours and flavours.

1 Make a light caramel (see page 109) and allow to cool slightly. Hold the fruit by the leaves or stalks, or use a cocktail stick, and dip into the caramel.

2 Allow excess caramel to drip off the fruit, then place the dipped fruit on baking parchment to set.

HALF-COATING FRUIT

Half-coating fruit produces a striking look. Submerge the fruit only half way, allow the excess coating to drip off and place on parchment to set. A plate of strawberries, some half-dipped in plain chocolate, others in white chocolate, makes a lovely presentation.

Try tinting fondant with food colouring, in pink, blue and green, for instance, for a jewel-like range of coatings.

STUFFED DRIED FRUIT

Dried fruits can be stuffed with a nut paste based on almonds, hazelnuts or walnuts. To fill 48 pieces of dried apricots, dates or prunes, heat 1 beaten egg and 100 g caster sugar in a bowl over simmering water until they begin to thicken. Beat in 100 g ground almonds and 100 g icing sugar until the mixture forms a paste.

1 Form the paste into ovals. Remove stones from dates or prunes and fill each with a generous portion of paste. Close the sides of the fruit around the filling.

2 Dip the stuffed fruit in fondant (see page 112) or in melted chocolate or caramel. Place on baking parchment and allow to set.

MINIATURE ICES

Ice cream petits fours are made using the same basic moulding and shaping techniques as for larger ensembles. The scale requires a slightly different decorative approach and a finer touch.

LAYERED ICE CREAM

Use petits fours cases as moulds for making layered ice cream in miniature. Make sure you choose ice creams that complement each other in flavour and colour. Unmould on to chilled biscuits or slices of kiwi. Here, they are topped with a shape of finely piped chocolate icing.

Place horizontal layers of different ice creams in petits fours cases using the same method as for bombes and ice cream gateaux (see pages 39–40) and freeze to set.

QUICK AND COLD

It is very important when preparing ice cream petits fours to work quickly, assembling the ice cream before it softens and becomes unworkable. Your hand heat and the room temperature will quickly soften the ice cream, so you can work on it for only minutes at a time. Prepare all the equipment in advance so that it is all ready when you need it. Chill all of your equipment such as spoons and baking trays before use. As soon as the ice cream becomes soft it should be replaced in the freezer. Work in small batches, moving on to your second batch while your first is being chilled.

COATED ICE CREAM BALLS

Use a melon baller to scoop ice cream balls. Spike each with a cocktail stick and freeze until firm. Dip into cooled melted chocolate – here, cherry ice cream is dipped in white chocolate and white chocolate ice cream has a dark chocolate coating.

Place the dipped ice cream balls on baking parchment at an angle, pipe finely with zigzags of colour-contrasting chocolate icing and freeze until set.

CHERRY BOMBES

Macerate glacé cherries for several hours or overnight in kirsch or brandy, then drain before assembling these white chocolate mini bombes. Using a teaspoon, press a little white chocolate ice cream into the base of a petit four case. Top with a cherry, then cover completely with ice cream, pressing it around the side of the fruit. Repeat with the remaining cherries and freeze until firm. For a striking presentation, give these white chocolate bombes a contrasting dark chocolate base.

PREPARING THE BASE
Cut chocolate discs slightly larger than the bombes and unmould the ice cream on to them. Remove the cases. Pipe chocolate around the base of each one and freeze until set.

MINI ICE CREAM KEBABS

Use a small melon baller to scoop three different ice creams into balls, here, strawberry, chocolate and vanilla. Thread one scoop of each flavour onto a wooden cocktail stick and place in the freezer until firm. Serve on fruit purée or chocolate sauce, on sponge fingers or in small curved Tuile biscuits.

FINISHING TOUCHES

CHOCOLATE DECORATIONS

·

USING SAUCES DECORATIVELY

·

FROSTING & CRYSTALLIZING

·

SUGAR DECORATIONS

·

MAKING SPUN SUGAR

·

DECORATIVE BISCUITS

·

FRUITS & NUTS

CHOCOLATE DECORATIONS

Chocolate in its melted form can be used to make beautiful decorations – from intricate, feathery shapes to bold marbled slabs which can change the look of a dessert. It can also be used to make edible moulded containers.

PIPING CHOCOLATE

A small paper piping bag is essential for piping fine decorations. Tape the paper join outside the bag to strengthen it.

1 Cut a 25 cm parchment square into triangles. Curl a point of the long edge of one triangle round to meet the point of the right angle, forming a cone.

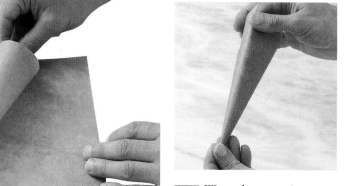

2 Wrap the opposite corner of the long edge around the cone to meet the other two points and tighten the cone.

3 Pull all three points tightly together to create a sharp tip and fold the flap inside, creasing it firmly to hold the bag in shape.

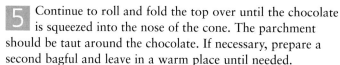

4 Fill the bag with melted, slightly cooled chocolate and fold the open top over to seal the bag.

5 Continue to roll and fold the top over until the chocolate is squeezed into the nose of the cone. The parchment should be taut around the chocolate. If necessary, prepare a second bagful and leave in a warm place until needed.

6 Just before you begin to pipe, snip off the tip. If you want fine lines of piping, cut it close to the tip.

PIPING MOTIF DECORATIONS

Shapes that have a repeated motif look spectacular in white and dark chocolate and can be used to add height to a dessert. You may find it easier to draw the shapes on baking parchment before piping, particularly geometric designs that require accuracy.

Lay your paper template on a cold, hard surface, such as marble, or pipe freehand on to acetate on marble. Try to obtain free-flowing marks.

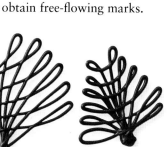

MESH CIRCLES

Circles of meshed chocolate can be applied decoratively to desserts or can form an integral part of them. Medium-sized discs with a dense mesh can be used instead of biscuits to sandwich ice cream or mousses for a delightful presentation. Press small discs into piped cream on top of cakes and other desserts.

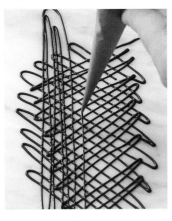

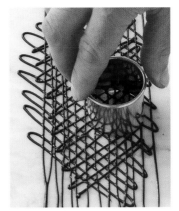

*Shapes with firm chocolate edges, such as the **mesh triangles** here, stand up on desserts more easily than these lovely **open-mesh circles**, which should be placed flat on the outer surface of a cake, for instance.*

1 Pipe chocolate lines on to acetate to make a mesh. The more lines you pipe the more dense the final mesh will be.

2 Before the chocolate mesh sets, press down into it with a circular pastry cutter to cut out discs to the size you require. Leave to set in a cool place until the chocolate has set completely.

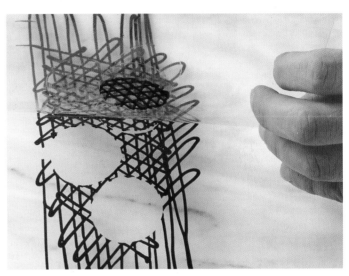

3 Turn both chocolate and acetate over so the acetate is uppermost and peel it away. The discs will lift off with the acetate. Loosen them carefully with a palette knife.

PIPING MESH TRIANGLES

To create geometric shapes with substance, pipe a wild mesh in chocolate and tidy the edges into more formal shapes. Pipe on to acetate laid over marble.

1 Create freehand patterns in melted chocolate using a small piping bag.

2 Pipe an outline of a triangle over the mesh in thicker piping and chill.

3 Once the chocolate has set, trim the shapes outside the thick outlines with a knife. Turn the acetate over with the shapes still on it, so that the acetate is uppermost. Peel it off. Chill the shapes until ready to use.

LACY CHOCOLATE CUPS

If your dessert calls for a light and elegant touch, try piping a decorative chocolate cup into a small container, such as a metal mould. When chilled the chocolate will retain the shape of the mould. Once you have tried the technique, experiment with your own ideas for alternative shapes, moulds and fillings.

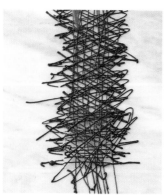

2 When the chocolate sets it contracts slightly and pulls away from the inner surface of the mould. This allows it to slip out easily. Chill until ready to use. Fill with fruits, ice cream or other chilled desserts.

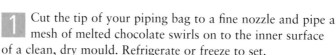

1 Cut the tip of your piping bag to a fine nozzle and pipe a mesh of melted chocolate swirls on to the inner surface of a clean, dry mould. Refrigerate or freeze to set.

TEARDROP CUP

A piped mesh cup can be used as a container in which to serve ice cream, mousses or other desserts that are soft enough to be piped or spooned into the cup, yet do not leak out of the mesh.

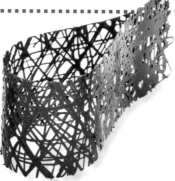

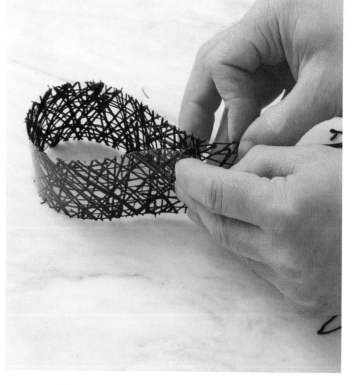

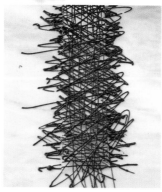

1 Lay a strip of acetate on marble and fill a piping bag with melted chocolate. Cover the acetate strip completely with a dense mesh of chocolate lines.

2 While the chocolate is still very slightly warm, trim the chocolate edges for neatness. Then pick up the acetate strip at one end and lift it away from the marble.

3 Bend the acetate strip, with the chocolate mesh on the inside, so that the ends meet. Press the ends together to form a teardrop shape and hold them together until they bond. Set in a cool place. Peel away the acetate before use.

CHOCOLATE SCIMITARS

Curled triangles can be made to any length and degree of curl. Shape the acetate and set the chocolate in a position that will create the shape of your choice.

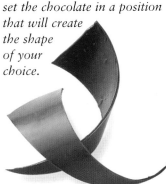

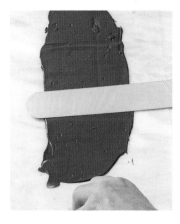

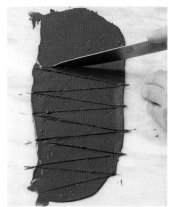

1 Lay acetate on marble and spread out some tempered chocolate (see page 110) on it.

2 Allow the chocolate to cool slightly, then cut zig zags from edge to edge to form the triangles.

3 Curl the sheet over and affix the edges of the acetate to the work surface with sticky tape. Chill to set.

CORKSCREW RIBBONS

Delicate spirals of chocolate make lovely decorations. If you are concerned about handling them, pick them up with a cocktail stick and arrange them on your dessert.

1 Spread melted tempered chocolate (see page 110) on to acetate and score with a wide-toothed scraper.

2 Allow to set just a little, then curl the acetate into a spiral and tape the ends to a tray.

3 Chill thoroughly, then carefully peel away the acetate from the chocolate to release the ribbons.

MARBLE SLABS

To prepare chocolate for marbling, melt both white and dark chocolate. Place the white chocolate in a bowl and add drops of dark chocolate to it with a teaspoon. Although they will mix a little, do not blend them together at this stage.

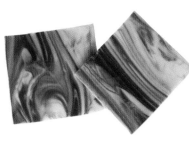

1 Lay a piece of acetate on to a cool surface and pour the chocolate mixture on to it. Pour quite freely, allowing the colours to mix a little as they leave the bowl.

2 Spread the chocolate out with a palette knife. Smear the two chocolates together, mixing them as you go to create the marbled effect. Make sure you keep the blade low and flat.

3 Cut the chocolate into your chosen shapes, here squares, and chill to set. Peel away the acetate and use the marbled squares to decorate or add structure to your dessert.

MOULDING JAGGED CUPS

Not every dessert has to look immaculately finished. A more natural look, such as the irregular effect of the chocolate cup here, will give your dessert a rustic charm. These chocolate cups are ideal for filling with ice cream, chilled fruit salad or mousses and can make a refreshingly simple presentation.

1 Melt some chocolate in a bowl. Cover one end of a wide-ended rolling pin with acetate and, holding the top of the acetate to the rolling pin, dip the end into the chocolate.

2 Dip several times more until you achieve the required thickness for your cup, then stand it firmly on a flat surface to level off the base. Allow to set slightly then remove the rolling pin. Chill thoroughly, then peel off the acetate.

CREATING FANS

Tiny ribbon-like fans can be made from gathers of chocolate and used for decorating cakes and topping desserts.

MAKING FANS
Spread melted chocolate out on to a hard surface and allow to set a little. Using a broad and flat blade, such as a clean wallpaper scraper, scrape up narrow lines of chocolate, which concertina into fans as you go.

MOULDING CHOCOLATE CUPS

When nothing but perfection will do, serve your dessert in an edible container. Mould chocolate cups in disposable plastic cups, which have the perfect shape. Base the size of the plastic cups and the thickness of the chocolate on the dessert you intend to serve in the finished chocolate cups. Thicker cups will keep iced desserts cooler for longer.

1 Melt some chocolate in a large bowl. Trim the plastic cups to the height you require and fill them to the brim with melted chocolate.

2 Pour out the excess chocolate. Chill the coated cups to set while you make the others. Stir the bowlful of chocolate now and again to keep it from setting.

3 Repeat until your cups reach the thickness you require. Level the rim with a palette knife. Chill to set and remove from the plastic cup, cutting it off if necessary.

ADAPTING THE DECORATIONS

- *By varying the colour of the chocolate or using chocolate that has been marbled or swirled, all the suggestions can be tailored to suit your dessert.*
- *Piped chocolate decorations can be made in practically limitless variety. You can draw any shape or use different pastry cutters to stamp out shapes.*
- *Dipped shapes, such as cups, can be created from almost anything, as long as there is an acetate lining.*
- *You can mould chocolate in most moulds. The more patterned the surface of the mould, however, the more difficult it may be to remove the set chocolate.*

CREATING CURLS

Chocolate curls vary from the long, thin and beautifully ragged caraque to the almost perfectly uniform white chocolate curls shown here. Both white and dark curls are ideal for decorating formal desserts and cakes.

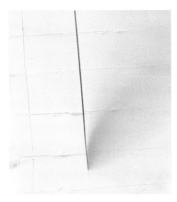

1 Spread melted white chocolate over a firm, cool surface such as marble or granite and allow to cool slightly. Using a sharp knife, cut the chocolate into squares of the same size.

2 Take a knife with a flat blade and scrape the squares off the marble. Work diagonally from corner to corner. The chocolate squares will curl over.

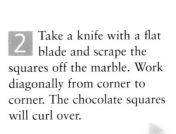

MAKING CARAQUE

Ragged, narrow chocolate curls are a popular decoration for chocolate cakes. They are usually used in abundance.

SCRAPING CARAQUE
Spread out chocolate thinly on marble. With a long-bladed knife, scrape up chocolate rectangles, keeping the pressure steady along the blade so that they curl.

CURLING CIGARETTES

A favourite decoration for ice creams and cakes, mousses and tarts, the two-toned cigarettes, shown here, will add even greater panache to your finished dish. Use plain and white chocolate – both melted and tempered (see page 110) – and work on a firm surface such as a piece of marble.

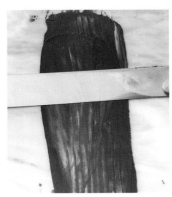

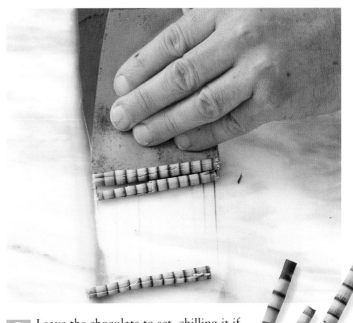

1 Spread a strip of white chocolate. The width of the strip will be the eventual height of the cigarettes, so keep the edges even. Drag indented lines along the strip with a toothed scraper.

2 Melt dark chocolate while you allow the white chocolate to set. Spread dark chocolate in an even strip over the white layer. Spread it gently to avoid blending the two chocolates.

3 Leave the chocolate to set, chilling it if necessary. Take a wide, flat blade and place it roughly 2 cm from a narrow edge of the strip. Facing this edge, scrape the chocolate off the marble using firm, even pressure and working slowly to form tight curls.

USING SAUCES DECORATIVELY

A sauce is a classic finishing touch that can influence the taste as well as the look of a dessert. Besides cream, yogurt and fromage frais, a fruit coulis or a custard may be used.

USING COULIS

The most successful choices are coulis that set off the flavours and colours of your desserts, whether you complement or contrast. Then you need to work out the design you wish to make with the coulis. The ideas below are a starting point.

DRIZZLING ON TO A PLATE
Overlapping rings of white chocolate sauce and raspberry coulis are drizzled from a spoon and allowed to blend.

POOLING COULIS
A dessert can be served sitting on a pool of coulis. Use the back of a spoon to spread out a circle of coulis on a plate.

OUTLINING

Serving a sauce in an unusual or interesting shape is an easy way to liven up a presentation. Pipe an outline using chocolate ganache and leave to set, then pour cream or another sauce into the centre of the outline.

DECORATIVE MIXING

FEATHERING
Drip a fine circular line of cream on a pool of coulis, near the edge. Using a cocktail stick, feather the cream across the coulis at regular intervals around the circle, one stroke inwards, the next stroke outwards.

HEARTS
Make a pool of coulis on a plate and drip equidistant dots of cream in a neat circle towards the edge. Use a cocktail stick to draw a line through each circle to spread the cream in a heart shape.

COMBINING SAUCES
Both sauces should be of the same, thick consistency. Spoon the sauces into the middle of their designated areas on the plate and allow them to spread into their joint shape. Using a cocktail stick, make a circular motion to feather one colour into the other.

FROSTING & CRYSTALLIZING

Some lovely decorative effects, which are easier to achieve than the
inexperienced cook may imagine, depend on sugar. Remember that in
most cases, a little sugar goes a long way – giving a shiny, sparkling finish.

FROSTING

*Leaves, flower petals and small
buds and the rims of bowls
and glasses can all be frosted
for decoration.*

1 Lightly froth some egg
white with a fork. Paint
a thin layer of this on to a
petal or leaf using a small
paintbrush.

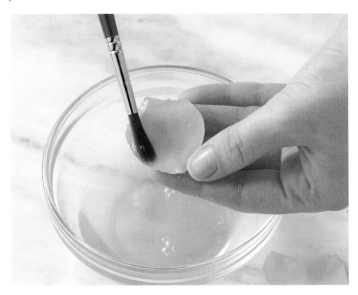

2 Sprinkle caster sugar
over the egg white to
cover it completely.

FROSTING FRUIT

*Fruits can be frosted using the same method as
that for leaves and petals. Redcurrants and other
berries are most suitable. A bright string of
redcurrants makes a lovely decoration
for a selection
of ice creams
or sorbets.*

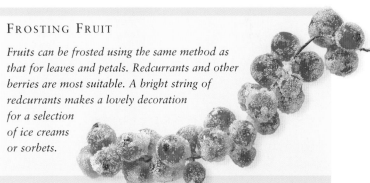

QUICK CRYSTALLIZED CITRUS JULIENNE

*Preparing crystallized peel by
the traditional method is a
long process, but this quick
technique creates fine shreds
of crunchy, sugar-coated rind.*

1 Use a vegetable peeler to
remove strips of citrus
peel, working down the fruit.
Take care to remove only the
rind, without any pith. Cut
the rind into long thin shreds.

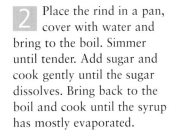

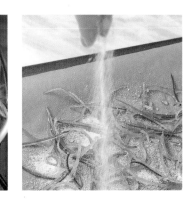

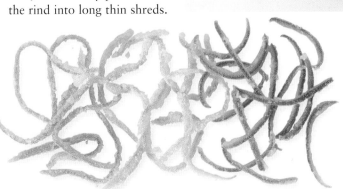

2 Place the rind in a pan,
cover with water and
bring to the boil. Simmer
until tender. Add sugar and
cook gently until the sugar
dissolves. Bring back to the
boil and cook until the syrup
has mostly evaporated.

3 Use a fork to lift the
rinds out and spread
them on non-stick baking
parchment. Dredge with
caster sugar and leave until
cold, when they will be crisp.
Store in an airtight container.

SUGAR DECORATIONS

Decorations made of sugar are ideal finishing touches for many desserts.
Whether you create complex patterns, or use very simple designs, the end
results will give your desserts an eye-catching, professional look.

USING POURED SUGAR

1 Bring sugar syrup (see page 108) to 165°C. Skim off frothy impurities.

2 Brush the sides of the pan with a wet pastry brush to avoid burning.

3 Cut out a square of parchment paper, slightly larger than your chosen mould. Lightly oil the mould and place it centrally on the parchment square on a flat surface. Remove the sugar syrup from the heat and pour it into the mould. Leave the sugar syrup to set.

4 As soon as the syrup has set, remove the mould and leave the sugar shape on the parchment paper until needed.

MARBLING POURED SUGAR

For a decorative marbled effect, add several drops of food colouring to the unset sugar syrup with a dropper. Using the tip of a knife or the handle of a small spoon, swirl the colouring into the sugar syrup to form the pattern.

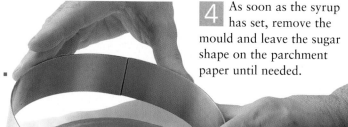

HEATING SUGAR

Sugar reacts very specifically to temperature, so you must be precise when heating sugar to ensure that your end product works as you want it to.

Poured sugar is heated to 165°C, beyond the hard-crack stage but before the stage for caramel, a difference of only a few seconds on a high heat.

At this precise temperature the structure of the sugar becomes very hard, but will soften again as it reaches caramel temperatures. This means that, although poured sugar has a beautifully smooth and shiny finish, a shape as large as the disc shown will be too hard and dense to be eaten and is for decoration only.

Caramel can be drizzled into some stunning shapes that bring emphasis to the presentation of your dessert.

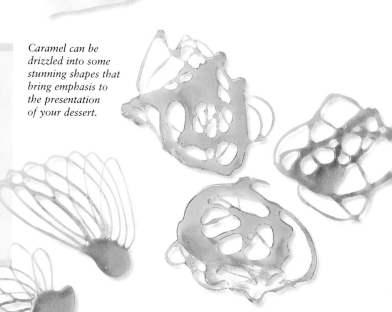

MAKING DRIZZLED SUGAR SHAPES

Edible sugar decorations can add a touch of elegance to desserts. The versatility of sugar syrup means that the shapes you make can be as simple or as intricate as you wish.

Spread a square of parchment paper on a flat surface. Make a sugar syrup and heat to 160°C. While it is still hot, dip a spoon into it. Hold the spoon over the parchment paper and allow the syrup to drizzle off the spoon. Move the spoon to create patterns and leave to set.

MAKING GOLDEN THREADS

1 Lightly oil a baking tray and drizzle horizontal lines of sugar syrup on to it.

2 Criss-cross with another layer of syrup. Leave to set. Use to top desserts.

MAKING A CARAMEL CAGE

1 Prepare a clean ladle by lightly oiling the back of it with oiled kitchen paper.

2 Drizzle strands of sugar syrup over the back of the ladle to form a cage.

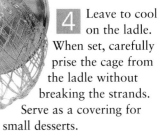

4 Leave to cool on the ladle. When set, carefully prise the cage from the ladle without breaking the strands. Serve as a covering for small desserts.

3 Drizzle a strand of sugar syrup around the edge of the ladle to seal off the edge of the cage. Snip off any overhanging strands.

1 Heat sugar syrup to 160–165°C. Place a piping bag in a wine glass for support. Pour in the syrup.

2 Fold in each side of the cone and roll the top over to secure. Take care not to touch the hot syrup.

3 Using a towel to protect your hands, remove the filled cone from the glass.

4 Carefully snip off the end of the cone to create an outlet from which to pipe the sugar syrup.

*Variations on a theme: **piped sugar decorations** with fruit and whipped cream make ideal toppings for meringues and ice cream.*

5 Pipe your design on to parchment paper or a baking tray. If you need a template, draw the shape on the reverse side of the paper first. If the syrup cools down and stops flowing, place the cone in a warm oven for a few minutes.

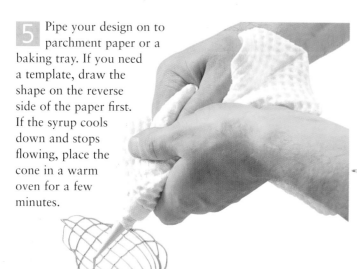

6 The syrup takes roughly 10 minutes to set. When it has, remove the shapes from the paper or tray using a palette knife. Test one of the syrup shapes for firmness before removing it completely so that you do not lose the shape.

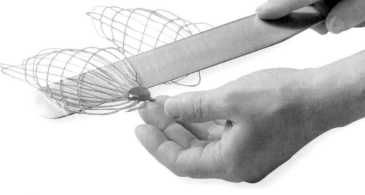

MAKING SPUN SUGAR

Supple and pliable but extremely delicate, spun sugar can be bent into many attractive shapes and used to garnish a plate or decorate a dessert. It is also extremely perishable, so should be made just before using.

MAKING SPUN SUGAR

It is important that your sugar syrup is at the correct consistency for making spun sugar. The sugar should fall away from the whisk ends easily, in strands that are fine enough to set as they fall. The surface on which you collect the strands should be clean and dry. Create your own special whisk for making spun sugar (see box, right), or hold two forks back-to-back so the prongs face away from each other and use as you would a whisk.

CUTTING A WHISK

A cut-off whisk will allow you to produce a number of thin strands at a time very easily. Buy a cheap whisk and, using a pair of sharp pliers, cut the curved ends off a the whisk to leave blunt-ended wires.

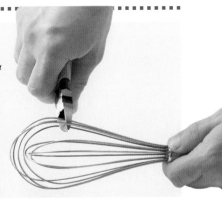

1 Heat the sugar syrup to 155°C then plunge into a pan of cold water to halt the cooking process.

USING SPUN SUGAR

Also known as angel's hair, this ethereal garnish can be shaped into an airy dome or halo and used on the top or to surround ice creams and mousses, or it can be patted into balls with cupped palms and used to adorn soufflés and festive cakes. The balls can be stuffed with spices or small sweets, although anything liquid will cause them to melt.

2 Cover your work surface with parchment paper. Holding a rolling pin in one hand over the paper, dip the whisk into the sugar syrup and flick it back and forth over the rolling pin so that trailing threads are formed.

3 Gently gather up the strands and fold them back over the rolling pin. Loosen and lift them or slide them off the pin gently.

4 Break the sugar in half and gently shape each half as desired in your hands.

DECORATIVE BISCUITS

A variety of crisp, edible decorations can be made to accompany many desserts, either as decoration or as containers. Biscuit pastes are simple to prepare and can be shaped easily.

DECORATIVE CHOUX SHAPES

Choux paste (see page 124) can be finely piped for delicate decorations for cakes.

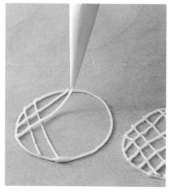

MESH CIRCLES
Draw circles of the size you require on parchment as templates. Pipe the outline, then add the central lines of mesh.

MESH OVALS
These pretty choux ovals make a fitting topping for fruit tartlets or ice creams. Draw oval shapes on a piece of parchment. Turn the paper over, then pipe the outlines using a fine nozzle or a finely-tipped piping bag.

SHAPING TULIPES

Tuile biscuits shaped into baskets make good containers for many desserts. 1 quantity of stencil paste (see page 127) will make 16 baskets. Bake 4 at a time in a 180°C oven for 5–8 minutes, until the edges are golden-brown.

1 Place 1 tbsp stencil paste on a greased baking tray or parchment and, using a palette knife, spread it outwards from the centre in a ring of overlapping petals. Bake as above.

2 Loosen the baked tuile with a palette knife. Place it in a bowl and shape it by weighting the centre with a biscuit cutter.

BRANDY BASKETS

To make these lacy brandy baskets, follow the recipe for brandy snaps (see page 126), but spread the mixture out into a flower shape instead of circles. Cook as for brandy snaps and shape as for tulipes, above. You can also place the biscuit over a convex object to mould it.

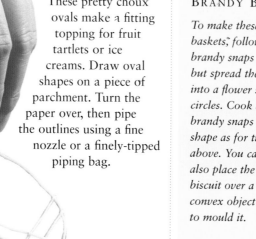

COCONUT TUILES

This is a delicious variation of the tuile biscuit. Follow the method given on page 70 to make this exotic and decorative accompaniment.

1 Once the egg whites, icing sugar, grated coconut and melted butter are combined, spread the mixture in an even layer on a baking tray, chill and bake for 3 minutes at 160°C.

2 Use a pastry cutter to cut biscuits of the size you require. For irregular shapes, spread spoonfuls of the mixture on a tray and bake for 3 minutes. Mould into shape whilst warm.

SILICONE MAT

A double-sided silicone-coated mat provides an excellent non-stick surface for baking fragile sponges and biscuits. The mixture is placed directly on to the surface, then the mat placed on a tray for support before baking. Silicone mats are available from specialist catering shops. Care should be taken when cleaning and storing these mats to retain their effectiveness.

LACE TUILES

70ml orange juice
Grated zest of 1 orange
50 ml Grand Marnier
250 g caster sugar
100 g unsalted butter, melted
200 g nibbed almonds
125 g plain flour

Mix the ingredients together in a bowl, then place small spoonfuls of the mixture on a greased baking tray, 5 per tray. Flatten them with a fork, then bake for 5 minutes at 180°C. As soon as they are baked, remove them from the oven and roll them around greased rolling pins to set their curved shape. Makes 25.

SHAPING TUILES

Use a template to make tuiles of any shape you like. Here, gentle cups with dramatic tails are made for serving ice cream quenelles (see page 42).

1 Cut a template from thin card and lay over greased parchment. Thinly spread stencil paste (see page 127) across the shape, remove the card and bake.

2 Loosen the baked tuiles from the tray with a palette knife and bend them into the shape you require with your fingers. Hold until set.

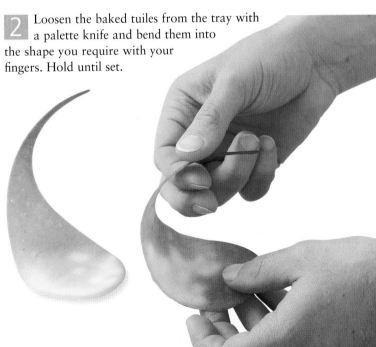

FRUITS & NUTS

Garnishes made from fruit or nuts can be used to complement many desserts. They are very simple to make, generally colourful and decorative in effect and also delicious.

CITRUS TWISTS

Lime, lemon and orange can be used on many different fruit desserts. Prepare them just before serving the dish to stop them becoming too dry.

Cut the fruit neatly into thin slices with a sharp knife, then cut from the edge into the centre of each slice. Twist the slice from the cut in opposite directions.

CITRUS KNOTS

These are great on petits fours. Peel citrus fruit avoiding the pith, then cut the peel into fine strips.

Simply tie a knot in each citrus strip.

APPLE & PEAR CRISPS

These delicately flavoured crisps, made from apples and pears, are a unique garnish idea and make perfect accompaniments for fruit desserts.

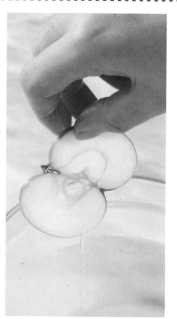

Make sure the fruit you use is firm-textured and not too ripe. Squeeze the juice of half a lemon into a bowl and dilute it with a little water. Using a Mandoline or a steady hand, slice apples and pears thinly to a thickness of about 2.5 mm. Dip the slices into the diluted lemon juice as soon as you cut them to stop discolouration. Mix 100 ml water and 100 g sugar in a pan. Place the slices into the syrup and boil. Remove the fruit, place on parchment and dry in the oven at 100°C for 4 hours, turning once half way through.

COCONUT CURLS

Use a vegetable peeler to shave long, curling strips from a large chunk of fresh coconut. Apply even pressure for regular curls. Toast them in the oven before sprinkling on a dessert as decoration.

DECORATIVE IDEAS

Enticingly transparent apple and pear crisps provide some architectural height to the flat canvass of a simple dessert and contrast creamy flavours. Shavings of fresh, toasted coconut spilling over exotic fruit salads or subtly curled on individual desserts look pleasing. Little knots of citrus peel add zest and colour to parfaits, cheesecakes and ices. These tiny decorations are ideal for petits fours.

CARAMELIZING NUTS

The flavour of caramel works particularly well with nuts, and the dark, lustrous coating it supplies gives the nuts a more decorative effect.

Make a caramel (see page 109). Push a cocktail stick into a nut, lift it by the stick and dip in caramel. Leave to dry on parchment. Repeat with each nut.

NUTS AND FRUITS FOR CARAMELIZING

Almonds, Brazil nuts, pecans, hazelnuts and macadamia nuts are all ideal for caramelizing. The flavour and texture of several fruits make them good choices for a caramel coating. The most widely known are toffee apples and bananas. Both are delicious plain or with a dollop of ice cream.

SHAPING NOUGATINE

To make nougat powder, cook 150 g sugar, 50 g glucose and 50 g flaked almonds to a light caramel. Pour on to an oiled baking tray, allow to cool, then chill. Process the hardened nougat to a powder in a food processor.

2 Carefully remove the paper template. Add flakes of nuts, or small pieces of chopped nuts to the shape, then cook at 170°C for about 5 minutes.

*Crisp **nougatine shapes** can be used to provide additional texture and flavour to a dessert. Use them as as decorative bases or toppings.*

1 Cut a template for the shape you which to achieve and place it on a sheet of parchment. Sprinkle the powdered nougat evenly inside the edges of the template.

3 Nougat will be soft when removed from the oven, but will harden to a crispness as it cools. If you wish to shape the piece, do so before it cools too much and becomes brittle. Here, it is wrapped around a rolling pin to give it a curved shape.

GLOSSARY

AGAR-AGAR A seaweed-based vegetarian alternative to gelatine.

BAIN MARIE A cooking utensil which allows heat to distribute evenly during cooking. Can be bought as a specialist piece of equipment or improvised by sitting a bowl containing the dessert in a larger pan of boiling water.

BAKE To cook food uncovered in an oven at a required temperature.

BAKE BLIND To part-cook a pastry shell before filling it when the filling requires cooking as well as the pastry.

BAKING PARCHMENT A non-stick paper that is particularly useful for lining baking tins.

BASTE To moisten food by spooning over or brushing on a liquid, in order to aid cooking and add flavour.

BATTER The uncooked mixture of crêpes, pancakes and cakes based on flour, milk and eggs. The term also describes a coating for foods to be deep-fried, such as fritters.

BEAT To mix ingredients using a quick, regular motion until smooth and evenly blended. Can be performed using a wire whisk, a spoon, a hand beater or an electric mixer. Also used to incorporate air into mixtures that will rise, such as soufflés and batters.

BLANCH A process for loosening and removing the skins of nuts and some fruits by plunging them first into boiling water and then into ice water to stop the cooking process. Blanching also sets their colour and reduces bitterness.

BLEND To mix ingredients until they are evenly combined.

BOIL To heat a liquid until bubbles break on the surface. To boil a food item is to cook it in boiling liquid (usually water). Water has a boiling point of 100°C but the boiling points of other liquids vary.

BRULEE To melt a sugar topping under a hot grill until it caramelizes to form a crisp crust.

CARAMELIZE To heat sugar and water together to 190°C until the syrup attains a rich brown colour and a consistency suitable for coating food. Sugar can also be caramelized once it is sprinkled on a dessert, by being melted under a hot grill (see also BRULEE).

CHILL To place food in a refrigerator or a bath of iced water to make or keep it cool or firm.

CHOP To cut food into small pieces, either manually or in a food processor.

COAT To cover the surface of a dessert, for example with icing.

COMPOTE Fruits, either one type or a mixture, cooked in a sugar syrup and often infused with flavours. Either dried or fresh fruit can be used.

CORE To remove the central core from fruits such as apples and pears. This can be done to either whole fruit or to fruit slices.

COULIS A sieved purée of fruits combined with a sweetener and a small amount of citrus juice.

CREAM To beat ingredients together until they have blended into a light, fluffy and smooth mixture. The term is usually applied to creaming sugar with a fat, such as butter.

CRYSTALLIZING Describes fruits or flower petals that have been coated in lightly beaten egg white, then sugar. These are used decoratively.

DETREMPE A French term that describes the initial paste made in the early stages of preparing puff pastry.

DICE To cut food into small cubes.

DOUGH A mixture based on flour and water that is soft and malleable, yet firm enough to hold its form.

DROPPING CONSISTENCY Describes the consistency of a mixture that can be dropped by the spoonful on to a baking tray, yet holds its shape once dropped.

DUST To cover a food with a light coating of a powdery ingredient, usually sugar or cocoa powder.

ENRICH To add cream, egg yolks or butter to a mixture or sauce to give it a richer texture or flavour.

FLAMBEE To coat a dish in alcohol that has been set alight to burn off the alcohol content but retain the flavour.

FOLD To blend a light ingredient with a heavier one. The lighter is placed on the heavier and the two are combined by a figure-of-eight motion with a metal spoon or rubber spatula. This retains air in the mixture.

FRITTER A small food item that is coated in a thick batter then deep-fried.

FRY To cook food in hot fat. Deep-fried foods are submerged in fat. Sautéed or pan-fried foods are cooked in just enough fat to coat the bottom of the pan and prevent food from sticking.

GELATINE A thickening agent that allows liquids to be set into a jelly. Available in leaf or powdered form.

GLAZE To coat food with a thin sweet liquid, such as melted jam or Apricot Nappage, that will set to a smooth, shiny finish. Also, to brush pastry with milk or egg wash for a shiny result.

GREASE To coat an item of equipment with a fat such as butter or oil, to prevent foods from sticking to it.

GRIDDLE A flat, cast iron, rimless pan used to cook batters for pancakes or dropped scones, for instance.

GRIND To crush dry foods to powder form or into tiny grains, using either a pestle and mortar or a food processor.

HULL Hulling describes removing the stalk and core from soft fruits such as strawberries.

ICE-BATH To immerse the base of a hot pan of ingredients in a bowl of water and ice cubes to suddenly arrest the cooking process.

IMBIBE To use a flavoured syrup or a liqueur to soak a cake in order to add flavour and moisture.

INFUSE To give flavour and aroma to a liquid by steeping it with flavourings such as zest or spices.

JULIENNE A fine strip of food, often used as decoration, for example a strip of orange or lemon peel.

KNEAD To fold and press dough, in order to mix it thoroughly, to make it smooth and firm and to incorporate air.

KNOCK-UP To press a series of flat depressions around the edge of a pastry crust of a pie, then tapping in between each depression with the blunt edge of a knife to create ridges.

LINE To give a tin a thin coating of a fat, such as butter or oil, or of flour, baking parchment, or a food item such as sponge fingers, in order to prevent the finished dish from sticking to the tin.

MACERATE To steep or marinate food items in a flavoured liquid, such as liqueur or spiced syrup, before cooking in order to soften them and give them additional flavour.

MARBLING A decorative effect achieved by partially mixing a cake batter or chocolate of two colours.

MARSALA A Sicilian fortified wine used to flavour some desserts.

MOULD Determining the shape of a dessert by placing a soft, malleable mixture into a mould and setting it into that shape by either chilling it, or using a setting agent such as gelatine.

MOUSSE A chilled dessert with a light and airy texture, consisting mainly of whisked milk, eggs and sugar .

PASTE Food that is ground to a fine texture and moistened slightly to make a fairly stiff, spreadable mixture.

PATE (pâte) The term used to describe a pastry mixture, as in Pâte Sucrée, Pâte Brisée and Pâte Sablé.

PITH The white layer of skin between the outer zest and the flesh of citrus fruits. The pith is bitter in taste.

POACH To submerge food in a liquid that is kept at just below simmering point in order to cook it. Water, alcohol, sugar syrup or poaching syrup can be used.

PRICK To pierce foods, usually pastry or unpeeled fruits, using a fork or a knife, so that air or moisture can be released during baking in order to retain a smooth finish on the dessert.

PUREE To reduce solid food, either cooked or raw, in a mouli or electric blender and to sieve it to form a smooth pulp which can then be used as a sauce or a base for other desserts.

QUENELLES Ovals of a soft mixture, such as ice cream or yogurt, shaped with two spoons and often used decoratively.

REDUCE To boil a liquid at a high heat in an uncovered pan to evaporate some liquid and concentrate the flavour.

RIBBON When a beaten egg and sugar batter runs from a spoon or whisk in a smooth, thick flow, it is said to be at ribbon consistency.

SCORE To cut the surface of a food item, such as an apple, prior to cooking, to enhance cooking and presentation.

SIEVE To pass ingredients through a sieve in order to thin the consistency or remove lumps from a mixture.

SIFT To sieve dry ingredients such as flour or sugar in order to add air and separate lumps from the fine powder.

SIMMER To keep a liquid just below boiling point so that the surface very gently bubbles. The term also refers to cooking food gently in that liquid.

SKIM To run a utensil such as a ladle over a simmering liquid in order to remove any gathered impurities.

SOUFFLE A light dish based on whisked egg whites, that is highly aerated. Cooked versions rise.

SWEAT To cook fruits gently in liquid until softened, but not browned. Often used to prepare fruit fillings for pies.

SYRUP A sweet liquid made by heating sugar with water. Syrups have a variety of uses depending on the ratio of sugar to water and the heating temperature.

TEMPER To melt, then cool chocolate in order to blend the fats within it, before making chocolate decorations.

VANILLA ESSENCE/EXTRACT Products made from vanilla that provide a reliable vanilla flavour without the need to include a vanilla pod.

WHISK To blend ingredients using a wire whisk in a beating action which allows air to be incorporated into the mixture. Mostly applied to liquid rather than dry ingredients.

ZEST The coloured outermost layer of citrus fruit skin.

INDEX

···· A ····

Agar-agar 128
Alcohol
  adding to jellies 128
  brandy
    butter 115
    parfait 39
    -preserved prunes 29
    snaps 126, 194
    syrup 28
  for flambéed fruit 17
  flambéeing 115
  in ice cream 36
  liqueur parfait 39
  mulled wine granita 33
  pink Champagne sorbet 32
  prunes in Armagnac 29
  rum
    babas 147
    and glacé fruit parfait 39
  summer Amaretto condé 183
  syrup, fruit in 28
  whisky and ginger ice
    cream 36
Almond(s)
  bavarois 49
  chocolate macarannade 178
  cream 153
  crumble topping 22
  custard 46
  ricotta cheesecake 79
  sponge 136
    cake 142
    pudding 146
Alsation plum tart 154
Amaretto condé, summer 183
American pancakes 87
Angel food cake 131, 134
Angel's hair 209
Apple(s)
  and almond cream 51
  baked 18
    fruit Charlotte 27
  corer 98
  crisps 212
  Eve's pudding 23
  grilled 16
  and pear tart 160
  preparing 101
  soufflé 60
  strudel 167
  stuffed poached 19
  tart, French 154
  Tarte Tatin 154, 156
  varieties for cooking 101
Apricot(s)
  glaze 88
  nappage 113
  palmiers with ice cream and
    poached 164
  sauce 184
  stoning 102
Armagnac, prunes in 29

···· B ····

Baked
  apples 18
  cheesecake 78
  custard 46
  custard, fried 48
  -custard pudding 48
  fruit Charlotte 27
  rice pudding 187
  rice with spiced fruit 187
  soufflés 58
Baker's chocolate 110
Baking
  beans 100
  blind 152
  an empty shell 152
  meringue 69
  sheet 100
Baklava, layering filo in 168
Baller 98
Bananas, grilled 16
Basic biscuit dough 126
Basics 97–128
Batters and Omelettes 83–96
Batter 125
  crêpe 84, 88
  fritter 125
  preparing yeasted 147
  puddings 92, 93
    clafoutis 92
    decorated 93
    fruit for 93
  waffle 91
  yeast 95
  yeasted 147
  See also Crêpe(s); Fritter(s);
  Pancake(s); Waffle(s)

Bavarian cream 49
Bavarois
  almond 49
  flavouring 49
  fruit 50
  preparing 49
  rich chocolate 49
  rose 49
  surprise 50
  three-fruit 50
Beignets 177
Berry(ies)
  in fruit compotes 15
  in fruit salads 10
  Summer pudding 25
  See also specific berries
Biscuit(s)
  brandy baskets 210
  brandy snaps 126
  chocolate and cinnamon 194
  choux shapes 210
  coconut tuiles 70, 211
  coffee brandy snaps 194
  crust, mousse in a 65
  crusts (for cheesecakes) 80
  cutters 99
  dough, basic 126
  Florentines 194
  lace tuiles 211
  shaping basic 126
  shaping tuiles 211
  shortbread 127
  tuiles 127
  tulipes 210
Blackcurrant(s)
  crumble 23
  ice cream 37
  moulds 11
  Summer pudding 24
Blanching nuts 107
Blender 100
Blending tool 123
Blini(s) 87
  pans 85
Bombe(s) 39
  cherry 196
  mould 39
Bowls 99
Brandy
  butter 115
  parfait 39

snaps 126
  coffee 194
  syrup 28
Bread and butter pudding 48
Buns, choux 170
Buttercream 117
Butterscotch sauce 114

···· C ····

Cakes and Gâteaux 129–150
Cake(s)
  almond sponge 142
  angel food 131, 134
  chocolate nut torte 141
  chocolate suprème 62
  entremet contemporain 52
  exotic fruit savarin 148
  exotic rice Imperatrice 70
  Nid d'Abeille 66
  nut torte 141
  Pain de Gênes 142
  Sachertorte 140
  savarin 150
  slice 99
  tins 100
  tipsy 141
  See also Gâteau(x); Sponge(s)
Caramel 109, 184
  cage 207
  mousse 52
  sauce 52
  syrup 52
Caramelized figs 76
Caraque 203
Cardamom whisked
  sponge 118
Champagne sorbet, pink 32
Charlotte(s)
  baked fruit 27
  Scandinavian 26
Cheese(s)
  desserts
    crémet de Touraine 74
    mascarpone figs 76
    Pashka 75
  for moulded desserts 75
  moulds 74
Cheesecake(s)
  almond ricotta 79
  baked 78

biscuit crusts 80
  flavouring 81
  fruit purée 81
  individual 79
  individual fruit 82
  lemon 80
  lime 81
  orange 81
  set 80
  toppings for 81
Cherry(ies)
  bombes 196
  clafoutis 92
  pitting 102
  strudel 167
Chibouste mousse 61
Chocolate
  bavarois 49
  caraque 203
  chestnut roulade 139
  chopping and grating 110
  cigarettes 203
  and cinnamon biscuits 194
  cream 178
  cream sauce 114
  crumble topping 22
  cups 42, 111
    moulded 202
    piped 200
  curls 203
  custard 46
  decorations 198–203
  -dipped meringues 69
  dipping and coating fruit 195
  fritters 190
  ganache 111
  glaze, 62, 132, 178
  ice cream 36
  icing 112
  macarannade 178
  marbling 201
  melting 110
  mousse 62, 132
    dark 64
    white 64, 142
  nut dome 132
  nut torte 141
  parfait 39
  piping 198
  praline cream 155
  and red wine sauce 20
  roulade sponge 139
  sauce 115
    white 115
  semolina, chilled 189
  shapes 111
  short pastry 123
  soufflé 57, 60

cups 57
  in hazelnut cups 59
  sponge puddings 146
  suprème 62
  tarts 155
  tempering 110
  types of 110
  and vanilla gâteau 134
  whisked sponge 118
Chopping
  chocolate 110
  nuts 107
Choux
  buns 170
  cases 176
  deep-fried 177
  deep-frying 124
  fillings for 171
  fingers 171
  ice cream fritters 177
  Paris-Brest 172
  paste 124
  piped shapes 172
  rings 171
  Saint Honoré 174
  sauces for 171
  shapes, decorative 210
  swans 173
  toppings for 171
Christmas pudding 30
Cinnamon
  date pastries 193
  shortcake 123
Citrus (fruit)
  cups 186
  julienne, crystallized 205
  knots 212
  meringue 72
  pancakes 90
  peeling and slicing 104
  segmenting 104
  short pastry 123
  squeezer 98
  twists 212
  whisked sponge 118
  zesting 104
  See also names of fruits
Clafoutis 92
Coating(s)
  fritters 94
  gâteaux 131
  with icing 113
  and icing Sachertorte 140
  meringue 68
  for roulades 138
  sponge shapes 137
Coconut
  curls 212

custard 47
  milk sauce 115
  rice with caramel-coated
    fruit 188
  soufflé 58
  tuiles 70, 211
Coffee
  brandy snaps 194
  custard 46
  espresso meringue 72
  granita 33
  ice cream 36
  parfait 39
  sauce 115
  soufflé 57
  whisked sponge 118
Compote(s)
  dried fruit 28
  serving 15
  fruit 15
Coring hard fruit 101
Cornflour sauce 114
Coulis 113
  raspberry 74
  using 204
Couverture 110
Cream cheese desserts 74
Cream(s)
  chocolate 178
    praline 155
  flummery 54
  fruit 51
  hazelnut 52
  honey 66
  mascarpone 76
  orange 88
  pistachio burnt 132
  of rice 70
  syllabub 54
  vanilla 62
  See also Crème; Custard(s)
Crème
  Anglaise 116
  au beurre 117
  brûlée 34, 46
  caramel 46
  Chantilly 116
  Chibouste 116
  patissière 116
  See also Cream(s); Custard(s)
Crémet de Touraine 74
Crêpe(s)
  batter 84, 88
  fillings for gâteaux 86
  fillings for soufflés 86
  folding 85
  French-style 84
  fruit-filled 85

gâteau, orange 88
gâteaux 86
  layered 86
  pans 85
  serving 85
  soufflé 86
  See also Blini(s); Pancake(s)
Crumble(s)
  fruit 22
  fruits for 23
  plum 22
  toppings for fruit 22
Crystallized citrus julienne 205
Currants strigging 103
Custards, Creams and
  Whips 45–54
Custard(s)
  baked 46
  buttercream 117
  coconut 47
  crème Anglaise 116
  crème au beurre 117
  crème Chantilly 116
  crème Chibouste 116
  crème patissière 116
  flavouring 46
  fried baked 48
  Indian 47
  moulded 49
  pudding, baked- 48
  spiced 47
  tarts 155
  zabaglione 54
Cutting
  hard fruit 101
  layers, for gâteaux 130
  pineapple from the shell 106
  sponges 130
  sponge shapes 137

••• D •••

Dacquoise 20, 62, 66
Dariole moulds 100
Date(s)
  pastries, cinnamon 193
  preparing 103
Decorating
  batter puddings 93
  soufflés 57
Decorations
  biscuit 210
  chocolate 198–208
  coulis 204
  fruit and nut 212
  sugar 206–209
  See also Frosting

Deep-frying
  choux 124, 177
  fritters 94
Dicing fruit 101
Dipping and coating fruit 195
Dissolving gelatine 128
Dough, basic biscuit 126
Dredger 98
Dried fruit
  compote 28
  pancakes 90
  stuffed 195
Drop scones 87
Dumplings, fruit 180

E

Eclairs 171
Egg wash 123
Electric beater 100
En papillote, fruit 19
Entremet contemporain 52
Equipment
  apple corer 98
  baking 100
  baller 98
  biscuit cutters 99
  blender 100
  blending tool 123
  bombe mould 39
  bowls and basins 99
  cake slice 99
  citrus squeezer 98
  crêpe pans 85
  electric beater 100
  food processor 100
  dredger 98
  grater 98
  ice cream
    maker 100
    scoop 98
  knives 99
  marble slab 98
  measuring 98
  moulds 99
  Mouli 113
  nutmeg grater 98
  ovenproof 100
  pastry
    brushes 98
    cutters 99
    wheel 99
  pestle and mortar 98
  piping 99
    nozzle 175
  pudding basin 145
  rolling pin 98

scissors 99
seasoning pans 85
sieve 98
silicone mat 211
slotted spoon 98
sorbetière 32
spatula 99
sponge tins 118
stoner or pitter 99
thermometer 98, 108
vegetable peeler 99
waffle irons 91
whisk 99
wooden spoons 99
zester 99
Eve's pudding 23

F

Feuilletés 165
Fig(s)
  caramelized 76
  flowers, preparing 103
  mascarpone 76
Filling sponge layers 130
Fillings
  for choux 171
  for crêpes and pancakes 85
  for crêpes gâteaux 86
  for feuilletés 165
  for omelettes 96
  for palmiers 164
  for roulades 138
  for soufflé crêpes 86
  for strudel 167
  for stuffed fruit 18, 19
  for sweet omelettes 96
  for turnovers 165
Filo pastry
  cinnamon date pastries 193
  fruit pies 169
  hazelnut pastries 193
  layering in baklava 168
  pastries, little 168
  topping, shredded 169
Finishing Touches 197–213
Flaking nuts 107
Flambéed fruit 17
Flambéeing 115
Flan(s)
  filling a cooked 153
  tin, lining 123, 152
  tins 100
  See also Pie(s); Tart(s)
Flavouring
  baked fruit 19
  baked rice pudding 187

cheesecake 81
crêpes 85
custards 46
fruit salads 10
fruit parcels 19
granita 33
grilled fruit 16
ice cream 39
  gâteau 40
meringue 72
omelettes 96
pancakes 90
parfait 39
poached fruit 14
savarin or babas 150
semolina 190
simmered rice pudding 182
soufflés 57
spiced custard 47
stuffed fruit 18
waffles 91
whisked sponges 118
yeasted fritters 95
Florentines 194
Flummery 54
Folding crêpes 85
Fondant
  dipping and coating fruit 195
  icing 112
Food processor 100
Fool, fruit 51
Freezing sorbet 32
French meringue 68
Fresh fruit minestrone 12
Fried baked custard 48
Fritter(s) 94
  batter 125
  chocolate 190
  choux ice cream 177
  deep-fried choux 177
  Oriental coated 94
  semolina 190
  stuffed 94
  yeasted batter 95
Frosting 205
Fruit Desserts 9–30
Fruit(s)
  in alcohol syrup 28
  Autumn pudding 25
  baked rice with spiced 187
  for battered puddings 93
  bavarois 50
  brûlée 17
  for caramelizing 213
  Charlotte, baked 27
  cheesecakes, individual 82
  compote, dried 28
  compotes 15

coulis 113
creams 51
crumble 22
  for crumbles 23
cups, citrus 186
cutting 101
decorations 212
dicing 101
dipping and coating 195
dumplings 180
en papillote 19
-filled crêpes 85
flambéed 17
flavouring
  for pancakes 90
  poached 14
fool 51
fritters 94
glazing soft 153
grilled 16
hollowed 32
ice cream 37
jelly 128
juicing 105
kebabs 16
minestrone, fresh 12
moulds 11
mousse 65
and nut tart filling 160
pan-fried 17
pancakes 90
peeling 101
pie 159
pies, filo 169
poaching 14
pudding 26
purée(s) 113
  cheesecake 81
  sorbet 33
salad 10
savarin, exotic 148
setting 11
soufflés, hot 60
spiced pears 20
stuffed dried 195
stuffing 18
Summer pudding 24
syrup sorbets 32
syrups for poached 14
tartlets 155
  red 193
toppings
  for cheesecake 81
  poached 81
Winter pudding 25
See also Citrus (fruit); names of fruit

··· G ···

Ganache, chocolate 20, 111
Gâteau(x)
  almond sponge 136
  assembling sponge
    shapes 137
  chequered 135
  coating 131
  coating sponge shapes 137
  crêpes 86
  cutting layers 130
  cutting sponge shapes 137
  folding sponges 136
  ice cream 40
  imbibing and filling
    layers 130
  loaf shaped 135
  mousse-filled 134
  orange crêpe 88
  de riz 184
  rolled sponge 138
  square and oblong 134
  See also Cake(s); Sponge(s)
Gelatine
  setting fruit 11
  using 128
Génoise sponge 70
Ginger
  ice cream, whisky and 36
  shortcake 123
Glacé icing 112
Glazes 113
  apricot 88
  chocolate 62, 132, 178
Glazing soft fruit 153
Grains 181–190
Granita 33
  mulled wine 33
Grapes, preparing 102
Grater 98
Grating 104
  chocolate 110
Griddle pancakes 87
Grilled
  fruit 16
  orange slices 186
Guava(s)
  grilled 16
  stuffed 18

··· H ···

Halving strawberries 103
Hard-ball syrup 108
Hard-crack syrup 108
Hazelnut

cups, soufflés in 59
parfait 19
pastries 193
whipped cream 52
Herbs, flavouring fruit salads
  with 10
Honey
  cream 66
  syrup 95
Hulling strawberries 103

··· I ···

Ice bowl 44
Ice cream 36
  balls, coated 196
  blackcurrant 37
  bombes 39
    cherry 196
  chocolate 36
  coffee 36
  cutting shapes 43
  fritters, choux 177
  fruit 37
  gâteau 40
  kebabs, mini 196
  layered 196
  maker 100
  meringue 37
  quenelles 42
  ratafia 36
  rich vanilla 36
  ripples 37
  scoop 98
  serving shapes 43
  shaping 42, 43
  slicing 43
  stamping 43
  textured scoops 42
  vanilla 36
  whisky and ginger 36
  working with 196
  See also Parfait
Iced Desserts 31–44
Iced
  soufflés 41
  yogurt 12
Icing
  chocolate 112
  coating with 113
  fondant 112
    glacé 112
Imbibing sponge layers 130
Indian custards 47
Indian-style rice pudding 186
Italian meringue 34, 68

··· J ···

Jalousie 166
Jelly, fruit 128
Juicing fruit 105

··· K ···

Kebabs, fruit 16
Knives 99

··· L ···

Lattice topping for tarts 158
Leaf gelatine 128
Lemon
  cheesecake 80
  mousse 61
  puddings 146
  soufflé 56
  yeasted fritters 95
Lime cheesecake 81
Linzertorte 158
Liqueur parfait 39
Lychees, preparing 103

··· M ···

Macarannade, chocolate 178
Mango
  and banana cream 51
  and passion fruit sauce 70
  peeling and slicing 107
Mangosteen, preparing 103
Marble slab 98
Marbling chocolate 201
Mascarpone 76
  cream 76
  figs 76
Measuring equipment 98
Melba sauce 115
Melon
  balls 105
  fool 51
  preparing 105
  varieties 105
Melting chocolate 110
Meringue(s) 48
  baking 69
  citrus 72
  coating 68
  drying out 69
  espresso 72
  exotic rice Imperatrice 70
  flavouring 72

French 68
  ice cream 37
  Italian 34, 68
  mini 192
  Nid d'Abeille 66
  Pavlova 69
  piping 68
  poaching 72
  pyramid 72
  quenelles 72
  shaping 68
  strawberry vacherins 34
  Swiss 68
  vanilla 72
Milk puddings 182
Millefeuille 163, 192
Mince pies 29
Mincemeat 29
Minestrone, fresh fruit 12
Mini
  meringues 192
  millefeuille 192
Moulded
  cheese desserts 74
  custards 49
  mousse 65
Mould(s) 39, 99
  fruit 11
  ice bowl 44
  parfait 38
Mouli, using a 113
Mousse
  in a biscuit crust 65
  caramel 52
  Chibouste 61
  chocolate 62, 132
    dark 64
    white 64, 142
  -filled gâteaux 134
  fruit 65
  lemon 61
  moulded 65
  serving 65
Mulled wine granita 33

··· N ···

Nectarines
  grilled 16
  skinning 102
  stoning 102
  stuffed 18
Nid d'Abeille 66
Nougat 160
Nougatine 109
  shaping 213

Nut(s)
  blanching and skinning 107
  caramelizing 213
  crumble topping 22
  decorations 212
  dome, chocolate 132
  hazelnut pastries 193
  nougatine 109, 213
  praline 109
  short pastry 123
  shortcake 123
  shredding and chopping 107
  tart filling, fruit and 160
  toasting and skinning 107
  torte 141
Nutmeg grater 98

••• O •••

Oat crumble topping 22
Oeufs à la neige 72
Omelette(s) 96
  fillings for sweet 96
  flavouring 96
  soufflé 96
Orange
  cheesecake 81
  cream 88
  custard 46
  flower water whisked
    sponge 118
  slices, grilling 186
  soufflé 57
  See also Citrus (fruit)

••• P •••

Pain de Gène 142
Palmiers 164
Pan-fried fruit 17
Pancake(s)
  American 87
  flavourings for 90
  fruit 90
  griddle 87
  Scotch 87
  stack 86
  See also Blini(s); Crêpe(s)
Pans
  blini 85
  crêpe 85
  seasoning 85
  See also Equipment
Papaya(s)
  grilled 16
  stuffed 18

Parfait 38
  brandy 39
  chocolate 39
  coffee 39
  flavouring 39
  hazelnut 39
  liqueur 19
  rum and glacé fruit 39
  serving 39
  vanilla 39
  See also Ice Cream
Pashka 75
Passion fruit sauce, mango
  and 70
Pastries 151–180
Pastries
  cinnamon date 193
  hazelnut 193
  little filo 168
Pastry
  baking an empty shell 152
  baking blind 152
  blending tool 123
  brushes 98
  cutters 99
  wheel 99
  See also Choux; Filo pastry;
  Pâte; Puff pastry; Short
  pastry; Strudel
Pâte
  brisée 122
    fruit dumplings 180
  sablé 122
    circles 162
  sucrée 122
Pavlova 68
Peach(es)
  crumble, dried 23
  grilled 16
  skinning 102
  stoning 102
  summer Amaretto condé 183
Pear(s)
  crisps 212
  crumble 23
  grilled 16
  preparing 101
  spiced 20
  stuffed poached 19
  tart, apple and 160
  varieties for cooking 101
Peeling
  citrus fruit 104
  grapes 102
  hard fruit 101
  mango 107
  pineapple 106
Pestle and mortar 98

Petits Fours 191–196
Pie(s)
  baking an empty shell 152
  baking blind 152
  definition 158
  fillings 153
  filo fruit 169
  fruit 159
  mince 29
  toppings 153
  See also Flan(s); Tart(s)
Pineapple
  grilled 16
  peeling 106
  rings 106
  soufflé-topped 60
Piping
  bag, using a 117
  chocolate 198
  choux shapes 172
  equipment 99
  meringue 68
  nozzle for Saint Honoré 175
  sorbets 32
  sugar 208
Pipping grapes 102
Pistachio burnt cream 132
Pitting cherries 102
Plum
  crumble 22
  tart, Alsatian 154
Poached fruit
  flavouring 14
  syrups for 14
Poaching
  fruit 12
  meringue 72
Pomegranate, preparing 103
Powdered gelatine 128
Praline 109
  Chantilly 178
  cream, chocolate 155
  soufflé 57
Prunes in Armagnac 29
Pudding(s)
  almond sponge 146
  Autumn 25
  baked rice 187
  baked-custard 48
  basin 145
  batter 92, 93
  bread and butter 48
  chocolate sponge 146
  Christmas 30
  clafoutis 92
  Eve's 23
  exotic rice 186
  fruit 26

Indian-style rice 186
individual sponge 146
lemon 146
milk 182
Queen of 48
Scandinavian Charlottes 26
simmered rice 182
simple semolina 189
steamed sponge 144
Summer 24
Winter 25
Puff pastry 120–121
  feuilletés 165
  jalousie 166
  millefeuille 163
    mini 192
  palmiers 164
  tranche 166
  turnovers 165
Purée(s) 113
  sorbet, fruit 33
  using a Mouli 113

••• Q •••

Queen of puddings 48
Quenelles
  ice cream 42
  meringue 72

••• R •••

Ramekin dishes 100
Raspberry coulis 74
Ratafia ice cream 36
Red wine sauce, chocolate
  and 20
Redcurrants
  Summer pudding 24
Rhubarb, preparing 105
Rice
  brûlée 183
  with caramel-coated fruit,
    coconut 188
  cream of 70
  gâteau de riz 184
  Imperatrice, exotic 70
  pudding
    baked 187
    exotic 186
    flavourings for 182
    Indian-style 186
    simmered 182
  with spiced fruit, baked 187
  summer Amaretto condé 193
Ricotta cheesecake, almond 79

Rolling pin 98
Rose bavarois 49
Rose water whisked
    sponge 118
Roulade(s)
    sponge, chocolate 139
    chocolate chestnut 139
    fillings and coatings for 138
Rum
    babas 147
    and glacé fruit parfait 39
    syrup 28

••• S •••

Sabayon sauce 114
Sablé cases 176
Sachertorte 140
    coating and icing 140
Saint Honoré 174
Salad, fruit 10
Sauce(s)
    apricot 184
    brandy butter 115
    butterscotch 114
    caramel 52
    chocolate 115
      cream 114
      and red wine 20
    for choux 171
    coconut milk 115
    coffee 115
    cornflour 114
    coulis 113
    mango and passion fruit 70
    Melba 115
    sabayon 114
    white chocolate 115
Savarin 150
    exotic fruit 148
Scandinavian
    Charlotte pudding 26
    waffles 91
Scissors 99
Scotch pancakes 87
Seasoning pans 85
Segmenting citrus fruit 104
Semolina
    chilled chocolate 189
    flavourings for 190
    fritters 190
    pudding, simple 189
Serving
    Charlottes 26
    cheesecakes 78
    Christmas pudding 30
    compotes 15

crêpes and pancakes 85
fruit
    crumble 22
    kebabs 16
ice cream shapes 43
hot folded sponges 136
mousse 61, 65
parfait 39
quenelles 42
sponge puddings 144
Setting fruit 11
Shaping
    basic biscuits 126
    chocolate 111
    ice cream 42, 43
    meringue 68
Short pastry 122
    pâte brisée 122
    pâte sablé 122
    pâte sucrée 122
    variations 123
Shortbread 127, 184
    cinnamon 76
Shortcake 123
    classic 162
    flavouring 123
Shredding nuts 107
Sieve 98
Simmered rice pudding 183
Skinning nuts 107
Skinning peaches and
    nectarines 102
Slicing
    citrus fruit 104
    ice cream 43
    mango 107
Slotted spoon 98
Soft-ball syrup 108
Soft Cheese Desserts 73–82
Soft-crack syrup 108
Soft fruit
    glazing 153
    sorbets 33
    stuffed 18
    See also Berry(ies);
    Blackcurrant(s);
    Redcurrants;
    names of fruits
Sorbet(s)
    freezing 32
    fruit purée 33
    pink Champagne 32
    piping 32
    simple syrup 32
    strawberry vacherins 34
    textural presentation 32
Soufflés, Mousses and
    Meringues 55–72

Soufflé(s)
    apple 60
    baked 58
    chocolate 60
      in hazelnut cups 59
    coconut 58
    cold 56
    crêpes 86
    cups, chocolate 57
    dishes 100
    finishing 57
    flavouring 57
    in hazelnut cups 59
    hot fruit 60
    iced 41
    individual cold 57
    individual hot 59
    lemon 56
    omelette 96
    -topped pineapple 60
    vanilla 60
Spatula 99
Spiced
    custard 47
    pears 20
Spices
    flavouring fruit salads
      with 10
    flavouring custards with 47
Sponge(s)
    almond 136
    chocolate roulade 139
    coating 137
    cooking times 188
    cutting 137
      layers 130
    enriching a 119
    fatless whisked 118
    fingers 119
    flavouring whisked 118
    folding 136
    Génoise 70
    glazing 113
    ice cream gâteau 40
    imbibing and filling
      layers 130
    layers
      assembling 137
      cutting 130
    pudding
      almond 146
      individual 146
      steamed 144
    rolled 119, 138
    savarin 148
    shapes, assembling 137
    whisked 118
    See also Cake(s); Dacquoise;

Gâteau(x); Roulade(s)
Spun sugar 209
Stamping ice cream 43
Star fruit, preparing 103
Steamed sponge
    pudding 144–145
Stoner or pitter 99
Stoning fruits 102
Strawberry(ies)
    halving 103
    hulling 103
    sorbet 34
    vacherins 34
Strigging currants 103
Strudel 167
    fillings 167
Stuffed
    dried fruit 195
    fritters 94
    guavas 18
    nectarines 18
    papayas 18
    poached apples 19
    poached pears 19
Stuffing fruit 18
Sugar
    crystal problem 108
    decorations 206–209
    heating 206
    piping 208
    poured 206
    shapes 207
    spun 209
    syrups 108
    thermometer 98, 108
    See also Syrup(s)
Summer
    Amaretto condé 183
    pudding 24
Sweetening fruit salads 10
Swiss
    meringue 68
    roll 119, 138
Syllabub 54
    cups 194
Syrup(s) 108
    alcohol 28
    caramel 52
    honey 95
    for poached fruit 14

••• T •••

Tart(s)
    Alsatian plum 154
    apple and pear 160
    chocolate 155

custard 155
definition 158
French apple 154
lattice topping 158
Linzertorte 158
Tarte Tatin 154, 156
See also Flan(s); Pie(s); Tartlets
Tarte Tatin 154, 156
Tartlets
fruit 155
red fruit 193
Tempering chocolate 110
Thermometer, sugar 98, 108
Tipsy cake 141
Toasting nuts 107
Topping(s)
for cheesecakes 81
for choux 171
for fruit crumble 22
poached fruit 81
shredded filo 169
Torte *see Cakes*
Tranche 166
Tuiles 127
coconut 70
shaping 211
Turnovers 165

••• V •••

Vacherins, strawberry 34
Vandyking melon 105
Vanilla
cream 62
ice cream 36
meringue 72
parfait 39
soufflé 60
whisked sponge 118
Vegetable peeler 99

••• W •••

Waffle(s) 91
batter 91
irons 91
Whisk 99
Whisky and ginger ice cream 36
White chocolate *see Chocolate*
Wine granita, mulled 33
Wooden spoons 98

••• Y •••

Yeast(ed) batter 95, 147
fritters 95
preparing 147
rum babas 147
savarin 150
Yogurt, iced 12

••• Z •••

Zabaglione 54
Zester 99
using a 104
Zesting citrus fruit 104

SPECIALITY SUPPLIERS

THE GROVE BAKERY
28-30 Southbourne Grove
Bournemouth BH6 3RA
Phone: 01202 422 653
Speciality: cake decorating Supplies (fondant icing)

KEYLINK LTD.
Blackburn Road
Rotherham S61 2DR
South Yorkshire
Phone: 01790 550 206
Speciality: chocolate
(ingredients, equipment, moulds)

PAGES
121 Shaftesbury Avenue
London WC2H 8AD
Phone: 0171 379 6334
Speciality: equipment

PETER NISBET
Sheene Road
Bedminster
Bristol BS3 4EG
Phone: 0117 966 9131
Speciality: mail order source, equipment

DIVERTIMENTI
(MAIL ORDER) LTD.
P.O. Box 6611
London SW6 6XU
Phone: 0171 386 9911
Speciality: equipment and ingredients

OVEN TEMPERATURES

CELSIUS	FAHRENHEIT	GAS	DESCRIPTION
110°C	225°F	¼	Cool
120°C	250°F	½	Cool
140°C	275°F	1	Very low
150°C	300°F	2	Very low
160°C	325°F	3	Low
170°C	325°F	3	Moderate
180°C	350°F	4	Moderate
190°C	375°F	5	Moderately hot
200°C	400°F	6	Hot
220°C	425°F	7	Hot
230°C	450°F	8	Very hot

VOLUME

METRIC	IMPERIAL	METRIC	IMPERIAL
25 ml	1 fl oz	500 ml	18 fl oz
50 ml	2 fl oz	568 ml	20 fl oz/1 pint
75 ml	2½ fl oz	600 ml	1 pint milk
100 ml	3½ fl oz	700 ml	1¼ pints
125 ml	4 fl oz	850 ml	1½ pints
150 ml	5 fl oz/¼ pint	1 litre	1¾ pints
175 ml	6 fl oz	1.2 litres	2 pints
200 ml	7 fl oz/⅓ pint	1.3 litres	2¼ pints
225 ml	8 fl oz	1.4 litres	2½ pints
250 ml	9 fl oz	1.5 litres	2¾ pints
300 ml	10 fl oz/½ pint	1.7 litres	3 pints
350 ml	12 fl oz	2 litres	3½ pints
400 ml	14 fl oz	2.5 litres	4½ pints
425 ml	15 fl oz/¾ pint	2.8 litres	5 pints
450 ml	16 fl oz	3 litres	5¼ pints

SPOONS

METRIC	IMPERIAL
1.25 ml	¼ tsp
2.5 ml	½ tsp
5 ml	1 tsp
10 ml	2 tsp
15 ml	3 tsp/1 tbsp
30 ml	2 tbsp
45 ml	3 tbsp
60 ml	4 tbsp
75 ml	5 tbsp
90 ml	6 tbsp

US CUPS

CUPS	METRIC
¼ cup	60 ml
⅓ cup	70 ml
½ cup	125 ml
⅔ cup	150 ml
¾ cup	175 ml
1 cup	250 ml
1½ cups	375 ml
2 cups	500 ml
3 cups	750 ml
4 cups	1 litre
6 cups	1.5 litres

WEIGHT

METRIC	IMPERIAL
5 g	⅛ oz
10 g	¼ oz
15 g	½ oz
20 g	¾ oz
25 g	1 oz
35 g	1¼ oz
40 g	1½ oz
50 g	1¾ oz
55 g	2 oz
60 g	2¼ oz
70 g	2½ oz
75 g	2¾ oz
85 g	3 oz
90 g	3¼ oz
100 g	3½ oz
115 g	4 oz
125 g	4½ oz
140 g	5 oz
150 g	5½ oz
175 g	6 oz
200 g	7 oz
225 g	8 oz
250 g	9 oz
275 g	9¾ oz
280 g	10 oz
300 g	10½ oz
315 g	11 oz
325 g	11½ oz
350 g	12 oz
375 g	13 oz
400 g	14 oz
425 g	15 oz
450 g	1 lb
500 g	1 lb 2 oz
550 g	1 lb 4 oz
600 g	1 lb 5 oz
650 g	1 lb 7 oz
700 g	1 lb 9 oz
750 g	1 lb 10 oz
800 g	1 lb 12 oz
850 g	1 lb 14 oz
900 g	2 lb
950 g	2 lb 2 oz
1 kg	2 lb 4 oz
1.25 kg	2 lb 12 oz
1.3 kg	3 lb
1.5 kg	3 lb 5 oz
1.6 kg	3 lb 8 oz
1.8 kg	4 lb
2 kg	4 lb 8 oz
2.25 kg	5 lb
2.5 kg	5 lb 8 oz
2.7 kg	6 lb
3 kg	6 lb 8 oz

MEASURES

METRIC	IMPERIAL
2 mm	1/16 in
3 mm	⅛ in
5 mm	¼ in
8 mm	⅜ in
10 mm/1 cm	½ in
1.5 cm	⅝ in
2 cm	¾ in
2.5 cm	1 in
3 cm	1¼ in
4 cm	1½ in
4.5 cm	1¾ in
5 cm	2 in
5.5 cm	2¼ in
6 cm	2½ in
7 cm	2¾ in
7.5 cm	3 in
8 cm	3¼ in
9 cm	3½ in
9.5 cm	3¾ in
10 cm	4 in
11 cm	4¼ in
12 cm	4½ in
12.5 cm	4¾ in
13 cm	5 in
14 cm	5½ in
15 cm	6 in
16 cm	6¼ in
17 cm	6½ in
18 cm	7 in
19 cm	7½ in
20 cm	8 in
22 cm	8½ in
23 cm	9 in
24 cm	9½ in
25 cm	10 in
26 cm	10½ in
27 cm	10¾ in
28 cm	11 in
29 cm	11½ in
30 cm	12 in
31 cm	12½ in
33 cm	13 in
34 cm	13½ in
35 cm	14 in
37 cm	14½ in
38 cm	15 in
39 cm	15½ in
40 cm	16 in
42 cm	16½ in
43 cm	17 in
44 cm	17½ in
46 cm	18 in
48 cm	19 in
50 cm	20 in

ACKNOWLEDGEMENTS

Additional editorial assistance Gerard McLaughlin
Additional design assistance Tracy Timson
Food consultants Cathy Man, Carol Handslip, Eric Treuillé
Food preparation Wendy MacDonald

Index Madeline Weston

Carroll & Brown would also like to thank the chefs of all the Le Cordon Bleu schools without whose knowledge and expertise this book would not have been possible, especially: Chef Laurent Duchène, (Paris) and Chef Julie Walsh (London). And for their invaluable editorial assistance: Susan Eckstein, Helen Barnard and Alison Oakervee.

Le Cordon Bleu London, 114 Marylebone Lane, London, W1M 6HH, England. Tel 44/171 935 3503. Fax 44/171 935 7621.

Le Cordon Bleu Paris, 8 Rue Leon Delhomme, 75015 Paris, France. Tel 33/1 53 68 22 50. Fax 33/1 48 56 03 96.

Le Cordon Bleu Tokyo, ROOB-1, 28–13 Sarugaku-cho, Daikanyama, Shibuya-ku, Tokyo 150, Japan. Tel 81/3 5489 01 41. Fax 81/3 5489 01 45.

Le Cordon Bleu (US Headquarters), 404 Airport Executive Park, Nanuet, NY 10954, USA. Tel 1/914 426 7400. Fax 1/914 426 0104 (Toll Free Number USA 1-800-457 CHEF).

Le Cordon Bleu Sydney, Ryde College of TAFE, 250 Blaxland Road, Ryde, Sydney, NSW 2112, Australia. Tel 61/2 808 8307. Fax 61/2 809 3346.